The Politics of Psychotherapy
New Perspectives

The Politics of Psychotherapy
New Perspectives

Edited by
Nick Totton

Open University Press

Open University Press
McGraw-Hill Education
McGraw-Hill House
Shoppenhangers Road
Maidenhead, Berkshire
England SL6 2QL

email: enquiries@openup.co.uk
world wide web: www.openup.co.uk

and Two Penn Plaza, New York, NY 10121–2289, USA

First published 2006

Copyright © Nick Totton 2005

Editorial matter and selection
individual chapters © the contributors

A catalogue record of this book is available from the British Library

ISBN-10: 0 335 21653 6 (pb) 0 335 21654 4 (hb)
ISBN-13: 978 0335 21653 6 (pb) 978 0335 21654 3 (hb)

Library of Congress Cataloging-in-Publication Data
CIP data has been applied for

Typeset by BookEns Ltd, Royston, Herts
Printed and bound in Poland by OZGraf S.A.
www.polskabook.pl

Contents

Acknowledgements

An earlier version of the chapter by Emanuel Berman first appeared in *Psychotherapy and Politics International*, 1(1): 1–16 (2003).

The chapters by Jocelyn Chaplin, Arlene Audergon and Lane Arye, and Katie Gentile and Susan Gutwill appeared in *Psychotherapy and Politics International*, 3(2): 133–9, 112–21 and 122–32 (2005).

The chapter by Andrew Samuels appeared in *Psychoanalytic Dialogues*, 14(6): 817–34 (2004).

Notes on contributors

Lane Arye, PhD teaches conflict facilitation, Process Work and Unintentional Music worldwide. He has worked with conflicts between Serbs, Croats and Muslims in the Balkans, between high-caste and low-caste Hindus from India, and with anti-Semitism in Germany and Poland, as well as racism, sexism, nationalism, homophobia and class issues in the USA and Europe. He is on the faculty of the Process Work Center of Portland's Master of Arts in Conflict Facilitation and Organizational Change. Author of *Unintentional Music: Releasing Your Deepest Creativity* (Hampton Roads, 2001), Lane has a private practice in the San Francisco Bay Area, where he lives with his wife, Lecia.

Arlene Audergon, PhD is a psychotherapist and conflict resolution facilitator. She teaches process-oriented psychology in the UK and internationally and her work has brought her to Croatia, Kosovo, Slovakia, Poland, Germany, South Africa, India, the UK and the USA. Arlene is co-founder of CFOR, an organization for community forums on preventive and post-conflict issues, diversity and democracy building. She lives in London, where she also works in theatre.

Emanuel Berman, PhD is a training analyst at the Israel Psychoanalytic Institute and a professor of psychology at the University of Haifa. He is also a visiting professor at NYU, the international editor of *Psychoanalytic Dialogues*, and a board member of the International Association for Relational Psychoanalysis and Psychotherapy.

Sandra L. Bloom, MD is currently President of CommunityWorks, a systems consulting firm. Dr Bloom served as founder and executive director of the Sanctuary programmes from 1980 to 2001, inpatient psychiatric programmes for the treatment of trauma-related disorders. She is a past-president of the International Society for Traumatic Stress Studies (ISTSS). Dr Bloom is the author of *Creating Sanctuary: Toward the Evolution of Sane Societies* (Routledge).

Jocelyn Chaplin is a psychotherapist in private practice in North London. She co-founded the Serpent Institute to train psychotherapists and counsellors in humanistic and psychodynamic approaches within a framework of natural spirituality. She has published widely including *Feminist Counselling in Action* (Sage, 1988, 1999). Jocelyn is currently writing a book on deep equality. She has been a supervisor at the Bridge Project for seven years.

Professor Petruska Clarkson, PhD, DLitt et Phil, FBPS, FBACP, CPsychol is a consultant philosopher and sexologist with more than 200 professional publications in 25 languages and 30 years of international clinical, supervisory, managerial, research and teaching experience as a psychologist, psychotherapist and management consultant trained and training in all major approaches. www.petruskaclarkson.com

Chess Denman is a consultant psychiatrist in psychotherapy at Addenbrooke's Hospital, Cambridge. She is a member of the Society of Analytical Psychology and a founder member of the Association of Cognitive Analytical Therapists. She has published papers and lectured widely on issues of sexuality and discrimination.

Dawn Freshwater currently holds the position of Chair of Mental Health at Bournemouth University. She is also Director of the Centre for Regional Development and Research and Professor of the Faculty of Regional Professional Studies at the Southwest Campus of Edith Cowan University in Australia. She has a PhD, holds diplomas in psychotherapy and clinical supervision and is a UKCP-registered psychotherapist. She is the Editor of the *Journal of Psychiatric and Mental Health Nursing* and has authored over 100 peer-reviewed papers and books and has co-edited texts relating to research, practice improvement, reflective practice and therapeutic nursing.

Katie Gentile, **PhD** is Assistant Professor of Counseling and the Women's Center Director at John Jay College of Criminal Justice in New York City. Her research focuses on gender, trauma and resistance from a cultural, feminist and psychoanalytic perspective. She has an upcoming book, *Creating Bodies: Bulimia as Time, Space and Resistance in One Woman's Diaries*, from the Analytic Press. She is also a psychoanalyst in private practice.

Susan Gutwill, **MS, CSW** is a supervisor and on the faculty of the WTCI and is in private practice in Highland Park, New Jersey. She is co-author of *Eating Problems: A Feminist Psychoanalytic Treatment Model* (Basic Books, 1994) and has presented widely on the intersection of the personal and political unconscious. She is on the board of Section 9, Psychoanalysts for

Social Responsibility of Division 39 and is active in Psychotherapists for Social Responsibility.

John Lees is a BACP senior registered practitioner who runs the Masters degree course in Therapeutic Counselling at the University of Greenwich. He also undertakes a small amount of client and supervisory work in both London and Sussex and is a consultant to a complementary healthcare organization in the process of self-regulating its practitioners. He is interested in developing research methods that are congruent with the principles of counselling and psychotherapeutic practice.

Hilary Prentice is an integrative psychotherapist, living and working on Dartmoor, in Devon. She has been centrally involved in the development of the ecopsychology movement in the UK over the last decade, organizing, writing, speaking, facilitating workshops and teaching. Diverse roots feeding into this work include years working in the addictions field and in mental health, activism in the women's peace movement, the radical worlds of self-help therapy and reevaluation co-counselling, the deep bodily knowledge of mutilation through invasive surgery and a lifetime of being in love with the 'greater than human world'. She increasingly understands the environmental crisis at this time to be our greatest teacher.

Mary-Jayne Rust is an art therapist and Jungian analyst living by the woods in North London. Her work on eating problems and body image at the Women's Therapy Centre, London, informed her interest in the psychology of consumerism. Her travels in Ladakh, India and Africa opened her eyes to the impact of globalization on our psyches, bodies and relationships. She has been involved with the ecopsychology movement in the UK for the last decade, interested in the interplay between nature, culture and psyche. Painting, cycling and swimming in wild places sustain this work.

Judy Ryde is co-founder and past chair of Psychotherapists and Counsellors for Social Responsibility, a senior trainer and supervisor of Bath Centre for Psychotherapy and Counselling (BCPC) and a trainer with the Centre for Supervision and Team Development. She is completing a PhD thesis at the University of Bath on the meaning and experience of being 'white' as a psychotherapist. Two years ago Judy set up a counselling service for asylum seekers and refugees in Bristol through BCPC.

Andrew Samuels is Professor of Analytical Psychology at the University of Essex, Visiting Professor of Psychoanalytic Studies at Goldsmiths College, University of London and a training analyst of the Society of Analytical Psychology. He is also co-founder of Psychotherapists and Counsellors for Social Responsibility and of Antidote, the campaign for emotional literacy, and a trustee of the Work–Life Balance Trust. Publications, which have been translated into 19 languages, include *Jung and the Post-Jungians* (Routledge, 1985), *The Father* (Guildford Press, 1986), *A Critical Dictionary of Jungian Analysis* (Routledge, 1986), *The Plural Psyche* (Routledge, 1989), *Psychopathology* (Routledge, 1989), *The Political Psyche* (Routledge, 1993) and *Politics on the Couch: Citizenship and the Internal Life* (Profile Books, 2001).

Nick Totton is a psychotherapist and trainer in private practice based in Calderdale, West Yorkshire. He has written several books, including *Psychotherapy and Politics* (Sage, 2000), *Body Psychotherapy: An Introduction* (Open University Press, 2003) and *Press When Illuminated: New and Selected Poems* (Salt, 2004) and edited others, including *Implausible Professions: Arguments for Pluralism and Autonomy in Psychotherapy and Counselling* (with Richard House; PCCS Books, 1997) and *Psychoanalysis and the Paranormal: Lands of Darkness* (Karnac, 2003). He is editor of the journal *Psychotherapy and Politics International*, published by John Wiley and Sons.

Introduction

*The ontological structure of the human being imposes
insurmountable constraints upon any form of social organization
and any political project.*

(Castoriadis 1999: 409)

Upstream runners and instream waders

There is an old Buddhist story (or if there isn't, there should be): two monks
are walking beside a fast-flowing river. Suddenly, they hear a shout and see
a man being carried helplessly downstream. Wading into the water, they
manage to pull him out and are tending to him on the bank when they hear
a woman's voice and realize that she too is struggling in the torrent. Again,
they manage to pull her out; but then they see a whole group of people
being swept along. One of the monks is about to wade in for the third time
when he realizes that his companion is not with him; instead she is running
upstream as fast as she can. 'Where are you off to?' he demands. 'These
people need help!' Without slowing, the other monk shouts over her shoul-
der, 'I'm going to find the bastard who's throwing them in!'

This pretty much sums up one central justification for bringing politics
together with psychotherapy: that it is not possible properly to understand,
or address, individual suffering (people being carried downstream) without
looking at the context of power relationships in which it occurs (someone
throwing them in). There are some complexities embedded in the story,
however. It is fairly clear what the 'upstream runner's' position is: it is less
important to relieve immediate drowning than to identify and resolve
underlying causative factors leading to drowning. But how would the
'instream wader' respond?

He might argue that what happens upstream is none of his business: he
is trained and specialized in rescuing drowning people, not in abstruse
analysis of how they got there. (For an explicit statement of this view, see
Johnson 2001a, b.) He might say that, as a compassionate human being, he
is compelled to try to save the drowning, whatever the reasons for their
being there (and he might prefer to supply life jackets rather than pull them

out of the water). He might take the view that, if someone is drowning, it is ultimately for internal rather than external reasons: if someone hadn't thrown them in, they would have jumped in themselves, or found another persecutor to do the job for them – and besides, they could always learn to swim! Another possible argument is that people get in deep waters because they are unwilling to adjust to reality and stay away from the bank.

The 'instream wader' might go further: he might suggest that if someone is indeed throwing people in, the real question is *why*. Given time, he might develop a theory (in the moments between rescuing the drowning) that those who throw people into rivers have themselves been thrown in at an early age and have a compulsion to repeat their own trauma; or alternatively, that the wish to drown others is an inherent aspect of human subjectivity. In fact, some of these ideas might appeal to the 'upstream runner' as well, and she might feel the need to sit on the bank and think about it all for a while. Meanwhile, struggling people are being washed downstream …

The politics of psychotherapy

The point I want to emphasize is that *all* these positions are *political* – in the sense of 'political' on which this volume rests: that is, related to issues of power and control in human society (see Totton 2000: 1–2). If we move from the river to the therapy profession, the view that psychotherapy has no business with the social causes of distress is just as much a political stance as the view that we do indeed need to examine those social causes. In more general terms, it represents a position on citizenship: that the job of the individual citizen is to stick to their last and leave politics to the 'experts', apart perhaps from election time (if the experts let us hold elections). It may well also incorporate an individualist and/or fatalist view of suffering – that people have a hard time because of their personal makeup/human nature/original sin.

All psychotherapists have a political view of their work; because all psychotherapy rests on a theory – explicit or implicit, conscious or unconscious – of *how people should be*. In assessing and working with clients, one is inevitably drawing on a sense of what is a desirable and appropriate state. Is happiness the goal for human beings? Or calm acceptance of the unsatisfactory nature of life? Is happiness attainable through following our own star, or through adapting to the society around us? Should we strive to be useful to others, or concentrate on fulfilling our own potential? One can hardly do psychotherapy without some way of positioning oneself around these and many other questions – even if one's position is that people should be supported in whatever goals they set for themselves. This, just like any other position on these questions about human nature and its needs, is a position not only about individual goals, but also about social and political ones; there is no line to be drawn between the two.

As I argue in Chapter 7 in this volume (and in Totton 2000), conservative political stances manage a smart piece of camouflage by presenting themselves as non-political: since they support the status quo, they can disappear into the default position, so to speak; what is, is natural, because it is. This is no more than sleight of hand, however – in the context of therapy as much as anywhere else. The view that the current situation is one to be approved and encouraged is as political as the opposite view. There have been times in the history of psychotherapy when its job was generally understood as being to support the status quo, and help clients adjust to it (for instance, in the USA in the 1950s); and times when its job was generally understood as being to challenge the status quo and help clients resist it (for instance, in the USA in the 1960s). In both cases, therapy was following and legitimating a powerful social trend.

I hope to have established that psychotherapy, far from being politically neutral, is shot through with political judgements. It is also a field of political *action*, a place where power is exercised and contested, as therapists try to affect clients' lives and clients acquiesce, resist or do both at the same time. (Again, this is argued more fully in Chapter 7.) If we add in the 'upstream runner's' view, that clients' problems can only be understood within a wider sociopolitical context, then there is surely serious need to explore the politics of psychotherapy – and also, perhaps, reason to be surprised that comparatively little work has been done in this field. (It would be more accurate to say that not a great deal of work has explicitly identified itself in this way. The recent creation of a journal, *Psychotherapy and Politics International*, has acted to crystallize a previously inchoate field, demonstrating just how much work is actually being done there.)

The psychotherapy of politics

But there are still further aspects of the interaction between these two fields. Not only – I would argue – do therapists need to examine the political nature of their professional work; there are also a number of ways in which psychotherapy as a field of knowledge and practice can contribute to the political sphere itself, both theoretically and concretely, and over a range of scales. In order to look at some of these within the space available, we will have to be willing to generalize enormously and to pretend that therapy is a far more monolithic enterprise than it actually is.

This imaginary, monolithic enterprise of psychotherapy, then, is perhaps uniquely able to address a central question of political theory: the articulation between macro and micro levels, between the social and the individual (Elliot 2004; Laclau and Mouffe 1985). It is clear that there is something in human culture that corresponds to Marx's perhaps crude dichotomy between 'base' and 'superstructure' – that individual subjects correlate, in however complex a way, with the conditions set by the ensemble of social relations. Quite how this comes about, however, is very hard to describe adequately.

Psychotherapy contributes to this description through its intensive focus on what Muriel Dimen calls 'the personal and interpersonal tangles of domestic intimacy ... Social theory leads right up to the bedroom door, to the hearth of family and psyche. Then it stops, defeated by the messy, tangled intangibles of domestic life' (Dimen 2003: 40). Therapy crosses that threshold and involves itself centrally with the family, the field within which infants become adults, 'the place where psychic structure is formed' (Poster 1978). Using both historical reconstruction and here-and-now investigation, psychotherapy studies minutely the workings of families, their micro-politics, the processes through which children develop in certain directions and styles, the resistance as much as the acquiescence that forge subjectivity. The pioneering work of Wilhelm Reich (1975) mapped out how the family constellation gives rise to character structure, conceived essentially as a political position, a relationship to power.

One radical perspective on the relationship of individual and society, then, can be summarized as follows:

> The encounter with the existing institutions is the encounter with the concrete Ego of the patient. This Ego is largely a social fabrication; it is designed to ... preserve, continue and reproduce ... the institutions which created it. These institutions are thus maintained not so much through violence and explicit coercion as through their internalization by the individuals in whose fabrication they participated.
>
> (Castoriadis 1997: 131)

Powerful though this picture is, however, psychotherapy charts not only the internalization of institutions, but also the *externalization* of psychic structures giving rise to those same institutions. This much richer account of a mutual, dialectical co-arising of individual and society goes beyond the many attractive dualisms available to us (Dimen 2003, 2004) – including that between instream waders and upstream runners.

Teamwork?

Mutuality, in fact, is the keynote of the relationship between psychotherapy and politics. One can sum it up as follows: *Psychotherapy and politics each problematize the other, and each contribute to solving problems that the other faces.*

For example, politics identifies difficulties with the therapeutic project that we would often rather not consider – issues such as discrimination, prejudice, domination and hierarchy; while psychotherapy shows politics its own unconscious – the structures of projection and identification that scaffold it, the 'motivational and affective bases of political action' (Hoggett 2004: 80). Politics shows how the roles of both client and therapist are socially constructed (Gergen 1994) and how therapy constitutes a regulatory discourse of social control (Foucault 1980). Therapy responds that something crucial is missing from this picture – the actual suffering of the subject, and the therapist's response to it (Burr and Butt 2000).

Through the mutual friction of therapy and politics, in fact, we start to uncover some of the deepest paradoxes in human experience; for example, the simultaneous reality and unreality of the self. Nikolas Rose suggests that 'psychotherapeutics is linked at a profound level to the sociopolitical obligation of the modern self. The self it seeks to liberate or restore is the entity able to steer its individual path through life by means of the act of personal decision and the assumption of personal responsibility' (Rose 1989: 253–4). By pulling someone out of the river, we simultaneously trap them within it, within the illusion of bourgeois personality. At the same time, however, therapy constantly and profoundly challenges this illusion, most directly through the very notion of unconscious process – which also throws into question the appearances of social and political life:

> Ideology is not a dreamlike illusion that we build to escape insupportable reality; in its basic dimension it is a fantasy-construction which serves as a support for our 'reality' itself: an 'illusion' which structures our effective, real social relations and thereby masks some insupportable, real, impossible kernel.
>
> (Zizek 1989: 45)

These are enormous issues, at the very edge of what can be spoken of. Psychotherapy and politics, in combination, offer new ways of speaking about them. As the chapters that follow show, they also offer important ways of exploring a whole range of significant themes in, between and beyond the two disciplines.

What follows

This book is divided into four loose and overlapping parts: 'Psychotherapy in the political sphere', 'Political dimensions of psychotherapy practice', 'Psychotherapy, the state and institutions', and 'Working at the interface: psychotherapy in political action'. The first part opens with a blazingly inspirational chapter by Andrew Samuels – really the founder of contemporary thinking about psychotherapy and politics (Samuels 1993) – bringing together many of the themes Samuels has highlighted over the last decade and a half: the stuckness of contemporary politics, the need for 'resacralization', the nature of political energy and political style, the shortcomings of therapy that keep the world away from its couch and much more. Samuels' chapter, as much as this one, is an introduction to all that follows.

What does immediately follow is Sandra Bloom's incisive take on a live issue of current psycho-politics, the concept of societal trauma. Whatever its shortcomings (Bracken 2002; Haaken 1998; Leys 2000), trauma is a tenacious, recurring and explanatorily powerful model in psychotherapy. Its extension to the social field is equally powerful, offering fresh traction on the whole question of social violence. Bloom applies her great learning to illuminating current issues around the so-called 'war on terror'. My own chapter on conflict, competition and aggression then surveys some of the approaches to this area from therapists of various schools and takes up the idea of societal trauma, asking how the cycle of retraumatization might have originated; it also considers some of the practical initiatives from within psychotherapy for addressing conflict in society.

Next, Hilary Prentice and Mary-Jayne Rust contribute a beautiful and passionate piece on perhaps the most recent psycho-political formulation, ecopsychology, which asks: how have we allowed the world to get into its current state of mess? How can we tolerate, even largely ignore, the environmental catastrophe surrounding us? How can we mend our relationship with the world and come more deeply to feel and express our love for it?

Part II is focused less on the movement from psychotherapy into politics and more on the energy flow from politics to psychotherapy. It opens with Chess Denman's brilliant synthesis of several major issues around sexuality and gender in psychotherapy – one can only gasp at how she tackles a vast theme in a small space without sacrificing subtlety and nuance. In a very real sense, gender and sexuality are where psychotherapy started; and the 'sexual politics' project has always drawn heavily on therapy for its inspiration. Yet therapy itself is affected by the universal tendency to confusion and trance around this issue and can use Denman's bracing precision as a wakeup.

Judy Ryde's chapter on 'working with difference' takes race as its primary focus, but, as she points out, much of it applies equally to other differences, such as gender or sexual orientation – or indeed (I want to interpolate) the ordinary differences between any two human beings. From an intersubjective perspective, Ryde maps out strategies for recognizing and respecting difference and understanding its impact on the therapy relationship. Her chapter is a model of how therapy can creatively take on political imperatives within the context of its own concerns and understandings.

My own chapter (7) on power in the therapeutic relationship follows on well from Ryde's, being also concerned with issues of difference – how the asymmetric roles of therapist and client can combine with social and individual expectations to create severe power imbalances. My suggestion, however, is that rather than seeking to eliminate such power issues (although we should, of course, try to minimize them), we need to centre our work on them, bringing to light clients' deep wounds around power and powerlessness.

Part III opens with Petruska Clarkson's coruscating intellectually and personally engaged analysis of the law and ethics in relation to psychotherapy, which challenges much received wisdom and calls for a personal ethical commitment by each individual practitioner, rather than reliance on institutional wisdom. As my own chapter (9) on therapy institutions underlines, such wisdom may be in short supply: the organizations that administer psychotherapy and counselling often function well below the average level of awareness shown by individual practitioners. I consider some of the reasons that therapy institutions are so often fractious, power hungry and fundamentally stupid and look at one or two attempts to challenge them.

John Lees and Dawn Freshwater use discourse analysis in a case study of one large institution, the British National Health Service, as it interacts with psychotherapy. Many of the issues they uncover are very widely relevant: the medicalization of therapy, the rise of 'evidence-based practice' and the alienation that can accrue for both client and practitioner. These phenomena are most apparent within what is, after all, a medical institution, but they are fast coming to dominate the practice of psychotherapy in every context.

The final part of the book seeks to ground us with four examples of 'psychotherapy in political action'. In Chapter 11, Arlene Audergon and Lane Arye describe their work in Croatia with survivors of vicious ethnic conflict; with vivid humour and deep compassion, they bring out the intensity and difficulty of this sort of work, also outlining the approach of process-oriented psychology, currently perhaps the most politically committed form of psychotherapy. In a classic piece of writing, Emanuel Berman then describes the campaigning work of Israeli psychotherapists opposed to Israel's policies on Palestine, incisively responding to some of the criticisms of therapists making themselves politically 'visible' and illustrating his arguments with clinical examples.

Jocelyn Chaplin's account of the Bridge Project in West London demonstrates that social activist projects of the 1970s can survive into the 21st century – and flourish! She also describes some of the ways in which this feminist counselling project has had to change and adapt over the years of its existence. Chaplin's chapter is centred around reinstating the deceptively simple concept of equality at the centre of psycho-political thinking. In the final chapter Katie Gentile and Susan Gutwill bring us right up to date with an account of activist US therapists' response to September 11th and the ensuing 'war on terror'. With great openness and honesty, they describe both the struggle against dominant political attitudes and the difficult internal dynamics of the group; creating a valuable resource for any group of therapists trying to take a radical position in the face of resistance from society, from their professional institutions and from their own internalized oppression.

I want to thank Shona Mullen and three anonymous referees for sharpening up the original proposal; and Colin Whurr and his team for offering a first home to the journal *Psychotherapy and Politics International*, which is proving so fruitful for this new(ish) discipline. There are many other topics, and many other authors, who could well have been represented here. These chapters, I feel, however, give a remarkable introduction to the field and a good base for further exploration.

Part I
Psychotherapy in the political sphere

1 Politics on the couch? Psychotherapy and society – some possibilities and some limitations
Andrew Samuels

As Robert Musil (1937: 17) put it:

> I am convinced not only that what I say is wrong, but that what will be said against it will be wrong as well. Nonetheless, a beginning must be made; for the truth is to be found not in the middle of such a subject but around the outside, like a sack which changes shape every time a new opinion is stuffed in, but grows firmer all the while.

The intention is to test and explore the boundaries that exist (we have been told) between therapy and politics, between the inner world and the outer world, between being and doing and even between what people still call 'feminine' approaches to life and 'masculine' approaches to life, no matter how problematic those words are.

This chapter is divided into a number of sections. It begins by addressing the questions, Why me? Why here? Why now? Then there follows a discussion of how, particularly after the 2004 US presidential election, politics in the west can be understood as changing in the direction of what I call 'transformative politics'. Third, the question, 'Can therapists really make a difference in the world today?' is asked. Fourth is a markedly experiential section entitled 'The inner politician'. I conclude with a few reflections on therapy, politics and spirituality.

Introduction: why me, why here, why now?

The bases for these remarks, which are grounded in clinical work with individuals, also lie in my involvement with a number of political organizations and recent political developments. I have carried out consultations and conducted workshops in Britain, Europe, the United States, Japan, Brazil, Israel, Australia, New Zealand and South Africa. These activities are designed to see how useful and effective perspectives derived from psychotherapy may be in forming policy, in creating new ways of thinking about the political process and in resolving conflict. It is difficult to present therapy thinking so that mainstream politicians, for example, a senior US Democrat senator or a British Labour Party committee, will take it seriously. And the problem is only slightly reduced when the politicians and organizations are alternative or activist.

I have also been involved in the formation of three organizations in Britain that are relevant to the themes of this chapter. One is Psychotherapists and Counsellors for Social Responsibility, an organization intended to help therapists and counsellors use their knowledge and experience to intervene as professionals in social and political matters. The second organization is Antidote, a psychotherapy-based think tank co-founded with Susie Orbach. It fosters multidisciplinary work and links are sought with people working in fields other than psychotherapy. Antidote has undertaken research into psychological attitudes toward money and economic issues and is also involved in trying to apply ideas about emotional literacy/intelligence to politics.

The third organization is called the St James's Alliance. Based at a beautiful Wren church in Piccadilly in central London, it consists of individuals from fields as diverse as politics, economics, ethics, religion, nongovernmental organizations, activist and pressure groups, the media and psychotherapy. It attempts to incorporate psychological, ethical and spiritual concerns into the political agenda and to facilitate dialogue between various single-issue and pressure groups. In the past, these groups were unsympathetic to other groups' goals – poverty workers did not have time for animal rights activists, for instance, and neither group seemed interested in the problems of the Middle East. But in a suitably facilitated environment, it has been possible to find whole areas of common ground in relation to politics and there are so many emotional and spiritual similarities to share. This is an experiment in gathering and using the shards of political energy that are normally split up and dissipated.

Politics in many western countries is broken and in a mess; we urgently need new ideas and approaches. Psychotherapists, along with economists, social scientists, religious people, environmentalists and others, can contribute to a general transformation of politics.

Today's politicians leave many with a sense of deep despair and disgust. They seem to lack integrity, imagination and new ideas. Across the globe and in response to the challenge, a search is on to remodel politics. Psychotherapy's contribution to this search depends on opening a two-way street between inner realities and the world of politics. We need to balance attempts to understand the secret politics of the inner world of emotional, personal and family experiences with the secret psychology of pressing outer world matters such as leadership, the economy, environmentalism, nationalism and war.

Our inner worlds and our private lives reel from the impact of policy decisions and the existing political culture. Why, then, do our policy committees and commissions not have psychotherapists sitting on them as part of a range of experts? This is not a call for a committee of therapists, but just as a committee will often have a statistician present (someone whose role may not be fully appreciated by the other members), there should also be a therapist at the conference table. We expect to find therapists offering views on social issues that involve personal and familial relationships or matters to do with mental health but they may also have ideas to contribute on the 'hard' issues of war, violence, poverty and the economy.

Is it possible to imagine a world in which people are encouraged to sharpen their half-thought-out, intuitive political ideas and commitments so as to take more effective political action? There are probably buried sources of political wisdom in many people, particularly those who do not seem likely to function in such a way. I have come more and more to see that one does not have to be politically active or knowledgeable and talkative about politics to have something creative to say. Poets and mystics, introverts, those who eschew politics and those who are ashamed at what they take to be their own ignorance often know something that the more overtly political do not. These anti-political citizens are a great aid in finding out how secret things, childhood experiences, intimate relationships, fantasies (including sexual fantasies), dreams and bodily sensations, may be reframed and turned to useful political ends.

Thinking about those who usually do not say much, I find that they make a profound contribution to what I call 'political clinics'. These are large-group events, often composed of persons who have nothing to do with therapy and psychology at all but come together to explore their emotional and feeling-based reactions to major political themes such as terrorism, the troubles in Northern Ireland, the conflict in the Middle East, racism and homelessness. I have discovered that those who say 'I am not interested in politics' are often deceiving themselves, caught in a reaction formation. As the political clinic unfolds, it becomes clear that they are indeed extremely interested, knowledgeable and wise about politics but have always doubted, because they have been taught to doubt, that the emotional reactions they are experiencing are a legitimate part of political process. We in western countries are taught, not to deny that we have emotions about politics, because that would be impossible, but to put those emotions rather low on the scale of what we value in official political debate and political discussion.

Sometimes at the conclusion of these political clinics, we start to talk in terms of citizens as 'therapists of the world' who have a large set of usable countertransferences to the political cultures in which they live. This idea constitutes an intellectual challenge to much psychological theorizing about citizens, especially in psychoanalysis, wherein the citizen is regarded as a kind of baby, who has a transference and a collection of fantasies toward the 'parental' society in which he or she lives. Turning that around, so that the citizen is seen as a kind of therapist or parent figure for the society, can have a radical, uplifting and empowering effect, overturning the tradition especially in psychoanalysis (for example, Richards 1984) in which the citizen is seen as the baby and society as the parent. This claim, that the citizen is capable of being the therapist (parent) of the world, is one that embodies many possibilities as we struggle to work out what functions citizens might perform in a society in which their voices are distorted by the mass media and their internal lives unfold in a highly fraught political climate dominated by corporations and cartels.

Transformative politics

Politics is slowly changing in western countries and we are at a very interesting moment in political consciousness. What used to be an elitist insight about how everything is secretly political is now becoming an element in mass awareness. For years now, feminists, academics, intellectuals and some therapists and analysts have lived happily with the idea that our personal, psychological and private worlds are full of political tensions, dynamics and energies. But, actually, this has been a superior form of knowing, a political gnosticism. We knew that politics has expanded its definition to include all the private stuff, but the masses did not. They have continued to be taught (but many now accept it less) that politics means official politics, party politics, congressional or parliamentary politics, power politics, the politics that money can buy and so on. What helped to accelerate the democratization of the personal-is-political insight were the huge eruptions of feelings about certain events or political trends in recent years, turning those events into what can be called archetypal or at least numinous experiences: I am thinking of disparate phenomena, ranging from grief at the death of Princess Diana, to global anger at the role of the United States in world politics, to intense debates about the role of women in societies across the planet. The most ruthlessly successful contemporary politicians (such as Tony Blair) have perceived this move into general awareness of the elitist, gnostic, private knowledge about how politics has changed and they now couch their utterances in the language of the emotions.

Another way in which politics has changed is that it has become more of a transformative process. By this I mean that engagement in political activity and processes of personal growth and development are seen increasingly as the same thing, or at least as the two sides of a coin. If one interviews people active in post-Seattle politics, in the environmental movements, in certain sectors of feminism or the men's movement or in ethnopolitics, one sees that what they are doing is in many respects self-healing in a positive sense that is familiar to psychotherapists. So politics starts to carry an overtly psychological, transformative burden. Sadly, this kind of transformative politics is not only progressive and left leaning, but it can also be spotted in many right-wing and reactionary movements, as the recent US election showed.

A third way in which politics has changed is that there is now something that can be called 'political energy' to be considered along with political power. Political power is what you would imagine it to be: control over resources such as land, water, oil – or indeed, information and imagery. Especially today, the issue of who controls information and imagery (for instance, on the internet and on television) is almost as important as the issue of who controls oil or water. Political power is held by those you would expect to hold it: men, white people, the middle and upper middle classes and those who run the big institutions of finance, the military and the academic and professional worlds, including the world of mental health.

Political energy is different. It is almost the opposite of political power. Political energy involves idealism and an imaginative and visionary focus on certain political problems with a view to making a creative impact on those problems (not necessarily with the goal of solving them). Political energy seeks more political energy, attempting to build to critical mass. It is different from political power because those who have political energy, imagination, commitment, idealism and real compassion almost by definition lack political power. Conversely, in contemporary societies, those who have political power tend to lack political energy. This is a fundamental and radical claim that I am sure will be much disputed.

Indeed, the very idea of political energy will upset some intellectual applecarts, because most analysts cannot entertain this notion. In their view, energy does not exist; it is only a mechanistic 19th-century way of looking at things. But there seems to be a possible middle position in which energy, in the sense of psychic energy, is maintained simultaneously both to exist and not to exist.

Jung suggested that, contra Freud's conception of libido, there is a neutral form of psychic energy that can run down various biological, psychological, spiritual and moral channels. My proposal is that there is also a social channel and that a subset of the social channel will have to do with politics and political energy. As indicated just now, I use the term energy in both a metaphorical and a literal sense.

Jung's idea that there is a specifically moral channel for psychic energy is extremely interesting, resonating with much evolutionary, ethological, genetic and psychoanalytic thought – Klein's idea of an innate superego; Winnicott's insistence that children have an inborn sense of guilt and hence are not born amoral; Milner's counsel that we stop seeing morality solely as something implanted in children by parents and society. Freud foreshadowed this train of thought with his remarks about the innate disposition of the self-preservation instincts to become more socially oriented (Freud 1905: 176). (See Samuels 1989: 194–215 for a fuller discussion of 'original morality'.)

People with political energy are doing something rather new and different in the western world today in comparison with what those who have political power are doing. This thought can be liberatory if you are working in a small neighbourhood group, in a social and political project with limited resources and support or with people who have been abused or if you are trying to build an environmentally informed movement for sustainable development and worldwide economic justice. If you are doing any or all of these things, then you probably do not have much power and it is very easy to judge yourself the way that the conventional political world might judge you: as a waste of time and space when it comes to real politics.

But the very notion of political energy is intended to shift this way of thinking. Very often when I talk about this, people say (as they did, for example, at a conference in Belo Horizonte, Brazil, in 2000), 'Yes and we wonder what would happen if our country valued political energy as much as it values political power.'

If political energy is not to be found in the sites of official politics, then where may we find it? Politics has left its home base and gone out into the world to redefine itself and find other and new places to settle. I am not advocating removing political energy from moribund formal institutions; this has been happening in western societies anyway over many years in one of the most significant sociocultural and collective psychological shifts to take place in the developed countries since the end of World War II. A striking feature of the past 20 years in such societies has been the spontaneous growth of new social and cultural networks. More and more people are now involved in such networks, increasingly aware that what they are doing may be regarded as political. The contemporary elasticity in our definition of politics is not something that has been worked out by intellectuals. Neither has there been a concerted effort to achieve such a shift, because the new social movements operate in isolation from each other. Yet, as we have found in the St James's Alliance discussed previously, they have something psychological in common. They share an emotional rejection of big politics – its pomposity and self-interest, its mendacity and complacency. They share a *Weltanschauung* and set of values based on ideas of living intelligible and purposeful lives in spite of the massive social and financial forces that work against intelligibility and purpose. Such new social changes include environmentalism; the formation of groups working for the rights of ethnic and sexual minorities, animal liberation, complementary medicine; spiritual and religious groups devoted to paganism and neo-paganism; rock and other kinds of music and art; finding God in the new physics; an explosive growth in the participation in sports; organic farming; and psychoanalysis, psychotherapy and counselling.

Elsewhere (Samuels 1993) I referred to the social movements as participating in a 'resacralization' of politics. Sacral means holy and the intent was to pick up on the attempt to get a sense of purpose, decency, aspiration and meaning back into political culture. When I consider attempts by analysts and psychotherapists to do their bit, I have no alternative but to count us as part of this general, worldwide resacralizing movement. Psychotherapists may want to be different and special, but in our attempts to work the borders between psychotherapy and society, we are part of something bigger, even if the rhetoric sometimes feels too New Age-y. Psychotherapists tend to share with other resacralizers a sense of disgust with present politics and politicians. In political clinics, this is often an actual physical disgust involving the gagging reflex, an ancient part of the nervous system that is absolutely necessary for survival in a world full of tangible and metaphorical toxins.

Let me conclude this section by accepting that a transformation of politics is not going to happen in any kind of simple or speedy way and, indeed, may not happen at all. There is an impossibility to the whole project because the social realm is as inherently uncontrollable as the drives and images of the inner world and the unconscious. Once human desire enters a social system – as it always will – that system cannot function predictably. There are no final solutions to social questions. The social issues that face western societies are as incorrigible, as unresponsive to treatment, as the psychological issues that individuals face.

Moreover, many will dispute that the cumulative public significances of these movements is positive. It can be argued that the proliferation of new networks and cultural practices is merely a further symptom of social malaise, a selfish retreat into personal, individual preoccupations, reflecting an abandonment of the aspiration to truly political values. It can also be pointed out that reactionary, fundamentalist, religious movements can be seen as attempting, in their own rather different terms, a form of resacralization. But what gets highlighted when religious fundamentalism is brought into the picture is the vastness of the energy pool available for the political reforms that are urgently needed.

Can therapists really make a difference?

Although I am enthusiastic about psychotherapy's role in the refreshing of political culture, I am also somewhat sceptical. So my answer to the question 'Can therapists really make a difference?' is both 'No' and 'Yes'. Let us deal with 'No' first, with the pessimism. James Hillman and Michael Ventura (1992) wrote a book called *We've Had a Hundred Years of*

Psychotherapy – and the World's Getting Worse. It is fairly clear what they were getting at: that psychotherapy makes little or no impact on an unjust world and that persons in therapy are cut off from taking responsibility for ame-liorating injustice (cut off from their political energy by therapy, which takes all available psychic energy for its own project of personal explo-ration). Yet I think that a much more accurate title for their book would have been *We've Had a Hundred Years of Psychotherapy, Trying to Improve the World, but the World has Stayed Pretty Much the Same*, because it is not new for psychotherapists to want to do something in relation to the world (Foster *et al.* 1996; Totton 2000). Freud wanted it, Jung wanted it and the great pioneers of humanistic psychotherapy, such as Maslow, Rogers and Perls, all wanted it as well. All these people and their followers invited the world into therapy, but the world didn't show up for its first session. There are good reasons that the world didn't show up, other than mere resistance. One reason is that therapists so much want and need to be right. (Me, too – this shadow issue of the analyst's maddening rectitude is not one I pretend to have fully dealt with.) Therapists want to reduce everything to the special knowledge that they have. This kind of reductionism gives therapy a bad name when it comes to political and social issues. For example, I remember reading in the *Guardian* an article, later the object of intense ridicule, by a Kleinian psychoanalyst about the phallic symbolism of cruise missiles going down ventilator shafts in Baghdad. My Jungian colleagues are just as bad when they tell us that the military–industrial complex is all the responsibil-ity of the Greek god, Hephaestos. The world will not listen to that level of explanation from psychotherapists and is right not to. The priority for psychotherapists is to embark on multidisciplinary work.

But other issues besides therapy reductionism have stopped us from being useful outside a few specific areas such as psychoanalytically influ-enced social casework or, in some countries, child welfare legislation. Overall, there is a fairly bad record to own up to. Psychotherapists have col-luded with oppressive regimes in Nazi Germany, the former Soviet Union, Argentina and South Africa. We have been involved in dubious activities such as sending soldiers suffering from shell shock and battle fatigue back to the line of battle in both world wars. There is also the ever-present col-lusion of many psychotherapists with all manner of normative and oppres-sive practices, ranging from the psychopathological stigmatization of lesbians and gay men (which still continues in many implicit ways in a wide range of locations: Davies and Neal 2000; Magee and Miller 1997). And therapists all over the world easily join in right-wing politicians' attacks on father-lacking lone-parent families. According to the right-wing reading, these families, totally responsible for spoiling our wonderful world, only need a father or father figure to come back and sort them out. I love fathers and was one of the first to write about what good-enough fathers actually do, especially with their bodies, to further the sexual, aggressive and spiritual development of their children (e.g. Samuels 1986, 1989, 1993, 1996, 2001). But I utterly loathe the damaging idealization of fathers that so many western politicians have gone in for, backed by complacent analysts, therapists and other mental health professionals.

Then there is the problematic matter of psychotherapy's implicit claim that western androcentric, middle-class values and ways of thinking hold and have value universally and are superior to/should be imposed on the values and ways of thinking of non-western cultures (M.V. Adams 1996; Kareem and Littlewood 1992; Luepnitz 1988). Clearly, these unspoken assumptions reflect the typical caseloads of analysts and therapists, especially in private practice, in many countries (but see Altman 1995). The treatment of women in much psychoanalytic thinking and practice has also been damaging to some. The rise of feminist and gender-sensitive psychotherapy has had an important impact in ameliorating this situation (for example, Eichenbaum and Orbach 1982). And what a lot of therapists and analysts say about men is also beginning to receive the same kind of critique that definitions of and generalizations about women used to receive.

Another reason that people are not so likely to listen to therapists who want to make a difference in the world is that therapists are completely crazy in their own professional politics and the way they organize themselves radiates that craziness. No profession has been quite as subject to splits as the therapy profession; no profession has so frequently used personal demonization and pathological pigeonholing to deal with and get rid of troublesome outsiders and those who question from within (Turkle 1979).

As I continue to look at why we world-oriented therapists do not have a client, I note that – for reasons I do not fully understand even now – the therapy world has tragically split its clinical project off from its sociocritical project. Frankfurt school writers and Lacanian theorists rarely talk of clients or in an ordinary way about people: mothers, fathers, families, marriages, dreams, symptoms, sexuality, aggression, the inner world of the imagination. And when we read most clinical texts, the external world is hardly mentioned. Much therapy still seems (or claims) to take place in a political vacuum. There are several delusional aspects of this virginal fantasy about what we do. One delusion is that there are no politics going on in the session itself, whereas many clinicians know how the power dynamics and imbalances of the typical therapy setup cannot be wished away by reference to parental transference or the law of the father. These power imbalances often involve the denial of difference of any kind between therapist and client, the bending of the client to the moral will of the therapist and the ongoing scandal of sexual misconduct (Samuels 1996).

Another delusion is that it is not possible to find a responsible way to work directly with political, social and cultural material in the clinical session. There is not sufficient space here for a full discussion of this topic (but see Samuels 1997, 1999a). Succinctly, my position is that it is time to think *together* about how we can change our practices and our thinking about clinical work in order to incorporate these taboo themes. To explore empirically what has been happening at the interface of psychotherapy and politics in the actual session, I surveyed 2000 analysts and therapists of many schools worldwide about which political issues their clients mentioned in therapy, how frequently the clients raised such issues, whether such mentions were increasing or decreasing and how the therapists reacted. Approximately 700 responded. I also asked the respondents about their own political views and histories. The survey revealed that the therapy profession is far more politically sensitive than one would think and that politics is a welcome theme in a significant minority of clinical offices. (It underlined the importance of shopping around for and interviewing a potential analyst or therapist.) The answers to the questions about which political and social issues are raised (published in Samuels 1993, 1994) also made it clear that clients are raising economic, environmental and gender-political issues (including issues that do not seem to affect them personally) in their therapy sessions much more than they used to. The respondents clearly wanted to honour and respond to this development, but almost all admitted that they lacked training, helpful texts and general encouragement to do it on a regular, professional, reputable basis. In fact, many felt that it would be regarded as bad practice, even though they wanted very much to engage more expertly with such material when clients bring it to the session.

There is a big difference between a mutual exploration of some huge external event that has dominated everyone's lives (such as the terrorist attacks on September 11 2001) and struggling to develop ongoing, ordinary ways of working in the session with the client's political selfhood (and that of the therapist) as it has evolved over a lifetime. Although it can be a fascinating and important moment in any therapy, responding to the impact on the analysis of a moment of high political drama that has affected everyone is not the same as extending what we regard as contemporary good practice to include all aspects of work on the political dimensions of experience. For example, the Psychoanalytic Dialogues' symposium entitled 'Reflections on September 11, 2001' (2003), although moving and insightful, did not refer to an ongoing need to develop clinical principles by which to explore the transformative aspects of what I call political discussion within the sealed vessel of an ordinary therapy relationship. Such work might include (but not be restricted to) the following:

1   exploration of the role played by the joint immersion in the social order on the part of analyst and client in making relationality possible in the first place, whether at a conscious level or at that of unconscious-to-unconscious communication: citizenship facilitating countertransference

2   considering the functioning of nonpersonal fields that cause distress in individuals who are not personally affected, for example, economic injustice, species depletion, domestic violence (my experience being that the strongest imaginable affects, disturbances in self-image and psychological conditions such as depression involve aetiologies at least partly rooted in such nonpersonal fields)

3   refining technique so as to work out ways of managing states in the analyst that are difficult to manage due to the presence of political viewpoints in the client that feel offensive, upsetting or disagreeable to the analyst (we all work with people whom we sometimes find unpleasant and we can build on this capacity so as to encompass our responses to what we find personally unpleasant in the political positions held by the client).

The inner politician

Where did your own politics originate? I think this is a question worth asking. What influence did your mother have on the politics you now have? Or your father? And what about differences between your parents in political outlook? Some people have been influenced in their political development by significant others in their lives, such as teachers, clergy, older friends at school. Were you? Your gender is really very significant in the kind of attitude to politics that you have and your sexual orientation is equally important. Lesbians and gay men live more closely to the political aspects and nuances of life than straight people do. Class and socioeconomic factors are obviously central, too, and so is ethnic, religious and national background. In western societies, the feeling of being oppressed by a domestic tyrant, whether male or female, or of seeing other family members as oppressed, can give rise to a sharp sense of injustice and embryonic revolutionary feelings.

Sometimes when I talk to people about what has formed their politics, they start to speak about an event or moment that they remember, their first political memory, the first time they became aware that there is a political system with power at its core, including disparities of wealth and influence. Did you explore these first political memories with your own analyst?

Another way to look at the notion of the inner politician is to imagine a political energy scale on which 10 stands for political fanaticism, even martyrdom and zero stands for absolute passivity, a total lack of interest in politics. Where would you place yourself right now in your life – what level of political energy do you have? Play around with the scale. When you're with people of the same sex, does the energy level go up or down or stay the same? Is it higher at home or at work? Are there some issues that send it skyrocketing and some that bring it down? Think of the last big interpersonal disagreement or fight with someone you love. Could it be that there was a different level of political energy at work in each of you?

Let us take this thinking right into the traditional heartland of psychotherapy. What was your mother's level of political energy compared with yours, or with your father's? What was your level compared with the typical level of those from the street or neighbourhood where you grew up?

Continuing to sketch the inner politician, I come to the question of political style. I have noticed in my conflict resolution work that those in conflict are often operating not only with very different levels of political energy, but also with very different political styles. Hence, in my work as a political consultant, I am using the idea of conflicting political styles in many settings. My inspiration in overall terms was Jung's model of psychological types: extroversion, introversion, thinking, feeling, sensation, intuition. As in life generally, for a variety of reasons (some having to do with personal backgrounds, some with inborn political constitutions), people live out the political aspects of themselves in different ways. Some are violent terrorists; some are pacifists. Some want empirical backup for their ideas; others prefer to fly by the seat of their pants. Some definitely enjoy cooperative political activity; others will suffer the nightmare of working in a group only because they passionately believe in the ends being pursued. As we begin to work out a psychologically driven transformative politics, let us not make the mistake of insisting that everyone do it in precisely the same way. If we are to promote political creativity, we need to value and honour diverse political styles and types and to think of ways of protecting such diversity. (I am indebted to Muriel Dimen [2002, personal communication] for the observation that political style and self-state have something in common as approaches to the diversity of personality.)

As I mentioned, the notion of political style is useful when addressing conflict, whether interpersonal or within organizations, or even between nations or parts of nations. Just as introverts and extroverts suffer from mutual incomprehension, people who employ a particular political style often have very little understanding of how others or other groups are actually doing their politics. This is not to say that political content *per se* is irrelevant, only that there may be more that divides opponents than their different views.

One might list words that evoke images of differing political types as follows, in a spectrum ranging from active styles to passive ones: warrior, terrorist, exhibitionist, leader, activist, parent, follower, child, martyr, victim, trickster, healer, analyst, negotiator, bridge builder, diplomat, philosopher, mystic, ostrich.

When working on questions of political style, it is not necessary to encourage anyone to stick to just one style. In fact, the opposite is true. The context in which the politics in question is taking place needs to be borne in mind. Some people will use one political style in one setting and quite another in a different one. A negotiator at work may be a terrorist at home. Some may have a superior political style, an inferior political style and auxiliary styles, to borrow the words of Jung's typological schema. Thus, a warrior may have neglected her philosopher or a diplomat his activist.

This approach was partially fashioned on the basis of my work with a mixed group of Israeli Arabs and Israelis of Jewish background in Jerusalem in the early 1990s. It became clear that, aside from the obvious irreconcilable differences in how the Middle East political scene was understood, there were individuals on both sides of the divide who were participating in the group in very similar or identical ways. I pointed this out and reorganized the spatiality and seating plan of the group along style lines rather than content lines. There were discernible improvements in comprehension and even, to a limited extent, in goodwill. The warring factions were presented not with an analysis of what they were saying (that came later), but with a panorama of the ways in which they were saying it, that is to say, with the style of politics they were using.

I have also found the same approach useful in addressing organizational and theoretical disputes in the psychotherapy field and, most recently, in work with senior administrators in Britain's beleaguered National Health Service.

Psychotherapy, politics and spirituality

Attempts are constantly made to improve things in the political world, usually by redistributing wealth or changing legislative and constitutional structures or defusing warlike situations. It is not that nothing is being tried to make things better. Equally vigorous attempts are made to resist and to contest such changes and most social systems have a gigantic, impersonal capacity to resist change anyway. But projects of reform are valuable and necessary and generate their own psychological changes. For example, the consequences of fair and effective minimum wage legislation or devolving power to the regions of a country or amending the constitution would have effects that would show up on any national emotional audit.

But a materialist approach deriving exclusively from economics or one that depends solely on altering the structures of the state will not refresh those parts of the individual citizen that a psychological perspective can reach. Our disappointment at liberal democracy's failure to deliver the spiritual goods and our growing realization that there are limits to what can be achieved by economic redistribution or altering constitutional structures, strengthen my overall argument: something is missing in contemporary western politics, something that involves a calamitous denial of the secret life at its core. We can change the clothes and shift the pieces around, but the spectre that haunts materialist and constitutional moves in the political world is that they only ruffle the surface. They do not (because alone they cannot) bring about the transformations for which the political soul yearns.

The perspectives advocated here may never, ever be applied to our political culture. Everything psychotherapists and analysts have said or done may fail to make one iota of difference in the condition of the world. So I conclude with a few words about failure by Samuel Beckett, who lived and struggled as intensely as anyone with what it might mean to be a good-enough citizen, involving a profound acceptance of the need to go on in the face of not being able to go on: 'No matter. Fail again. Fail better.'

2 Societal trauma: democracy in danger
Sandra Bloom

Introduction

The overly simplistic explanations of human behaviour that guide so many organizational and political decisions regularly fail to take into account one of the most important determining factors in human experience – the presence throughout human history of exposure to overwhelming, repetitive, multigenerational traumatic experiences and the potentially negative impact of those experiences on individual, group and political processes.

The last 20 years have seen the birth of a new way of understanding human behavioural pathology from a complex biopsychosocial and existential viewpoint that we call 'trauma theory'. Trauma theory establishes a more coherent, scientifically grounded and complex chain of cause and effect for human behaviour that enables interconnections of meaning between individuals, groups and political systems without necessarily sacrificing centuries of established wisdom. Trauma theory makes it clear that individual, social and political policy decisions are intimately connected to people's experience of – and exposure to – traumatic experience. The field of traumatic stress studies has arisen out of advocacy and a global movement toward guarantees of basic human rights and for those working with trauma survivors, the personal and the political are irrevocably connected (Bloom 2000).

Trauma theory is grounded in an exploration of the evolved biological responses to overwhelming stress. Failing to recognize that as human beings we are still profoundly affected by our evolutionary roots, including the powerful evolutionary pressure of group behaviour, puts us at the mercy of unconscious forces that can be exceedingly destructive. Leaders and the people they lead may be guided – or driven – by rational self-interest, by economic considerations, by greed and the other deadly sins. But deeper, instinctual forces also drive individual and group behaviour. The study of traumatic stress has expanded our understanding of those unconscious – or less than fully conscious – forces that impact individuals and groups and may also help shed some much needed light onto the political stage as well.

In this chapter, we will look at the parallel processes that develop between stressed individuals, the groups that they form and the societies that result. Leaders stand at the interface between these levels of social organization, representing, simultaneously, their own development as individuals and the needs, both conscious and unconscious, of the group or groups they represent. Under conditions of great stress, the behaviour of leaders will be greatly determined by the impact of stressful conditions on them and the people they govern. Likewise, crisis provides an opportunity for leaders to actively manipulate the emotions and behaviour of the group to help them carry forth their own agendas.

The parallel-process nature of traumatic reality is a particularly important issue in today's world where entire cultures may be profoundly traumatized. Trauma shatters basic assumptions and in the unstable period immediately after such an event, individual, organizational and national decisions may be made that alter destinies and fortunes (Janoff-Bulman 1992). Since September 11 2001 the United States has offered an opportunity to witness the post-traumatic uses and abuses of fear at the hands of people in power and the threat that this poses for democracy. In the long term, the negative impact of exposure to trauma can severely impair individual and organizational skills necessary for the exercise of democratic processes.

Understanding the impact of acute trauma

Individual response to immediate danger

The stress response is a total body–mind mobilization of resources (Horowitz 2003). Powerful neurochemicals flood our brain and body in service of survival. Our attention becomes riveted on the potential threat and our capacity for reasoning and exercising judgement is negatively impacted by rising anxiety and fear. Decision making becomes dichotomous and extremist, providing us with a minimum of possible options for action and thereby increasing the odds of survival by decreasing the time it takes to actually make a decision (Janis 1982). In this heightened state of aggressive preparedness, defensive action is more likely to be violent. Taking action appears to be the only solution to this extraordinary experience of tension, so we are compelled to act on the impulses that often guide us to aggressively defend ourselves rather than to run away (Bloom 2003).

More closely resembling our animal ancestors, we become less attentive to words and far more focused on threat-related signals in the environment – all the nonverbal content of communication. As fear rises, we may lose language functions altogether as the verbal centres of the brain become compromised: a phenomenon recognized as 'speechless terror' (Van der Kolk *et al.* 2001). Without language, we can take in vital information only in nonverbal form – through our physical, emotional and sensory experiences – elements Bion termed 'beta elements', by which he meant the sensory impressions that remain in their raw state, unsymbolized and unable to be thought about or sublimated (Biram 2003). As the level of arousal increases, 'dissociation' – the loss of integrated function of memory, sensation, perception and identity – may be triggered as an adaptive response to this hyperaroused state, physiologically buffering the central nervous system and the body by lowering heart rate and reducing anxiety and pain while simultaneously shutting off troubling feelings, memories or thoughts about unfolding events, including even ethical standards for behaviour. This internal state of 'freeze' helps to temporarily reduce the overwhelming nature of the stress response and allows us to stay calm and function rather than experience emotions that are more than we can bear.

Each episode of danger connects to every other episode of danger in our minds, so that the more danger we are exposed to, the more sensitive we are to danger. With each experience of fight–flight–freeze, our mind forms a network of connections that is triggered with every new threatening experience. If people are exposed to danger repeatedly, their bodies become unusually sensitive so that even minor threats can trigger this sequence of physical, emotional and cognitive responses. We can do nothing to control this reaction – it is a biological, in-built response, a protective device that only goes wrong if we are exposed to too much danger and too little protection.

When overly stressed, human beings cannot think clearly; neither can we consider the long-range consequences of behaviour. It is impossible to weigh all the possible options before making a decision or to take the time to obtain all the necessary information that goes into making good decisions (Janis and Mann 1977). Decisions tend to be based on impulse and on a perceived need to self-protect. As a consequence, such decisions are inflexible, oversimplified, extremist, directed towards aggressive action and often very poorly constructed (Janis 1982). This tendency toward extremist thinking will be exacerbated in those individuals who are have strong authoritarian personality traits because they are unlikely to examine existing evidence, think critically about what they are experiencing, or reach independent conclusions (Altemeyer 1996). This state of extreme hyperarousal associated with stress serves a protective function during the emergency, preparing us to respond automatically and aggressively to any perceived threat, preferentially steering us toward action and away from the time-consuming effort of thought and language.

Group response to immediate danger

Under severe stress, if our powerful fear-driven emotional responses are not buffered by others through social contact and physical touch, our central nervous system is left exposed to unrelenting over-stimulation. This reaction can do long-lasting harm to our bodies as well as our psyches. As a buffer against such danger, human beings developed a network of attachment relationships, living in extended kinship groups throughout most of our evolutionary developmental period. Our capacity to manage overwhelming emotional states is shaped by our experience with early childhood attachments and is maintained throughout life by our attachment relationships. This development of extended social networks increased the likelihood that vulnerable offspring would be protected and, in combination with our expanding intelligence, made hunting and food gathering far more successful. Threat triggers an increase in social bonding. Under threat, human beings will more closely bond together with their identified group, close ranks and prepare for defence of the group.

A leader rapidly emerges within such a group, a complex process that is an interaction between the individual characteristics of the leader, the needs of the group and the contextual demands of the moment. Under such conditions, the vast majority of human beings become more suggestible to the influence of a persuasive, charismatic, strong, assertive and apparently confident leader who promises the best defence of the group, thereby containing the overwhelming anxiety of every member of the group (Cohen *et al.* 2004). In this manner, stress favours authoritarian social structures because, as research has demonstrated, individuals who are high in authoritarian traits are more likely to readily submit to legitimate authority figures (Altemeyer 1996).

In this state it is difficult for the members of a stressed group to discern the difference between a confident, intelligent leader and an arrogant blowhard and those with authoritarian dispositions are unlikely to question anyone who has the outer trappings of legitimacy. This is particularly true when a social group is at a point in its history when it has lost confidence in the old solutions to life problems, generating a state of helplessness and uncertainty (Werbart 2000). Decisions are made quickly, often autonomously, by the leader with relatively little input and the input that the leader receives is likely to be significantly coloured by the pressure everyone feels to conform to standards of group cohesion and unanimity. As stress increases, the leader is compelled to take action to reduce the threat while the followers simultaneously become more obedient to the leader in order to ensure coordinated group effort.

However, even with stern authoritarian leadership, individual and group conflict and competitive strivings are always present in a group and pose a threat to rapid, unified action. Therefore, efforts must be made to minimize the normal tensions, conflicts and aggressive behaviours that inevitably arise and that are exacerbated by the stress response itself. The group solution is to find an external enemy on which the group can project its own negative emotions and desires in service of group cohesion. The aggression of those individuals with strongly authoritarian personality traits can be most easily directed by authority figures against any perceived enemy (Altemeyer 1996). The greater the consistency between this psychosocial need and actual events, the easier it becomes to define friend and foe. The greater the perceived differences between 'us' and 'them', the greater the ease in labelling the enemy and doing whatever it takes to defend 'us'. The greater the previous injury experienced by the group at the hands of the enemy, the easier it is to flame the fires of revenge. Under conditions that provoke fear of death, stereotyped images of the enemy are likely to be even more fervently clung to by a threatened group (Schimel *et al*. 1999; Volkan 2002).

When danger is real and present, effective leaders take charge and give commands that are obeyed by obedient followers, thus harnessing and directing the combined power of many individuals in service of group survival. The basic programming for social functioning is 'tit-for-tat' and therefore, within the human species, a desire to seek revenge for real or perceived injury is a powerful motive force. The leader mobilizes the shared group need to wreak vengeance and directs these powerful forces toward attack on the perceived enemy. Longstanding interpersonal conflicts seem to evaporate and everyone pulls together toward the common goal of group survival, producing an exhilarating and even intoxicating state of unity, oneness and a willingness to sacrifice one's own well-being for the sake of the group. This is a survival strategy ensuring that, in a state of crisis, decisions can be made quickly and efficiently, thus better ensuring survival of the group, even while individuals may be sacrificed. Fears of mortality are buffered through a strengthened allegiance to whatever ideological framework the culture endorses, be it religious, philosophical or political and anyone who threatens to undermine or criticize that framework is considered deviant, if not dangerous, and is likely be forcefully extruded from the group (Bloom 2004a, b; Pyszczynski *et al*. 2003).

When fear becomes chronic

Individual response to chronic threat

The human stress response is an evolutionarily designed survival strategy that is extraordinarily effective under the conditions for which it was originally designed. The tragedy is that human beings are no longer particularly well suited to the environments we have created for ourselves, environments within which our most dangerous enemies are frequently members of our own families, while the institutions we have created to sustain and protect us often turn out to be the engines of our own destruction.

The tragedy of this magnificent evolutionary success for the individual emerges most fully when a human being is repeatedly traumatized, particularly when that exposure begins in childhood. Under such conditions, these evolutionary mechanisms that are so adapted to human survival become dangerous threats and impediments to further growth. After prolonged and/or repetitive exposure to serious stressors, the brain becomes hypersensitive, a state now recognized as *chronic hyperarousal*. In this state, people may perceive danger everywhere, even when there is no real danger, because their body is signalling the arousal response to even minor provocation. As a result, their ability to think clearly and rationally can be chronically and erratically impaired.

Although the fight–flight–freeze state of physiological hyperarousal serves a vital survival purpose in times of danger, when hyperarousal stops being a state and turns into a trait, human beings lose their capacity to accurately assess and predict danger, leading to avoidance and reenactment instead of adaptation and survival (Perry and Pate 1994). Prolonged hyperarousal can have disastrous physical effects as our biological systems become progressively exhausted. Hyperarousal leaves us physically and emotionally exhausted, burdened with hair-trigger tempers, irritability and a tendency to perpetuate violence. Our need to rescue ourselves from this untenable physiological state means that we will do anything, use any device, to calm ourselves down. If we cannot get relief from our fellow humans, we will turn to any substance or behaviour that does bring relief.

Childhood exposure to trauma, particularly repetitive exposure to interpersonal violence such as sexual abuse, has even more dire consequences than when an adult experiences a traumatic event for the first time. Children's brains are still forming. The release of powerful neurohormones, particularly during critical and sensitive moments in development, is thought to have such a profound impact on the developing brain that the brain may organize itself around the traumatic event in a 'use it or lose it' strategy (Perry *et al.* 1996). High-quality decision making may never develop and, instead, extremist thinking prevails, frequently accompanied by a willingness to uncritically accept the opinions of established authority. Attention to threat remains chronic and therefore all kinds of information not considered threatening are unlikely to be integrated or synthesized. Aggression becomes chronic and may become the preferred method for dealing with any kind of stress, even the stress of uncertainty or confusion. Dissociation may also become chronic, with progressive fragmentation of important mental functions and bodies of information paired with an inability to put feelings into words (*alexithymia*) and a tendency to act out distressing feelings instead (Krystal 1988).

Perhaps the most tragic element of the human response to chronic threat resides in the human capacity to adjust to adverse conditions, the consequence of which may be to inadvertently repeat a traumatic past. Fear precipitates the compulsion to fight or flee but when you can do neither, the biologically induced state of hyperarousal with its accompanying feelings of fear and aggression is toxic to mind and body. Like animals in a cage, with enough exposure to helplessness, human beings will adapt to adversity and cease struggling to escape from the toxic situation, thus conserving vital resources and buffering the vulnerable central nervous system against the negative impact of constant overstimulation (Seligman 1992). But later, rather than change situations that could be altered for the better, we will change our definitions of 'normal' to fit the situation to which we have become adapted, regardless of how controlling, abusive or repressive these conditions have become.

'Traumatic reenactment' describes the lingering enactment and automatic repetition of the past related to a history of trauma. It has long been recognized that 'history repeats itself', but never before have we so clearly understood *why* history does so. The very nature of traumatic information processing determines the reenactment behaviour. As human beings, we are meant to function at our maximum level of integration and any barrier to this integration will produce some innate compensatory mechanism that allows us to overcome it. Dissociating traumatic memories and feelings is life saving in the shortterm, but prevents full integration in the long term because the nonverbal images, feelings and sensations remain unintegrated. Assigned no category, no context, no point in time, these fragments of experience intrude on consciousness without warning, haunting the victim who thus remains trapped between the past and the present.

We are destined to reenact what we cannot remember (van der Kolk and Ducey 1989). And, as the reenactment unfolds, the adaptations we have made to cope with the original stressful events compel us to perceive the reenactment as perfectly 'normal' and human beings resist changing anything that feels normal (Bloom in press).

Group response to chronic threat

The tragic nature of human evolution emerges in social systems when groups of individuals develop a group identity – family, tribe, organization or nation – and then are repeatedly threatened by internal or external forces, thus arousing the conditions that lead to family wars, tribal wars, civil wars and international wars. Human beings are fundamentally emotional creatures, innately endowed with a biological system that is hardwired for affective experience. Put human beings together in groups and this effect is multiplied as a result of the powerful force known as 'emotional contagion' (Hatfield *et al.* 1994). A fundamental developmental challenge for all individuals and for all human groups is to learn how to appropriately manage emotional arousal.

How does a group normally 'manage' emotional states? It does so through the normal problem solving, decision making and conflict resolution methods that must exist for any human group to operate effectively. Although most organizations within our society function in a fundamentally hierarchical, top-down manner, in a calm, healthy, well-functioning system there is a certain amount of natural democratic process that occurs in the day-to-day operations of solving group problems, making decisions in teams and resolving conflict among members of the organization. For 99 per cent of the time our species has been on this planet, we lived in small hunter-gatherer clans of 40–50 people and in these groups, the ratio of adults to children under six was at least three to one (Perry 2002). Containing powerful emotions and resolving conflicts within the group were necessary for group survival and in such close quarters as we lived, children had frequent opportunities to watch adults develop effective skills.

The more complex the work demands, the greater the necessity for collaboration and integration and therefore the more likely that a system of teamwork will evolve. For a team to function properly, there must be a certain level of trust among team members who must all share in the establishment of satisfactory group norms. These are the norms that enable the group to: tolerate the normal amount of anxiety that exists among people working on a task; tolerate uncertainty long enough for creative problem solutions to emerge; promote balanced and integrated decision making so that all essential points of view are synthesized; contain and resolve the inevitable conflicts that arise between members of a group; complete its tasks.

For groups, as for individuals, emotions routinely inform the thought processes of the group and are critical to group learning and judgement; therefore group emotional processes must be constructively managed and contained. This is frequently the critical job of leadership. The more at ease the leader is with promoting democratic processes and transparency while minimizing the potentially negative impact of hierarchical structures, the more effective the group problem solving is likely to be. In exerting democratic leadership he or she is thereby reducing the abusive use of power while promoting more creative problem solving and diverse input, enabling the evolution of far more complex strategies. The greater the availability of conflict resolution techniques, the greater the willingness on the part of all group members to engage in, and even welcome, conflict as a stimulant for creativity and change. When there is less conflict avoidance there are likely to be far fewer longstanding and corrosive buried resentments.

In groups under stress, however, this healthier level of function is likely to be sacrificed in service of facing the emergency. Militaristic hierarchies can respond more rapidly and mobilize action to defend against further damage. Leaders give orders and followers follow those orders, uniting a group as one. Problems occur, however, when this emergency state is prolonged or repetitive, problems not dissimilar to those we witness in individuals under chronic stress. Groups can become chronically hyperaroused, functioning in crisis mode, unable to process one difficult experience before another crisis has emerged. Hierarchical structures concentrate power and, in these circumstances, power can easily come to be used abusively and in a way that perpetuates rather than attenuates the concentration of power. Transparency disappears and secrecy increases under this influence. Communication networks become compromised as those in power become more punishing and the likelihood of error is increased as a result. In such a situation, conflicts tend to remain unresolved and tension (and resentment) mount under the surface of everyday group functioning. Helplessness, passivity and passive–aggressive behaviours on the part of the subordinates in the hierarchy increase while leaders become increasingly controlling and punitive. In this way, the organization becomes ever more radically split, with different parts of the organization assuming the role of managing and/or expressing different emotions that are then subsequently suppressed. This is not a situation that leads to individual or organizational health but, rather, to increasing levels of dysfunction and diminished productivity.

The chronic nature of a stressed atmosphere tends to produce a generalized increased level of tension, irritability, short tempers and even abusive behaviour. The urgency to act in order to relieve this tension compromises decision making because group members are unable to weigh and balance multiple options, arrive at compromises and consider long-term consequences of their actions under stress. Decision making in such groups tends to deteriorate with increased numbers of poor and impulsive decisions, compromised problem-solving mechanisms and overly rigid and dichotomous thinking and behaviour. Interpersonal conflicts that were suppressed during the initial crisis return, often with a vengeance, but conflict resolution mechanisms, if ever in place, deteriorate under stress.

Problem solving is also compromised because, under these conditions, group members are likely to turn to leaders who urge action and, in this condition of tension, virtually any action will do to alleviate the immediate need to respond. Extremist thinking tends to dominate discussion. Leaders may become increasingly autocratic and dogmatic, trying to appear calm and assured in front of their subordinates while narrowing their circle of input to a very small group of trusted associates. As the leader becomes more threatened, sensing the insecurity of his decisions and his position, these small groups of associates feel increasingly pressured to conform to whatever the leader wants. In this process, judgement and diversity of opinion are sacrificed in service of group cohesion and, as this occurs, the quality of decision making becomes progressively compromised, an insidious process that has been termed 'groupthink' (Janis 1983).

Under conditions of chronic threat, escalating control measures are used to repress any dissent that is felt to be dangerous to the unity of what has become focused group purpose, seemingly connected to survival threats. This encourages a narrowing of input from the world outside the organization. It also encourages the development of split-off and rivalrous dissenting subgroups within the group who may passive–aggressively or openly subvert group goals. As group cohesion begins to wane, leaders may experience the relaxing of control measures as a threat to organizational purpose and safety. They may therefore attempt to mobilize increasing projection onto the designated external enemy who serves a useful purpose in activating increased group cohesion while simultaneously aggressively suppressing dissent internally. But the suppression of the dissenting minority voice has negative consequences. As dissent is silenced, vital information flow is impeded. As a result, the quality of problem analysis and decision making deteriorates further. If this cycle is not stopped and the group allowed opportunity to recuperate, the result may be a group that becomes as rigid, repetitive and ultimately destructive as do so many chronically stressed individuals (Bloom 2004a, b). In the process, the group will have lost the democratic processes that are so critically important to the ability of the group to respond to complex, ever-changing environments.

The erosion in previously held democratic norms within a group does not happen overnight. There is an insidious process of adjustment and readjustment as control measures are instituted, the numbers of rules and regulations are increased and punitive measures for responding to infractions in these rules are instituted. Because the change is gradual, not sudden, the entire group adjusts to the adverse conditions that are always created in the name of 'safety' or 'security' from some perceived negative environmental force or in order to exert 'control' over negative influences within the corporate body itself. As the changes are accepted they become the new social norms and therefore the very definitions of normal, expectable conduct within the social group change, even while actual behaviour is becoming increasingly aberrant and even ineffective. When someone mentions the fact of the changed norms, about the differences between the way things are now and the way they used to be (when the organization was more functional), the speaker is likely to be silenced or ignored. As a result there is an escalating level of acceptance of increasingly aberrant behaviour toward subordinates and leaders within the in-group as well as the out-group(s). Meanwhile, the past becomes romanticized and calls for stricter 'moral values', defined as the repression of freedoms perceived as dangerous, rise. This necessitates a call for 'purification' from whatever forces are considered to be contaminating group unity (Volkan 2002). Those who believe that the present reality could be changed for a freer, more just and progressive future are first ignored and ridiculed, then labelled as divisive and even dangerous malcontents who should be censured or are simply called naive, absurd 'utopians', wishing for a society that can never exist.

Within a social framework we call memory 'history'. Some modern philosophers believe that all memories are formed and organized within a collective context. According to them, society provides the framework for beliefs, behaviours and the recollections of both (Halbwachs 1992). Later, present circumstances affect what events are remembered as significant. Much of the recording and recalling of memories occurs through social discussion. This shared cohesiveness of memories is part of what defines a culture over time. Shared language also helps a society organize and assimilate memories and, eventually, forget about the events. Individuals are destined to reenact what they cannot remember and so, too, are groups. There is reason to believe that maintaining silence about disturbing collective events may have the counter-effect of making the memory even more potent in its continuing influence on the organization or society much as silent traumatic memories continue to haunt individuals (Pennebaker *et al.* 1997).

Organizations can forget the past just like individuals do and the more traumatic the past, the more likely it is that a group will push memories out of conscious awareness. Corporate amnesia has been defined as the loss of collective experience and accumulated skills usually through the trauma of excessive downsizing and layoffs (NewsBriefs 2000). Analogous to the division in individual memory between verbal, explicit and situational, implicit memory, literature in the corporate world refers to explicit and implicit (or 'tacit') corporate memory, the latter referring to vital, organizationally specific knowledge that is cumulative, slow to diffuse and rooted in the human beings who comprise the organization, in contrast with the explicit corporate memory that is embodied in written documents, policies and procedures. It is this valuable tacit memory that is profoundly disturbed by the loss of personnel in downsizing (Hazell 2000).

Groups can also distort memories of the past as individuals can. Organizations may selectively omit disagreeable facts, may exaggerate or embellish positive deeds, may deny the truth. They may manipulate linkages by focusing on one cause of an event while ignoring or denying other causes. They may exaggerate the misdeeds of an enemy or competitor and minimize the group's own misdeeds toward that very competitor or simply blame 'circumstances' and thereby minimize their own responsibility (Baumeister and Hastings 1997). Groups may engage in what has been termed 'organizational nostalgia' for a golden past that is highly selective and idealized and, when compared to the present state of affairs, surpassingly better. It is a world that is irretrievably lost, with all the sense of inexpressible grief associated with such loss and the present is always comparatively poorer, less sustaining, less fruitful, less promising. In this way the organizational past – whether accurately remembered or not – can continue to exert a powerful influence on the present. In fact, one author has noted that: 'Nostalgia is not a way of coming to terms with the past (as mourning or grief are) but an attempt to come to terms with the present' (Gabriel 1993: 132).

Critical events and group failure change us and change our groups, but without memory – without history – we lose the context. Studies have shown that institutions do have memory and that once interaction patterns have been disrupted, these patterns can be transmitted through an organization so that one 'generation' unconsciously passes on to the next norms that alter the system and every member of the system. But without a conscious memory of events also being passed on, organizational members in the present cannot make adequate judgements about whether the strategy, policy or norm is still appropriate and useful in the present (Menzies 1975). This process can be an extraordinary resistance to healthy group change.

An organization that cannot change, like an individual, will develop patterns of reenactment, repeating the past strategies over and over without recognizing that these strategies are no longer effective. With every repetition there is, instead, further deterioration in functioning. Knowledge about this failing is available but it tends to be felt before it is cognitively appreciated, but without the capacity to put words to feelings a great deal of deterioration may occur before the repetitive and destructive patterns are recognized. Healthier and potentially healing individuals enter the group and may even vie for leadership, but are rapidly extruded as they fail to adjust to the reenactment role that is being demanded of them. Less autonomous individuals may also enter the organization and are drawn into the reenactment pattern. In this way, one autocratic and abusive leader leaves or is thrown out only to be succeeded by another.

Reenactment patterns are especially likely to occur when events in the past have resulted in behaviour that arouses shame or guilt in the group's representatives. Shame and guilt for past misdeeds are especially difficult for individuals and groups to work through. The way a group talks to itself is via communication between various 'voices' of the corporate body. If these voices are silenced or ignored, communication breaks down and is more likely to be acted out through impulse-ridden and destructive behaviour.

Conclusion

Endangering democracy

An evolutionarily based, biological understanding of human behaviour has broad implications for national and international leadership. The world is now so obviously interconnected and ecologically interlinked that destruction of others is, in an increasingly real sense, self-destruction. The need to address repetitive crises is of global concern since every crisis presents us with complex dilemmas. Yet under conditions of national and international stress the quality of thought processes is likely to deteriorate to dichotomous 'good and evil' thinking. All that is required to mobilize aggression and hatred against those defined as enemy is the incitement to vengeance paired with sufficient fear to disarm coherent thought processes. Unable to engage in complex decision making, governmental problem solving becomes compromised, making it more likely that we will turn to leaders who appear strong, decisive and who urge immediate action and a satisfaction of the growing lust for violent action. Unfortunately, such leaders are likely to be charismatic authoritarians, frequently right-wing fundamentalist authoritarians. Authoritarianism is known to increase under the threat of violence and when such an ascendance occurs, critical thinking, the ability to collaborate with others and the search for nonviolent solutions to complex problems are likely to evaporate (Altemeyer 1996).

In a time of national tension, virtually any action will do to alleviate the immediate pressure to respond. Under conditions of stress, we are more likely to be swayed by the influence of a group we are identified with and pressures for conformity increase at the moment when we are most desperately in need of diverse opinions. This leads to an increase in territoriality and aggression that, to some, may feel satisfying in the long run but is likely to compound existing problems. Although intended to decrease the sense of danger and insecurity, premature and poorly considered action tends to increase danger. As leaders focus exclusively on physical security, we may sacrifice other forms of safety and well-being in order to achieve an elusive sense of physical security that remains threatened. Unfortunately, focusing on only physical safety while ignoring the other domains of human existence that constitute sustained security tends to procure exactly what we seek to avoid – more danger.

Using violent means to achieve nonviolent ends is oxymoronic action bound to involve a group in the escalation of ever more dangerous forms of offensive behaviour. As a species we cannot escape our evolutionary heritage, tied as it is to our biological makeup. We can, however, learn to more effectively understand and manage our impulses, desires and instincts.

3   Conflict, competition and aggression
Nick Totton

Introduction

Since its foundation, psychotherapy has discussed conflict between human beings. The themes of those early debates are little different from contemporary discussions, which perhaps suggests how little has been achieved. They boil down to three questions about aggression (without which neither conflict nor competition would be serious problems):

- Is aggression an innate human trait, or is it the product of specific conditions?
- Is aggression wholly negative, or does it have positive aspects and expressions?
- Can therapy contribute either to minimizing aggression or to supporting its positive aspects?

I shall examine the varied answers given to these questions by different theorists within the field of psychotherapy; and also look at the application of these answers to destructive 'isms', such as racism and sexism.

Is aggression innate?

Sigmund Freud saw aggression as both innate and dangerous. *Civilisation and Its Discontents* insists that:

> men are not gentle creatures who want to be loved … they are, on the contrary, creatures among whose instinctual endowments are to be reckoned a powerful share of aggressiveness. … *Homo homini lupus* [man is a wolf to man]. … In consequence of this primary mutual hostility of human beings, civilized society is perpetually threatened with disintegration.
>
> (Freud 1930: 302)

In order to rein in aggression, Freud believed, civilization must repress sexuality and transform its energy into a sort of libidinal social cement. 'Civilized man has exchanged a portion of his possibilities of happiness for a portion of security' (1930: 306). He criticises communists for their social interpretation of aggression: 'Aggressiveness was not created by property. It reigned almost without limit in primitive times … and it already shows itself in the nursery' (304).

Freud's most eloquent contemporary opponent on this issue was Wilhelm Reich, who believed that Freud wrote *Civilisation and Its Discontents* specifically to oppose his own position (Reich 1967: 44). Reich argues that human beings are exactly what Freud says they are not, beings whose 'deepest and most natural feelings' are 'natural decency, sponta-neous honesty, mute and complete feelings of love' (Reich 1983b: 186); we are born to seek the 'natural pleasure of work and activity' (1983b: 8). The violence, malice and hatred that Freud interprets as 'primary mutual hos-tility', Reich ascribes entirely to culture's distortions: 'antisocial actions are the expression of secondary drives' – the intermediate character layer between our superficial, inhibited 'niceness' and our authentic core, 'pro-duced by the suppression of natural life' (1983b: 7).

The contrasting positions of Freud and Reich, with correspondingly contrasting implications for political activism, are the poles between which most other interested psychotherapists have placed themselves. Reich's view of human nature attracted many radicals in the 1960s and 1970s, echoing the 1930s independent thinking of Ian Suttie, who argued in *The Origins of Love and Hate* (1936) that hate and destructiveness are secondary reactions when 'primal love' is threatened and that social and cultural life derive from love itself, not from sublimated sexuality.

Projection

Freud's version of aggression has influenced many attempts by therapists to understand social behaviour. Melanie Klein's theories, in particular, have been taken up by politically interested therapists; she outlines a complex alchemical sequence of introjections and projections, splittings and recom-binations, through which the infant (and the later adult) attempts to manage what she sees as a terrifying 'innate conflict between love and hate' (1975: 180). We try to eliminate our own hate by treating it as *not* ours, but belonging to other people – whom we can then freely hate. 'First we project our destructiveness into others; then we wish to annihilate them without guilt' (Segal 1988: 51).

For Kleinians, the solution is the 'depressive position', where we can integrate our positive and negative feelings. In some ways, this is obviously an unfortunate name for a set of attitudes portrayed as positive and creative; but it does accurately convey something about how Klein views adulthood, as a renunciation of deeply held wishes that she believes to be unrealistic. Reich's attitude then exemplifies the refusal to give up these goals (for an extended critique of Reich along just these lines, see Chasseguet-Smirgel and Grunberger 1986). Samuels strongly disputes the Kleinian view: 'The object-relations consensus suffers from a norm-making enmeshment with the numinous images of the bodily relationship of mother and infant, leading to the moralistic advancement of the depressive position as a nostrum for social and cultural ills' (1993: 285).

Klein links the depressive position with the task of 'reparation' – 'the variety of processes by which the ego feels it undoes harm done in phantasy, restores, preserves and revives objects' (1975: 133). These ideas have been used towards a psychotherapeutic politics that claims to be both radical and realistic, based on a continuous mature compromise between our loving and destructive impulses (Alford 1990; Young 1994: 133ff) and using as a key tool the concepts of projection and of 'projective identification', where not only are unacceptable feelings put onto someone else, but that person also *experiences those feelings as their own*. Social groups facilitate such processes: 'Group helps its members defend against anxiety by sanctioning the projection of internal persecutors outward onto a hated group. At the same time the group heightens individual anxiety' (Alford 1990: 18; cf. Hopper 2003).

These ideas can clearly help us to understand political phenomena such as leadership, scapegoating and xenophobia; we shall consider later how they can help us think about racism and sexism. Perhaps their most highly developed use in a political context has been by the 'psychohistory' movement, which argues that 'leaders are personalities able to become containers for the bizarre projective identifications of group-fantasies' (DeMause 1982: 138) and offers practical tools for analysing this material as it appears in political speeches, writings and cartoons (DeMause 1982: 193–230, 301–17).

Andrew Samuels perceptively critiques Kleinian politics:

> The concept of projective identification, invaluable though it is in many respects, tends to feed into an approach to politics in which the irreducibly social nature of humanity has less prominence. This is because [it] just does not get hold of the collectivity of persons, of where they are already joined together on a psychosocial level, of where things are shared.
>
> (Samuels 1993: 277)

This accurately describes how projective identification is often used. However, one can also see it as encapsulating our ambiguous status as simultaneously individual and collective, with feelings and ideas 'floating' through a family, group or society, creating experiences of both community and alienation. An emphasis on *re-owning* projected material, as for example in Worldwork (see later), suggests the possibility of *non*-projective identification and real collectivity.

Racism, sexism and hatred of difference

The concept of projection is not tied to belief in innate aggression. If we hold that hate and destructiveness are acquired reactions to environmental pressures, we can still use projection and projective identification to understand how these forces operate. In fact, similar and overlapping concepts exist in other therapeutic traditions under different names – for example, the Jungian shadow or the Lacanian Other (see S. Clarke 2003 for an attempt at synthesis).

The black African Franz Fanon employed the concept of the Other in the first serious psychotherapeutic analysis of racism, *Black Skin, White Masks*, in the early 1950s (Fanon 1986), describing how white culture identifies the black man with the 'dark', 'animal' quality it fears in its own sexuality:

> European civilization is characterized by the presence, at the heart of what Jung calls the collective unconscious, of an archetype: an expression of the bad instincts, of the darkness inherent in every ego, of the uncivilized savage, the Negro that slumbers in every black man.
>
> (Fanon 1986: 187)

Fanon's theory has led to a wider picture of how people can project onto difference a broad range of negative psychological material.

> To the extent that we wish to believe that our violence, our greed, our exploitativeness, our passivity, our dependence is 'out there', not 'in here', then the 'other' group, the group that is 'different' can easily come to represent what Harry Stack Sullivan called the 'not me'.
>
> (Altman 2003: 96)

Kovel (1995: 218) describes a process of 'segregated mental essences' – difference as a means of separating out, a psychic ghettoization into different kinds of being: sex roles, gender roles, social roles in general. Along with other writers, notably Rustin (1991), Kovel has clarified the mechanisms involved and linked the psychological aspects of racism to its economic and political aspects – the payoff of racism. Kovel, Rustin and Altman all argue that modern racism's real source is capitalist society's destructive effects on its members, leaving many in need of something onto which to project their own painful feelings.

This approach can be applied equally to other 'isms' that project negativity onto difference, for example, sexism and religious fundamentalism. Kovel argues that 'as the western mentality began to regard itself as homogeneous and purified ... it was also led to assign the negativity inherent in human existence to other peoples' (1995: 212) – women and children as well as non-westerners. What Altman says about blacks applies equally to many other groups:

> To the extent that black people represent the objectified human being, the objectified part of all of us human beings, people defined as black become suitable containers for our sense of oppression and for all aspects of ourselves from which we wish to create distance, from which we wish to disidentify.
>
> (Altman 2003: 96)

Slavoj Zizek's parallel Lacanian account shows how Nazi society used the Jews to represent the 'Real' that it could process:

> Society is not prevented from achieving its full identity because of Jews: it is prevented by its own antagonistic nature, by its own immanent blockage and it 'projects' this internal negativity into the figure of the 'Jew'. In other words, what is excluded from the symbolic (from the frame of the corporatist socio-symbolic order) returns in the Real as a paranoid construction of the 'Jew'.
>
> (Zizek 1989: 127)

He deepens our understanding of what is projected into the Other:

> We always impute to the 'other' an excessive enjoyment: he wants to steal our enjoyment (by ruining our way of life) and/or he has access to some secret perverse enjoyment. In short what really bothers us about the 'other' is the peculiar way he organizes his enjoyment ...: the smell of 'their' food, 'their' noisy songs and dances, 'their' attitude to work.
>
> (Zizek 1993: 202–3)

Racism and sexism are not contingent features of our society, but essential to it, leading to 'a continuous reinstitutionalization of the material basis of racism [and sexism] and a continuous reproduction of racism [and sexism] itself' (Kovel 1995: 218–19), often in new forms and guises. These projections bind a tremendous charge, always liable to explode into violent backlash if challenged. 'The situation in which the subject is split off from the object is highly unstable. The disavowed position is always there, requiring continual warding off' (Altman 2003: 96). The only way forward is to re-own the disavowed position, which is experienced as a threat to hard-won identities.

It is worth noticing that this understanding of 'otherism' also warns us against polarizing our own position as *against* any particular form of bigotry, however tempting this may be. Writers from a therapy perspective can fall into this trap as easily as anyone else:

> The racist defence ... is part of the hatred of all that modernity brings – of its terrors and disconnections, of its promise and its fertile creativity. Racism, consequently, is not just anti-Semitic or anti-black; it is anti-world, anti-desire, anti-modernity itself.
>
> (Frosh 1989: 243)

Stamp out intolerance, in other words!

Beyond the dichotomy

The argument over innate versus acquired aggression can seem very familiar: replaying a traditional debate over Original Sin versus Free Will. In failing to transcend the Judaeo-Christian paradigm, this argument may simply provide another dualistic screen for projection onto difference. As in the equally stuck nature–nurture debate (Ridley 2003), we need to find a way to answer 'both': aggression is both innate and acquired; we are born with a capacity, a potential to fight fire with fire, which will be expressed in different ways and degrees depending on our life circumstances.

This is plain enough: our capacity for rage lets us defend ourselves against attack, our assertiveness and competitiveness are part of any living organism. Recognizing this means withdrawing our negative projection *onto aggression itself*: acknowledging that, although aggression, competition and conflict can and do cause terrible harm, they are not intrinsically evil. For Wilhelm Reich:

> Every positive manifestation of life is aggressive, the act of sexual pleasure as well as the act of destructive hate, the sadistic act as well as the act of procuring food. Aggression is the life expression of the musculature, of the system of movement.
>
> (Reich 1983b: 156)

Fritz Perls correlates aggression with the natural processes of biting and eating (Perls 1969; Perls *et al.* 1973: 386). Aggression contributes to discrimination – chewing things over and biting them off, swallowing and incorporating nourishment and spitting out what we don't like; hence, 'morality and aggression … are essentially linked', both forms of discrimination between 'good' (for me) and 'bad' (for me). Survival and flourishing require aggressive assertion of our boundaries. 'It is not aggression, any more than sex, that is responsible for the neuroses, but the unfortunate organization of aggression that occurs in our institutions and families' (Perls 1955: 33–5).

Similarly Andrew Samuels says 'aggressive competition can be understood as lying at the heart of a pluralistic approach to politics' (Samuels 2001: 176), arguing that just as aggression in relationships is sometimes a clumsy attempt to reconnect, 'aggression, which is so prevalent in modern societies, often masks the deepest need for contact, dialogue, playback, affirmation' (2001: 198); aggression can be 'a politically reparative drive' (Samuels 1993: 56). These more positive versions of aggression imply a positive reading of conflict itself, on personal and political levels, as a necessary precursor to growth through its signal that the current situation is incomplete and needs to change. Thus for Arnold Mindell, 'engaging in heated conflict instead of running away from it is one of the best ways to resolve the divisiveness that prevails on every level of society' (Mindell 1995: 12).

Hence, paradoxically, one of therapy's key contributions is to *affirm* aggression, to *support* conflict, to *speak up for* competition – while also affirming, supporting and speaking up for the victims of alienated and destructive expressions of these qualities. This is the starting point of Mindell's 'Worldwork', perhaps the most dynamic and exciting therapeutic response to conflict so far: 'Value trouble. Accept nature. Make peace with war' (Mindell 1995: 241).

However, we still need an account of cruelty, of oppression, of what Berke (1989) calls 'malice'. How do healthy aggression and competition frequently become vicious and destructive dehumanization of opponents? It is insufficient to say, for example, that competition over resources leads to war; this assumes what it seeks to explain, human capacity for cruelty. Unless we fall back on the concept of innate aggression, a further explanatory tool is needed.

There is now a strong consensus within psychotherapy around the concept of individual and societal trauma (see Chapter 2). Trauma works in two ways to create destructive cruelty: first, through dissociation and disconnection from the world, it attacks empathy founded on embodied presence. And, second, traumatized people or societies try, through projection, to get rid of their own pain and oppression onto the Other, whoever that may be in each situation. I free myself from my internal destroyedness by destroying the enemy. We each have an internal reservoir of bodily violence in our experience of birth, available for this purpose (DeMause 1982).

Several people have studied specific social conflicts as responses to trauma: for example, the ongoing revenge scenarios and ethnic cleansings of former Yugoslavia (de Levita 2000), the similar if less extreme conflict in Northern Ireland (Elliot *et al.* 2004) and the role of collective Holocaust trauma in Israeli treatment of Palestinians (Bunzl and Beit-Hallahmi 2002). It seems that societal trauma can be transmitted through childrearing approaches based on violence, sexual repression and deprivation of tenderness (DeMause 1982; Prescott 1975) and through traumatizing birthing procedures (DeMause 1982; Reich 1983b). Analysing cross-cultural data, Prescott (1975) demonstrated that the physical affection withheld from children accurately predicts levels of adult physical violence, while repressive attitudes towards extramarital sex correlate with violence, authoritarianism and militarism. But if the concept of societal trauma is to be really effective, it needs a scenario for how the whole machine got kick-started – otherwise we are back with the Judaeo-Christian model of the Fall. Once in existence, aggressive, dominating, traumatized societies have a tremendous edge over more peaceful cultures. But where did they originate?

The best description so far of how aggressive, patriarchal societies might originate is the 'Saharasia' theory (DeMeo 1991). DeMeo argues that patriarchy developed in and spread outwards from the hyperarid belt encompassing North Africa, the Near East and Central Asia – 'Saharasia' - after c.4000 BCE, when a major ecological transition occurred from grassland forest to dry desert. Harsh and impoverished conditions required a psychosocial shift to a harsher attitude towards self and others (Turnbull 1972); once in place, trauma transmission through the mistreatment of babies and children would tend to maintain it, even when living conditions changed – just as individual trauma survivors respond as if still under threat.

Can anything be done?

If we accept this picture of aggression and conflict – accept, at least, that it is possible to form *some* picture of how our aggression has been distorted by trauma – then psychotherapy may have several important roles to play. It can develop and disseminate a model of how, individually and collectively, we project our own traumatic experience onto others as a way of trying to manage our pain and of how this is transmitted down the generations. This needs to be combined with explicit support for aggressive, assertive and competitive impulses as in themselves healthy and creative.

A second role for psychotherapy is helping survivors of conflict manage and heal their traumatic experience, so that it is not simply passed on generationally as a revenge imperative (de Levita 2000). Such work is already happening in many conflict areas, with groups (Chapter 11, this volume;

Audergon 2004, 2005) and individuals (Heinl 2001; Linden and Grut 2002); it no doubt needs expansion and development.

A third task is developing group process methods that enable conflict to be handled and resolved. The key to this is simple, yet difficult: if those in conflict can stay together for long enough to hear one another out, then resolution can and will begin to take place – first emotionally and, later, rationally. So the job of facilitation is primarily to offer a container that allows and encourages this to happen. The longest established and best known such structure is encounter, developed by Carl Rogers and others in the late 1940s. The essence of the encounter group is that it is *unstructured*: the facilitator does not tell people what to do:

> Often there is consternation, anxiety and irritation at first – partic-ularly because of the lack of structure. Only gradually does it become evident that the major aim of nearly every member is to find ways of relating to other members of the group and to himself [sic] ...
>
> (Rogers 1973: 15–16)

(On a different theoretical basis, exactly the same is true of the classic ana-lytic group.)

Thousands have been positively touched by encounter; the model has influenced and/or been appropriated by several other approaches and the name is now almost generic for many forms of group work, including some using more active facilitation. Encounter groups responded in the 1960s to a perceived 'hunger for relationships which are close and real' (Rogers 1973: 18); they were then used experimentally in specific conflict situations, on the theory that 'open and honest communication, of feelings as well as thoughts' could only be helpful. Encounter groups have been used in indus-try and business, in educational institutions, in churches, in government departments and in situations of racial conflict (Rogers 1973: 138–50).

The encounter approach has been sharply criticized by Jacoby (1977: 64) for acting 'as if "the Person" existed in a no-man's-land of free-floating interpersonal relations and not in a society'. Certainly one can question a style that claims to be equally applicable to all without distinguishing explicitly between different social positions and access to power, as if oppressive institutions can be cured not through structural change but through more 'real relationships' – as Jacoby sarcastically puts it, 'not the dissolution of dehumanization but its humanization' (1977: 64). However, Rogers stresses that encounter 'is not simply a means of damping down ten-sions', but a way of bringing them into the open so that the whole com-munity has to address them (1973: 142). He emphasizes (1973: 88) that encounter groups can be deeply challenging for institutions.

In many ways similar is M. Scott Peck's community building. Peck defines 'community' as 'a group of individuals who have learnt how to communicate honestly with each other, whose relationships go deeper than their masks of composure' (1987: 59); he speaks of the need to 'go beyond democracy' and 'transcend differences in such a way as to include a minority' (1987: 63), by employing our 'natural yearning and thrust towards health and wholeness and holiness'; this above all requires safety – 'when we are safe, there is a natural tendency for us to heal and convert ourselves' (1987: 68). Safety does not mean the absence of conflict, but 'a place where conflict can be resolved without physical or emotional bloodshed' (1987: 71).

Peck believes that 'the process by which a group of human beings becomes a community is a lawful process' (1987: 83). He defines four stages: 'pseudocommunity', when a group basically fakes agreement and avoids conflict; 'chaos', when conflict insists on emerging; 'emptiness', when in desperation or despair the group members drop their prejudices and assumptions, their need to solve and control; and 'community', rebirth out of a subjective 'group death'.

The deep learning is experiential: a group takes itself to community, with only minimal help from designated facilitators. Peck believes community building lets us move beyond our personal cultural values 'toward the notion of world community and the possibility of ... belonging to a planetary culture' (1987: 202). He criticizes the US governmental system as 'oblivious to the rules of community' and stuck in the fight model and the avoidance of communication wherever possible.

By far the most politically engaged therapeutic approach to conflict is Arnold Mindell's Worldwork: an approach to all group conflict situations, based like Mindell's work in general (Chapter 11, this volume) on the concept of 'dreaming', a fundamental process expressing itself in actual dreams and also in bodily symptoms, relationship conflicts and group conflicts. For Mindell, conflict indicates unprocessed dreamlike material – usually, some minority experience that is not being adequately represented. Worldwork introduces into the process 'deep democracy', which is 'the realization that everyone is needed to represent reality' (Mindell 1992: 155), 'the inherent importance of all parts of ourselves and all viewpoints in the world around us' (1992: 5) or 'our sense that the world is here to help us become our entire selves and that we are here to help the world become whole' (Mindell 1992: 96).

In Worldwork large groups of people meet, representing as wide a range as possible of situations and experiences. This can be within a neighbourhood, city or political situation; or seminars can draw hundreds from many countries, ethnic groups, classes, genders and sexual orientations (participants from disadvantaged groups get considerable financial support to attend). At first, everyone expresses the attitude they came with, whatever this may be. Conflicts emerge, mirroring conflicts in the larger world – for example, between women and men, black and white, third world and first world, rich and poor, gay and straight – often generating much anger, grief, terror, outrage, frustration and despair. As each experience is attended to, acknowledged, accepted, fought against and worked with, hopefully new roles come into being. In theory at least, silent roles are every bit as important as noisy ones – those who feel helpless, who listen and feel, who create the space within which other people can be more visibly active.

This work is painful and demanding – sometimes terrifying, as several hundred people enter chaos. It takes nerve to 'sit in the fire of conflict and not be burned' (Mindell 1995: 18). But what is striking – and, of course, other group situations work similarly – is that, given the willingness to sit with what is happening, to support how people are acting and feeling, however unpleasant this may be, to maintain awareness to the point of completion – conflicts do tend to complete themselves, generating an extraordinary sense of mutual recognition and respect. The core recipe for conflict resolution is that people stay and listen. Clearly objective conflicts around power and economics cannot be resolved purely psychologically; but people can come away from such an experience and act differently in the world.

'Deep democracy' reframes of the concept of leadership:

> If we understand the leader as just another role, we see that the power projected upon our leaders is apparent, not absolute, since real leadership comes from those who are aware of the process trying to happen in their community. The apparent leaders are representations of field roles, which are parts each of us can and sometimes must fill.
>
> (Mindell 1989: 88)

In a Worldwork seminar, the leadership in the room shifts from person to person, often in very surprising ways. One facilitation task (and this, too, is a field role not always residing with the designated facilitators) is to notice where leadership is: sometimes with people who are being very quiet or frightened or apparently outside the action.

In a striking demonstration of its own principles, Worldwork, having unreservedly taken on the standpoint of oppressed minorities, then found the space to recognize that 'mainstream' experience also had to be validated if deep democracy were to mean anything:

> [T]hose of us who want to facilitate should not fall into one-sided support of minority positions ... That makes the majority feel marginalized. The facilitator's task is not to do away with the use of

rank and power, but to notice them and make their dynamics explicit for the whole group to see.

(Mindell 1995: 37)

Mindell explicitly recognizes a major problem in combining real political analysis with support for all parts of the situation:

> The paradox of group process is this: to be useful, it must address everyone's social and rank issues. It's got to deal with the issue of who has the money. At the same time, a community dies if it focuses on only what is right or wrong about each side.

(Mindell 1995: 181)

Uncompromising in its support for minorities oppressed for their gender, colour, sexual orientation or economic position, Worldwork connects all these in a coherent analysis, which also criticizes some of the assumptions of psychotherapy:

> It is devastating to assume, as some Western therapies do, that certain races and myths are more primitive than others. And most therapists assume that the only conscious human beings are ones who think about themselves all the time. Such apparently 'harmless' assumptions are so full of naive prejudices that it is not surprising that our Western therapies and group and organizational practices are not solving city and international problems.

(Mindell 1992: 4–5)

Worldwork is a so far unique attempt to apply psychotherapy in the sphere of political conflict without privileging the therapeutic over the political – without falling into the error, for which Jacoby criticizes Rogers, of treating conflict as something that occurs and can be resolved simply on the level of individual human beings, rather than that of social structure.

Conclusion

Conflict, competition and aggression are perhaps the most fundamental problems human beings now face (and also key elements in our attitude towards the rest of life on this planet). It would be naive for therapy to claim that it has solutions. It does seem likely, however, that some central concepts of psychotherapy have a significant role to play in getting to grips with these issues. Using other people and groups – and indeed the non-human world in general – as dumping grounds for our unwanted feelings, is plainly not the way to go; it also appears that in dumping what we do not want, we are also getting rid of valuable aspects of our own being. By re-owning the Other we enrich ourselves.

History is indeed a long nightmare, a feverish sleep shot through by jumbled dreams of violence and abuse and, equally, by glorious dreams of freedom and peace. We are all, individually and collectively, punchdrunk from repeated traumatic blows to the head and body, and our confusion renders us unable to see where the blows are coming from and to protect ourselves. But we are perhaps finally coming to understand our situation; which allows us some faint hope of transforming it.

4 The breast-milk of the Inuit mother: a tale of micro- and macrocosm, shadow and light
Hilary Prentice and Mary-Jayne Rust

Introduction

> *Until the late twentieth century, every generation throughout*
> *history lived with the tacit certainty that there would be*
> *generations to follow. Each assumed, without questioning, that its*
> *children and children's children would walk the same earth, under*
> *the same sky. Hardships, failures, and personal death were*
> *encompassed in that vaster assurance of continuity. That certainty*
> *is now lost to us, whatever our politics. That loss, unmeasured*
> *and immeasurable, is the pivotal psychological reality of our time.*
> (Macy 1995: 241)

In the mid-1980s a university scientist from Quebec went north seeking a 'pristine' group to compare with women in southern Quebec who had poly chlorinated biphenyls (PCBs) in their breast-milk. Instead, he discovered that Inuit mothers had breast-milk with PCBs that were five times higher.

PCBs are classified as persistant organic pollutants (POPs), chemicals that are highly toxic, bioaccumulative and capable of undergoing long-range transport. These pollutants migrate to colder climates and precipitate in places like the Arctic. The Inuit are hit particularly hard because they eat a diet rich in fat from sea mammals. The fat is loaded with a variety of long-lived toxic chemicals that become more concentrated as they move up the food chain, reaching humans at the top. POPs come from insecticides, electrical insulation, pesticides and industrial waste. They can cause a range of problems such as hormonal imbalance, brain damage and learning difficulties. As a result, Inuit mothers are being advised not to breastfeed their babies.

This shocking piece of news illustrates beautifully the interconnectedness of all living systems and the complexity of the social and environmental crisis we face today. Our consumer habits have reached a land that is so far away, a place so white and pure. Our toxins intervene into the most tender of early relationships, into that most vulnerable of places in a woman's body, so symbolic of mother love. Now we know that there is no pristine place left untouched. Our wild spaces, both inside and out, in matter and psyche, are affected. The land, our bodies, the air, our spirit, the sea, our unconscious and our dreams, our mother's milk and the groundwater of Mother Earth – all are affected and seamlessly interwoven.

We write this chapter in the wake of the tsunami disaster amidst the continuing bloody war in Iraq. These events are symptoms of a world in crisis. The fight for the Earth's diminishing natural resources becomes more desperate. As global warming becomes a reality we face increasing numbers of 'natural' disasters. Yet change seems slow and hard to make. Denial of our situation is rife, inertia hard to shift. How do we make the collective sea change in the service of life?

The work of psychotherapy is dedicated to deep change. Can we use our skills to help illuminate our collective crisis and strengthen the sea change in our attitudes and lifestyles?

Microcosm and macrocosm: mapping individual psychological insights onto the collective

Psychotherapists and environmental activists, ecologists and counsellors and a host of others have been coming together in recent years to try to shed psychological light on our current ecological crisis. Many environmental activists have been coming to the conclusion that our ecologically destructive behaviour is ultimately a question of human consciousness and are caused to wonder: can anything that has been learned in the proliferation of psychotherapies over the last century help us to understand what we are doing, to wake up and change, fast? Conversely, there are many psychological workers who are very aware of the significance of climate change, pollution, over-fishing, habitat destruction, the loss of rainforests … and no longer wish to work in an anthropocentric, a human-chauvinist way that partakes in the massive cultural denial of the situation we are in. How to do this? Perhaps we psychological workers also have much to learn from ecologists and others immersed in sustainability issues – about sustainability in the human psyche, about the relief and joy of moving towards ecological balance, inner and outer, about 'nature', outer and inner.

The ecopsychology movement that has been emerging around these questions, these impulses, involves much energetic debate, some shafts of insight and any number of practical initiatives. We shall first briefly describe some of the latter, as they are inspiring and informative, before going on to look at some of the knottier issues about changing consciousness. Many involve helping people to 'reconnect' directly with the other-than-human natural world, by time and attention spent in gardens or going into the (relative) wild, trusting and variously supporting the healing process that then often spontaneously seems to occur. Increasing numbers are now taking part in 'vision quests' or in 'wilderness therapy' journeys (C. Adams 1996) (related work has included time in the wild as an alternative to custody for young offenders in South Africa and the USA). Practitioners are developing horticultural therapy around hospitals and in mental health settings, doing psychotherapy on allotments (Linden and Grut 2002), 'ecotherapy' wherever you are, and the burgeoning world of adventure therapy often takes place outdoors. 'Nature therapy' with various groups including autistic children and psychiatric patients is taking off in Israel. Research has established significant improvement to recovery times for patients in hospital with a 'natural' view compared to those without, and gradually more hospital gardens are planned and established (Cooper Marcus and Barnes 1998).

Time with 'nature' seems to be simply good for us and, where there is space for this, much often also takes place at the levels of metaphor and synchronicity, if only we are prepared to be open to this, to look and listen and stay aware. The world around us seems uncannily to mirror what may be going on for us in our inner worlds and, furthermore, often seems to have something rather useful to say to us about it. This resonance, these moments of synchronicity can be healing at many levels; the content of the learning involved being added to by the very magic of the thing; we are part of a world, a universe, that can speak to us in such ways – we are, after all, part of a quite extraordinary web of life and that web is infused with meaning.

Reconnecting 'psyche' with 'ecos' at any level is surely a valuable part of what Thomas Berry has called the 'Great Work' (Berry 1999) that faces the generations alive today – the shift from an unsustainable and destructive, to a sustainable, life-enhancing, human presence on the planet and the change of consciousness that must attend that.

However, a great deal of ecopsychological exploration involves the attempt to understand deeply what is occurring in the *collective* psyche and we thus tend to find ourselves using concepts and tools from individual psychological work and applying these to the 'big picture'. We shall attempt here to begin to discuss the possibilities, limits and growing edge of such an approach. (For the purposes of exploring how models from individual psychology may be mapped onto collective processes, we shall refer to the 'human species', when in fact we are talking about current human behaviour in the developed western world; the 'industrial growth society', which is in many ways now dominant on the planet and increasing its dominance and spread constantly. There are, of course, many within that dominant culture who strive to live differently and many indigenous societies have lived, and strive still to live, in ecological balance with the living beings that surround them and in full conscious participation with 'all that is' (Abrams 1997; Armstrong 1995; Norberg Hodge 1991; Prechtel 2002; Some 1998).)

It is quickly apparent that understandings and insights from individual and family work do map fairly easily onto the apparent collective psychological aspects of our environmentally destructive society. For example, if psychological work might start with an initial assessment of risk factors – risks of suicide, self-harm, danger to others, substance abuse/active addictions – we find an immediately urgent, risky situation. The species is not consciously suicidal (although we find it amazing how many ordinary people, once you start talking about environmental issues, express the view that 'we' are rather a bad lot and if we make ourselves extinct, which is seen as quite possible, then the planet would probably be better off anyway). Yet it is behaving with reckless abandon, as though unaware that it is destroying all that it depends on for its life; atmosphere, rainforest, clean oceans full of life, weather systems, habitats, biodiversity, soil structure, water tables – and poisoning the food chain throughout the planet, as we have seen. Evidently it is a danger to others (other species) – it is actively ecocidal and showing a psychopathological lack of empathy or remorse about this. Others are seen as without consciousness or the capacity to suffer, having no intrinsic value, just here to serve us, no loss if harmed or damaged – after all there are plenty more (species) – just expendable objects.

If it is without empathy, presumably its capacity for intimacy, for relationship other than abusive and using, is negligible? Exactly so; the dominant culture has no loving relationship with 'nature', but exploits the imagery of nature (wild places, beautiful sunsets, wild animals) and our repressed longing to be in true communion with these, in order to sell ever more goods – the very goods whose production is destroying ever more of those wild places, wild creatures, peaceful lakes, alighting butterflies, honking geese. And sells it to us directly in packaged holidays, as the lethal air miles build up.

If the apparent lack of remorse is reminiscent of the psychopath, the lack of empathy, and the using of others is characteristic of narcissism. In narcissism, a lacking in the core sense of self leads to a process of using others to bolster appearance, bolster a secretly low self-esteem and there is an obsession with self-image, with self in the superficial sense. As though all the 'resources' of the planet become a giant fur coat that we throw around ourselves and temporarily hope to share the glory of, but unsatisfyingly so, for the animal is dead and died in vain.

Anyone who has worked in mental health would guess that this being must be an addict and, of course, this is so. It is not new to look at the psychological processes of consumerism through the lens of addiction (Kanner and Gomes 1995). Ever more 'stuff' is used, but the brief high does not hold, as what is really being sought for (perhaps confidence, spiritual uplift, the capacity for easy intimacy, a sense of wildness, feelings of true power, true freedom, safety, comfort ...) cannot be found in this stuff and what is being avoided (painful feelings, perhaps also a sense of emptiness, having in some sense profoundly lost the way) cannot forever be avoided by consuming the stuff. Addictions are mean – the longer you pursue them, the more the painful feelings build up and push to be expressed – and the further you get from what you really wanted. When an addict faces up to the situation, s/he finds him/herself more out of control, less free and with relationships in a worse state than they would ever have thought possible.

We could go on. See for example, Paul Shepard (1995) for a developmental model of our having collectively derailed the conditions of the wild tribal childhood in which we developed psychologically over thousands of years and thus being collectively, chronically immature, full of unresolved early omnipotence, with little sense of limits. Probably our readers could go on also – mapping the psychological models and ways of working to which they have allegiance onto the broad outlines of our collective situation.

The knotty question that then arises and that we would here like to acknowledge and at least begin to address is, of course, *and then what*? How do we respond to this situation? The question is arguably central to the whole territory where psychotherapy and political process meet. What do we do, for example, with clear insights about the projection of shadow issues onto so-called 'enemies' in international relations, the need to create enemies? With the 'war on terror', the repression and demonization of the feminine in deeply patriarchal situations, the developing world culture of self-righteousness, complacency and guilt, resentment and murderous rage?

On the one hand, to wonder how we might respond to such huge issues risks grandiosity and the accusation of grandiosity. We psychological workers are not the answer to the problems of humanity; if we have something to offer it will be as 'plain members' of the human as well as of the biotic community, alongside activists and gardeners, indigenous peoples and economists, farmers and spiritual leaders. On the other hand, who are we to avoid responding, perhaps even taking the stance of 'bystanding' (Clarkson 1996) in a situation of holocaust?

It is also, arguably, not an entirely new thing to attempt. Ecophilosopher, anthropologist and magician David Abrams spent time studying with shamans – magicians and healers – in Indonesia and Nepal and quickly noticed that these people tended to live 'at the spatial periphery of the community, or more often, out beyond the edges of the village – amid the rice fields, or in a forest, or a wild cluster of boulders'. Abrams realized this was significant and symbolic:

> For the magician's intelligence is not encompassed within the society; its place is at the edge of the community, mediating between the human community and the larger community of

beings upon which the village depends for its nourishment and sustenance. This … includes … diverse plants, myriad animals … winds and weather patterns … and the various landforms, forests, rivers, caves, mountains.

(Abrams 1997: 6)

As he goes on to spell this out, it is as though he is describing precisely the territory that modern-day ecopsychologists are attempting to explore, or perhaps 'remember':

The traditional tribal shaman … ensures that the relation between human society and the larger society of beings is balanced and reciprocal and that the village never takes more from the living land than it returns to it.

(Abrams 1997: 7)

Furthermore, his/her work as a healer of individuals, arises *from* the afore-mentioned work:

Only those persons who, by their everyday practice, are involved in monitoring and maintaining the relations between the human village and the animate landscape are able to appropriately diag-nose, treat and ultimately relieve personal ailments and illnesses arising within the village.

(Abrams 1997: 7–8)

We return to the question: what practices might 'ecopsychologists' adopt that could help mediate the currently terribly disrupted relationship between human community and the wider community of beings, knowing that such was honourable work over thousands of years? On what ground might *we* stand as we attempt to do this, living, as we do, in the 'belly of the monster', in every sense part of what is occurring?

Perhaps some elements of the answer to this question are beginning to appear. We may find that our individual work begins to change, as our own consciousness changes. A senior analyst once told one of us that in years of therapy the cutting down of the tree in her childhood garden had *always* been interpreted as being about her father, never about the tree in its own right and her relationship to it. How different, we wonder, might her therapy and her life have been if her grief – her actual experience – about that beloved being in her young life had been really heard, acknowledged and supported?

We may find that we are drawn to begin to work with our clients out-doors, allowing those processes of metaphor and synchronicity back in. A friend was wondering whether to attend a men's workshop, following the traditions of 'rites of passage', to take place outdoors, in a wild place. He had never done anything remotely like this before and was understandably wary. As he sat outside and talked about it with a friend who would be there, a robin landed on the tip of his boot and perched there, suspended in midair at the end of one of his long, crossed legs. Neither man moved a muscle, or scarcely dared breathe, as the sense of the sacred, of the magic and mystery of life surrounded them, brought by the most friendly and reassuring of messengers. Needless to say my friend attended the workshop and much was to follow for him.

Perhaps we trust that the very work of individual therapy in simply supporting personal and spiritual growth is part of a broad move from outer to inner, from unsustainable to sustainable values and pursuits in life.

Another modality is intentional group work, as 'ecotherapy' and 'wilderness work' and 'nature therapy' gatherings add themselves to 'deep ecology' workshop practices (Macy and Brown 1998). The power of such collective 'setting of intention', together with our allowing ourselves to reconnect with the greater wilder consciousness surrounding us and the return to working through ritual, music and art that seems spontaneously to arise in such settings, is a potent new/old force.

More contentiously, is it also possible to speak to the broader collective psyche? In group therapy, the therapist may make an observation, or perhaps an interpretation, from a place of witness that so accurately mirrors what is being experienced that the whole group process moves on. Such interventions would never usefully have a tone of criticism, blame or accusation, yet how hard it is to talk about our current behaviour at a planetary level without such a tone creeping in! The useful intervention, rather, will be entirely without judgement and is likely to be highly empathic to the predicament, experience and process that is being thus witnessed and reflected.

Collecting the shadow: bulimia and the collective

Some forms of writing, speaking, filmmaking, theatre, art (and more) do mirror the collective process; storytelling and commentary have been likened to a psychotherapeutic process. Would we learn anything new if we tried a more deliberate form of mirroring?

We have tried an experiment here, using bulimia to echo aspects of our collective crisis. Bulimia reflects consumer culture, with its fast food, quick-fix, disposable habits. Although the twists and turns of recovery are different each time, there are patterns to be found over the course of time as individuals change. For example, through years of working with bulimic women, I (Mary-Jayne) have witnessed repeated healing of destructiveness towards the self. We wanted to use this to tease out how our collective destructiveness might be spoken to and transformed.

The individual and collective voices are interwoven, with the collective voice written in italics.

A bulimic woman is a food addict; she feels out of control around eating, hates her body and resorts to bingeing to avoid certain unbearable feelings and states of mind. Terrified of getting fat, she vomits the binge so that on the surface all appears well. Yet underneath, there is physical deterioration such as hormone imbalance, tooth decay and damage to internal organs. Meanwhile, all the mess is flushed away.

We consume fast and beyond our means, damaging our very life support systems, disposing of our undigested waste into vast landfill sites. We abuse our Earth body. Are we bingeing in order to avoid the lurking shadows of our collective past? We seem unable to reflect on, let alone repair, the damage we have done. Craving deep soul nourishment, we remain stuck in a vicious circle of indigestion.

A bulimic woman arrives for therapy when her habit has become more trouble than it is worth. Her therapy journey will be a bumpy ride as she negotiates her way through previously forbidden territory, forever tempted to fall back into the immediate comfort of food.

Industrial growth culture has not yet arrived for therapy and it is possible that we will reach a dangerous level of collapse before deep change can happen. How long do we have to wait until consumer habits become more trouble than they are worth?

The bulimic woman (often?) has an early experience of abandonment by mother, as well as being used for her mother's unmet needs. In her childlike way, she concludes her needs are too much and tries to become a 'good girl', splitting off her needy, messy self and flushing it away. Food becomes more of a reliable mate than mother.

We live in a Hollywood culture of fast food, where slow, dark, needy feelings are unacceptable. We must be efficient, bright, fast and logical to be successful in the west. Our growing alienation from Mother Earth leaves us dangling as if we were separate objects floating in space. In desperation, we turn to material comforts, confusing matter, mater and mother love. We have lost our ability to commune with our fellow Earth community, believing ourselves to be a lone intelligence in the universe. There is unacknowledged abandonment in the early experience of our species.

cont.

It is sometimes necessary for the therapist to actively 'pull' the secret bulimic symptoms into awareness. The bulimic woman has great difficulty in spitting out the difficult things within the relationship. Instead, she holds onto them and may vomit her feelings before or after the sessions. If the lurking shadow material is not picked up, the client may leave suddenly, often without paying. There is the need to be on the lookout for what is on the edges, what is not being said.

Who is able to watch and speak the shadow material in our culture? The shamans were the ones who could communicate with the web of life, speak with nature spirits. In psychotherapy we learn to work with the dark material, to integrate it with the light. How does this weave into our cultural space?

Destructive symptoms, however ugly, hold meaning. They serve a function. Some bulimic women have prevented themselves from going quite mad in their early life by channelling the pain into their bodies, despite the harm they may have caused. When the symptoms recede, the old madness lurks and care must be taken not to move too quickly. There is a great deal of stored up and unprocessed material that needs to be listened to carefully. Retelling the story, often many times, is an attempt to find a truth that fits.

Western culture tells our collective history in a particular way: that we have made great progress since living in caves, that our scientific and technological achievements give us longer and safer lives. But these achievements have also brought us to the most dangerous point that homo sapiens has ever known in its life: our species is now in danger of becoming extinct. Living with a story that does not fit gives rise to great dissatisfaction, bewilderment and lack of meaning. Retelling that story takes time.

Destructiveness can be about a need to repeat something from the past, in order to do it differently this time around. Bulimia can be a way of dealing with past sexual abuse. The abuse has moved from the hand of someone else, to the hand of the victim. Talking about past relationships enables links to be made and slowly some sense can be made out of madness. Secrets will out and the abusers can no longer use threats to maintain the status quo to their advantage. At times, the client may experience the therapist as the hated parent, the abuser; although uncomfortable, this can enable past feelings to be worked through in the present.

Abuse at the hands of those in power is, more often than not, covered up. What is wrong in the collective gets converted into an issue of personal ill
cont.

health. Past abuse at the hands of those in power needs to be publicly exposed so that individuals can see the links and know the difference, between personal and collective pain. How do we rework this damage? Is it our leaders that need to be strong enough to cope with negative projections, understanding them enough to be able to respond with wisdom, to make sense of our predicaments, rather than trying to spin?

The bulimic woman has cut off from her body and is trying to rule it with her mind. She will respond to almost any strong emotion with food and starve herself as a way of punishing her body for being too needy. Her distrust of her intuition and instinct, as vital guides, causes inner chaos. She fears that her body, her senses, will simply lead her astray. Recovering trust in the body is about listening and deep attunement. Using a tender and acute mindfulness, she can learn to differentiate between, and respond to her array of different emotions and bodily sensations. As her emotional literacy develops, she discovers her body to be a useful antenna to let her know what is going on in her environment; if she trusts her body to tell her what she needs, she will settle at a sustainable weight. In part, her self-harm has been a frustration with her strange and unknown nature that she cannot control. The more she attempts to discipline and control her body, the more it fights back. Getting to know her nature, with respect, is the turning point.

Here lies a hotbed of a cultural past, where Christianity and other patriarchal religions have developed a transcendent spirituality, moving up and out of the body in order to control our wild nature – and nature herself. For nature has been turned from feeling subject into inanimate object. Our fears of nature need naming and addressing. Changing direction requires a climbing down from an inflated position of all-knowing humans, recognizing the damage we have done. Seeing ourselves as an equal part of the web of life is both terrifying in its loss of control and magnificent in realizing its capacity to hold and guide us. Destructive behaviour is likely to cease when we can feel the presence of nature as larger and more powerful than humans, as subject not object; at last we are no longer alone in the universe – we have a container and guide, if we can allow attunement with the body and the body of the Earth.

As the layers peel away and the war with food and her body ceases, the struggle with intimate relationships begins. For now we are in the territory of the unknown other, of that which is out of our control, with whom we must negotiate, listen to, speak with, learn about, survive loving and hating. Destructiveness only comes when that process

cont.

becomes so blocked that no other way seems possible. Destructiveness ceases when 'the other' – that alien body, those alien parts of ourselves, become knowable, become our allies instead of threats.

If we peel away the layers of war on terror, war with nature, we face the nakedness of intimate relationships. We can no longer live as if we were separate beings. Destructiveness ceases when all who inhabit this earth are experienced as interconnected, necessary and fascinating parts of the web of life ... transient guests on the earth.

One of the most striking things for us in this experiment is that it highlights a process that therapists are familiar with, but that may seem paradoxical to the wider world: rather than locking up destructiveness and keeping a tight control over it, it needs to be spoken to, with loving tenderness. It needs to be attuned to, loved and understood for how it came into being and what it wants. Only then will it grow and change into something else.

Many people are concerned that the move towards sustainability will involve loss of material wealth and power. This feels like an enormous deprivation. Of course, all change involves some loss. But what we arrive at in the end is so much more satisfying. The bulimic realizes that food could never satisfy her soul hunger, in the same way that we know deep down that endless material wealth cannot make us happy. Yet we fight like mad in the face of this process, fearing loss of control and hardship. We desperately need a different kind of leadership that can contain our fears and speak to the terror in our hearts – rather than a president who expects that to wage war on terror will somehow destroy it!

... and light: environmental crisis as spiritual teacher

As well as denial about our destructiveness and the danger we are in, there is also arguably a taboo in our dominant culture about being too hopeful, about really believing that a profound transformation of human behaviour is possible, about having the temerity to see light in the darkness. In speaking or writing about the situation, it is easy to run into either defence, as they stand like huge guardians at the threshold. Too dark and people recoil from a 'doom and gloom' approach, literally turning off their televisions in millions in the 1980s, leading to a major change in environmental broadcasting. Too hopeful and the accusation would be of naivety and a lack of compassion for the suffering that wracks our planet.

Nonetheless, as we attempt to listen in to collective process, we keep tuning in to the need for hope, as all of us endeavour to stay sane and functional in the midst of overwhelmingly distressing news, every day, day after day. A 'story' that we find inspiring is the idea of our current predicament as *teacher*. Such a story can balance meaninglessness with meaning, despair with tender encouragement to become all we can be.

The 'environmental crisis' is certainly a crisis of human consciousness and as such it challenges us to face up to ourselves and to grow, very fast. As with any potent story of life-as-teacher, most of the pain arises from our resistance. If we don't resist, the learning is perhaps fairly clear, although each one of us will, of course, be aware of different aspects of what we are being called to learn, how we are being challenged to grow.

For example: organizing our lives and society around getting materially richer is ravaging our planet, dividing us from each other, creating wars and largely failing to make us any happier (Durning 1995). However, if we look for what is deeply important to us, *represented* by what we materially consume, we find sources of value that are much more 'inner' than 'outer' (love, intimacy, freedom, creativity, joy, wisdom, purpose, play, compassion) and are infinitely sustainable, so we have a double reason to transform ourselves and our societies.

As well as a move from an 'outer' to an 'inner' focus, many searching conversations about environmental issues seem to arrive repeatedly at the similar insight that our lives need to become *simpler* and we need to *slow down*, both of which seem to be very desirable at the point of insight and also tremendously hard to attain. Speeding up seems to have much to do with avoiding pain and with the desire to feel in control; again, the insight repeatedly arises that letting go into *trusting* life, trusting ourselves, rather than struggling to control nature, outer and inner, is part of the journey.

In seeing that we destroy ourselves when we are in unbearable pain, it becomes clear that we must focus on our healing.

As we become increasingly aware of the consequences of our actions, we are perhaps challenged to practise mindfulness in our everyday lives. Spending less time 'lost' in the past or future, we arrive in the present, where life is to be found.

In the attempt to live sustainably, we get to reconnect with and to deepen our understanding of our dependence and interdependence, we get to wake up to our place in an infinitely beautiful web of life, to remember mystery.

Perhaps most crucial of all, we simply *have* to learn to replace destructive competition with cooperation and love, to really learn that we are not separate, that what we do to others we do to ourselves. We will have to learn to grow beyond greed and violence to become compassionate and skilled peacemakers, able to nourish ourselves and each other well and safely. The ecology of our Earth tells us that there really is no other choice and that time, for us, is short.

Part II
Political dimensions of
psychotherapy practice

5   The politics of sexuality, gender and object choice in therapy
Chess Denman

Introduction

Therapists cannot practise for long without a sharp appreciation of the political implications of these topics as they affect both their patients and the practice of therapy. Indeed, the politicization of sex and sexuality in our culture is so strong as to amount to policing (Foucault 1981). There are in our culture as in almost all cultures very sharp limits on the permissible social forms in which sexual expression and activity may occur and fairly sharp limits on the ways in which gendered identity may be expressed.

There are probably both biological and cultural reasons for the intense politicization of gender and sexuality. Sexual expression and consequently gender dimorphism are under strong evolutionary control since it is by conferring reproductive advantage that variations in sexuality and reproduction itself are spread through a species. Darwin (1859) thought that the evolutionary mechanisms involving sexuality were so important that he termed them 'sexual selection' and contrasted them with 'natural selection'; he showed how some characteristics of animals – especially those in which the two genders differ – are the result of sexual selection within rather than between species. In the case of peacocks, for example, male peacocks compete for females with ostentatious displays of their tail feathers. The phenomenon of sexual selection extends also to behaviour, with some animals displaying complex patterns of stereotyped behaviour that precede mating and that generally function to govern competition for mate selection.

Unlike animal behaviour, human behaviour is characterized by a high degree of plasticity and freedom from biological control. It is therefore likely that the control of human sexual behaviour is partly under biological but also partly under cultural control. Even where there are commonalities in the cross-cultural control of sexual behaviour, these may stem from the time when humans moved from a primarily hunter–gatherer mode of existence to a more agrarian economy involving raising livestock (Taylor 1997). Once human societies concerned themselves with animal husbandry and breeding, they perforce took an interest in controlling the sexuality of their animals and extended the same concerns to themselves.

If sex, sexuality and gendered identity are politicized, therapy will inevitably concern itself with the politics of these activities. Therapists need to consider how general political issues in relation to sexuality and gender affect patients in their struggles and difficulties. Samuels (1993) has extended this question usefully to remind therapists that they should spend some time considering the political developmental needs of patients and this is as true in the areas of sexuality and gender as it is in any other political domain. A second raft of questions concerns the impact that political issues have on the practice and organization of therapy itself.

The domain of sexuality and gender is vast. For this reason, a single book chapter cannot even begin to cover the domain. So this chapter discusses only a limited number of topics in the three areas of gender, sexual orientation and sexual expression. Its aim is, as it were, to whet the appetite. Readers who would like to extend their knowledge of the field of sexuality and gender more widely can refer to the key texts cited in this chapter and to be found in the bibliographical listing at the end of the book.

The politics of gender

Feminism

Although early feminists were critical of psychoanalytic psychotherapy, seeing it as a male-derived instrument of social control, many female psychotherapists have been profoundly influenced by feminism. Juliet Mitchell (1974) was instrumental in trying to show the potentially radical nature of psychoanalytic theory and demonstrating its value to feminist theorists and its potential as a political tool of use to feminists. Later therapists developed explicitly feminist therapies, for example Ernst and Maguire (1987). But possibly even more importantly, a group of psychoanalytically inspired theorists were able to develop psychological theories that described and attempted to understand the structural power inequalities that centre on gender in our culture.

Both Chodorow (1978) and Dinnerstein (1999) analyse the power differences in our culture between men and women as founded in the asymmetrical distribution of the sexes in childrearing. They account for what Chodorow describes as the 'reproduction of mothering' by giving differing developmental trajectories for little boys and little girls as they relate to a caregiver who is for boys the opposite and for girls the same gender as themselves. Chodorow argues that experiences of merger with their primary caregiver are crucial in conditioning the development of children. These experiences are much less prominent in boys, who are related to as separate by their mothers and are encouraged to separate. Girls, by way of contrast, are allowed to remain merged with mother to a much greater extent. The consequence of this is that male identity remains rather precarious, being based on negation, whereas female identity is more secure, but this security is achieved at the price of continuing merger with mother. The ultimate effect of this asymmetric childrearing is that children grow up to reproduce the gendered division of labour that their parents display, girls being socialized to motherhood and boys fitted for the labour market. Jessica Benjamin (1988) and Contratto (1987) have extended these theories usefully to incorporate ideas about the role of fathers in enabling and liberating or constraining their daughters' development

The founding of the London Women's Therapy Centre by Orbach and Eichenbaum represented a practical attempt to bring this kind of therapeutic and political analysis to bear on the lives of individual women. Refreshingly, Orbach and Eichenbaum (1987) argued that women are the stronger and are depended on by men for emotional support. The consideration of psychopathologies such as eating disorders, which are commonly associated more with women than men in our culture, and an analysis of female predisposition to these disorders in terms of the politics of the female body have extended the work of earlier feminists in important and fruitful ways.

As a result of the work of these and numerous other theorists, few therapists in practice today, whether male or female, can fail to be aware of the politics of gender and particularly of gender inequality as they impact on women in treatment. And the position of women in culture has advanced; but not as far, I think, as might have been hoped in the heady days of earlier feminist enthusiasms. Inequities in pay rates, glass ceilings (as apparent in the upper echelons of psychotherapy as elsewhere) and uneven distribution of childcare responsibilities are still the norm in our culture one of the most pro-feminist cultures worldwide. There is also increasing pessimism about the plasticity of gendered social arrangements and an increasing reliance on the idea of inherent differences between male and female natures.

The men's movements

An advantage for men of the hegemony of male gender is that all theory applies to them as the default gender. Thus the term 'issues of gender' often refers in a coded or politically correct way to feminism. However, while the policing of male gender in our culture may not, because of all the advantages it confers, chafe as much as that of female gender, it is as intense as the policing of female gender. Furthermore, gender deviation in men, being read against the dominant male hegemony, can only be in a female and implicitly an inferior direction. Thus for men to wear stereotypically female clothing is a far more transgressive and politically difficult act than for women to dress up the power structure into male clothing.

Those men who express or live out their dislike for aspects of the current organization of masculinity may be seen as effeminate or treacherous. The men's movements (for there is not one but rather several related political ideologies to consider) are attempts to deal with this state of affairs. (For a good history of this movement, see Newton 2004.)

The men's movements are, in fact, very varied. Some groups' primary aim is to reassert male dominance or aspects of male experience that are thought to be at risk of being occluded in our culture. Examples of this kind of group would be organizations dedicated to ensuring fathers have rights to see their children. Related organizations such as the Christian-inspired 'promise keepers' also wish to retain traditional family structures. Other parts of the men's movement have tried to recover, for men, aspects of experience that are traditionally seen as female and some of these have had explicit roots in therapy. An important group of this kind has been called the 'mythopoetic men's movement'. This concentrates on the use of myth and stories to reclaim aspects of masculinity that have been suppressed in western culture.

Case example: Peter and Ruth[1]

Peter and Ruth were both successful self-employed barristers. Their 10-year marriage was a model of equality with apparently even-handed childcare and mutual respect. But, secretly, Peter felt crushed and constrained by his marriage and longed to paint. At an evening life class, he met and fell in love with Andrea, another woman in the class, and then agonized over a decision to leave Ruth.

Both partners sought individual and couple therapy to help them decide to stay together or split up and ultimately Peter left Ruth to be with Andrea. It transpired that he had been repeatedly unfaithful to Ruth throughout their marriage but concealed this from her.

Ruth was furious with Peter and Peter was hangdog, guilty but defiant, but both were determined to 'keep the children out of it'. Even so, when Peter moved out the children stayed with Ruth and it was her business

cont.

---

[1] The case examples given in this chapter are highly fictionalized. See Denman (2003) for a discussion of the advantages and disadvantages of this approach.

interests that suffered. Over the months that followed Peter often appealed to the needs of his business as reasons for changing arrangements about having the children at short notice. He would point out that if his work took a downturn Ruth would get less maintenance. In practice, he saw less and less of the children and, in truth, although this lack pained him at times, he found the freedom of not having to care for two small children suited him well.

Peter stayed on in therapy dealing with a wide range of issues related to difficulties in his emotional development. He explored alternative therapies including the mythopoetic men's movement but, sadly, his relationship with Andrea did not last long. For a while he felt bitter and cheated despite having initiated the break-up in the relationship. Even though his standard of living improved rapidly as his career took off, he felt cheated by the money he had to pay Ruth and saw this as money given to her rather than to his children. Furthermore although he had quite a number of casual relationships, he often said he felt lonely and at sea.

Ruth did not need further treatment. After the ending of the marriage, she was furious first with Peter and then with herself for being blind. She turned to her large circle of female confidantes with whom she felt free to talk and renewed her relationship with her mother who moved in to help with childcare. The main stress in her life remained her financial worries. She found it difficult to return to work and often had to hassle Peter for maintenance.

Peter and Ruth's story exemplifies many of the modern issues of gender and power that therapists will meet either while treating couples or individuals. The presence of children in a relationship often heightens the tension and sense of moral risk involved in managing relationships and children are often the pivots around which moral and political policing of gender and human relationships is enforced. Peter and Ruth's subsequent differences in adaptation to their situation also illustrate one variant of the differing fortunes of men and women emotionally and practically after the ending of relationships.

Transgendered and intersexed patients

Two groups of patients can present with particularly difficult issues in relation to gender. These are people who feel they would like to change their gender (transgendered people) and people whose gender at birth is uncertain. That the ruthless surgical assignment of gender for intersexed patients was based for quite a while on the single consideration of whether sufficient tissue existed to form a viably long penis is a powerful illustration of the enforcement of social gender norms. Against this must be the increasing acceptance of and political liberalization towards transgendered people. While transgendered people still face frequent prejudice (not least in the psychotherapeutic community: Denman 2003), the rudiments of social acceptance are beginning to be offered to them. Possibly one reason for this is that they are less politically disquieting than intersexed individuals, because even though they wish to change genders, they do not pose any fundamental challenge to the concept of mutually exclusive categories of gender. That this may be the case can be seen when disapproval of them is reinstated if they appear to make any gender nonconformist choices in their gender of assignment, for example, a male-to-female transgendered patient choosing to wear trousers, continuing to masturbate or preferring a female sexual partner.

The politics of gender in the practice of therapy

The political organization of therapy with its inevitable power differential between patient and therapist will evidently intersect with culturally driven power distribution between men and women. Thus the overt and unconscious gender (not to mention declared and unconscious sexuality) of the analysing couples can give rise to myriad intersections of power and gender. (Some of these are covered in Denman 2001, 2003; others in Person 1999; Samuels 1989; Schaverien 1995.) In addition to considering how the politics of gender will impact on patients in therapy, it is also possible to ask a wider question about how the gender of therapy impacts on its organizational politics.

The existence of gender inequity within the professions that practise psychotherapy has already been pointed out. While women are preponderant among the practitioners of therapy, they are still underrepresented at the highest levels. Some of this inequity is related to underlying inequities in the professions that contribute their practitioners to the profession of psychotherapy; other parts are related to the difficulties women still have in pursuing careers in our culture; but the possibility of institutional sexism in psychotherapy organizations cannot be entirely ruled out.

But there is a more fundamental way in which the politics of gender may impact on the practice of therapy. In some ways, therapy is itself a gendered activity, even if its gender is rather uncertain! On the one hand, psychotherapy was founded by and remains dominated by white heterosexual men. Its theories apply generally in the default to white men, and other genders or sexual orientations, while increasingly theorized, are still routinely contrasted to the white straight male template.

Yet, on the other hand, there are both homosexual and feminine trends in the process and practice of therapy and these were discernible even in the early years of the psychoanalytic enterprise. Freud's issuing of a special ring to those in his inner circle and his intense relationship and subsequent bust-up with Jung have homosocial if not homosexual overtones. More generally, the whole activity of speaking intensely in a close confiding dyadic relationship is one that is distributed asymmetrically in relation to gender in our culture. Most men, when asked who their closest confidant is, will, if they are married, name their wife. Women asked the same question do not name their husbands but instead a close female friend or relative. Thus in confiding relationships in our culture, the one confided in, if not the one doing the confiding, is stereotypically female (O'Connor 1992).

Perhaps the dominant feature of gender as it manifests in the politics of therapy is gender confusion. Overtly straight heterosexual males lead a profession that engages them in activities that in some ways are both feminine and homoerotic. Samuels (1989) has argued that in individuals, gender confusion and gender certainty are in a reciprocal relationship to each other. If there is conscious gender confusion then gender certainty may be an unconscious feature and vice versa. It is intriguing to find a similar dialectic between gender confusion and gender certainty on the larger political arena.

The politics of object choice

Political struggles over homosexuality

The organization of therapy and its practice were for a long period of time in grim synergy over gay and lesbian sexuality. Homosexuals were unwell. Their sexual orientation needed correction and they should not, on account of their illness, be trained as therapists. This attitude has largely died out and remains acceptable only in the higher reaches of the analytic community (see, for example, Kernberg 1992).

In its place has come a large literature from homosexual and lesbian therapists offering a gay-affirmative approach to therapy and also beginning to theorize gay and lesbian sexuality from a range of therapeutic perspectives. (See, just for a start, Isay 1996; Lewes 1989; O'Connor and Ryan 1993.) At its most exciting this literature has relevance not only to the specific interests of gay and lesbian therapists and patients but also to a wider heterosexual audience, as insights derived from the margins (gay and lesbian experience) are turned to inform and provide a critique of the mainstream. This theoretical device has been exploited most extensively by theorists whose ideas draw on deconstruction and, in relation to gay and lesbian literature, the body of thought developed is often termed queer theory.

Queer theory

In the most general way, the use of the margins to provide a critique of the mainstream is a central feature of much postmodern thought on which queer theory draws. Queer theory aims to show how the sexual margins are a necessary creation of heterosexuality, even as it disavows them. A critique from those margins could break down the very mainstream/margin distinction itself. Foucault's (1981) political analysis of the body as a centre of biopower (an object of state regulation, contested social meaning and potential social change) set the agenda for queer theory as a political as opposed to a theoretical project. A good example in this respect is Monique Wittig, whose claim (1981) that lesbians are not women derived from her theoretical position that masculinity and femininity are defined in binary opposition to one another and therefore that a woman who relates to women cannot be defined this way. She argued that heterosexuality is the requirement of a political regime based on the oppression of women rather than of a sexual object choice. Patriarchy therefore requires enforced heterosexuality. Radical lesbians took up this project and sought to overthrow the political regime of 'heteropatriarchy'. There are advantages to this analysis in therapy where both lesbians and straight women can be helped to explore how their assumptions (derived from mainstream views) of heteropatriarchical norms confine and constrain them.

Paula, a straight married woman, always felt anxious with male friends. She worried her husband would misconstrue any closeness. In therapy, she wryly remarked that she was far more likely to have a lesbian than a straight fling but she never worried about spending time alone with her female friends.

For gay men, calls for radical self-exposure and self-definition have forced an examination of the policing of male sexuality. The acceptable gay man who assimilates into the straight world by being 'invisibly visible' (Bersani 1995) may be accepting this policing too easily. The revolutionary rather than the friendly and assailable elements of gay sex are emphasized by queer theorists such as Hocquenghem (1978) or Mohr (1992), both of whom are able to celebrate less assimilable elements of gay sex such as anal sex, anonymous sex or having multiple sexual partners. For these writers there is explosive and liberating power in gay sex, which has the potential to disrupt the gendered and sexual certainties of the established order.

But can any identity be secure? As might be expected, queer theorists have problems with any naive notion of identity and Judith Butler (1990) has done most both to problematize and to re-theorize identity. She argues that gender is a performance rather than a given and relentlessly questions any settled identity or identification that might provide a secure basis for launching a political or therapeutic project. Such a stance has evidently as much unsettling potential for heterosexual as for gay and lesbian identities and makes a secure foundation for political action difficult to find. Unsurprisingly, then, queer theory has been criticized for undermining by its stance of restless uncertainty the basis of any form of concerted political action. Similar criticisms have also been made of psychotherapy (Voloshonov 1976), which stands accused of relocating political conflict (the social) within the mind of individuals (the personal). A way out of this difficulty both for queer theory and psychotherapy is to understand the identity-making and identity-shaping value of political action. Thus engaging in political activism may be therapeutic both for the individual and society.

Case example: Gaynor

Gaynor had left her husband for a lesbian relationship. This had involved leaving behind her two daughters as she felt that she would be unable to win a custody battle. She struggled to maintain contact with them and to bear their rage and incomprehension over her decision. Often during access visits the children were extremely badly behaved and Gaynor did not know how to control them.

Gaynor was also both a mental health worker and a patient with quite a serious mental health problem. She entered therapy after difficulties with a work colleague, which she felt were rooted in homophobia. She was pressed into seeking treatment by her workplace and, in therapy, she explored the idea that the institutional response to these work difficulties might also be homophobic. As time passed she also came to see that the way work had dealt with her embodied its prejudice against people with mental health problems, a pretty irony for a mental health treatment service. Gaynor used therapy to explore her identity as a mental health service worker, a patient and a lesbian but she also became more politically active, setting up a group for mental health workers who were also users of mental health services. Some users of this group broke the confidentiality on which all had agreed and Gaynor found herself in the role of trying to keep order, but in general the group was successful and supportive. The responsibilities of running this group led to a re-evaluation of her own rebellious and wayward childhood. She felt more able to empathize with her mother and wondered to what extent the relationship would have gone better if she had been aware of herself as having a lesbian identity at that age.

cont.

> Gaynor's exploration of her rebelliousness allowed her to consider her own children's difficulties with her in a new light. She commented that she was both stricter with discipline and more permissive with them than she had been before.

The case of Gaynor illustrates the way in which issues of political oppression still face gay and lesbian patients, even in a middle-class enclave that might be expected to be at the liberal end of the political spectrum. However, it also shows the way in which a weaving of political and personal issues in and around therapy can stimulate at one and the same time political development, therapeutic growth and social action.

The politics of sexual activity

All cultures regulate sexual activity. Some early Freudian and Marxist therapists (Marcuse 1970, for example) argued that this was because of the revolutionary potential of sexual activity to disrupt social structures. So therapists find themselves dealing with political questions as much as sexual ones when patients consult with sexual difficulties.

Therapists have tended to side with the political mainstream by pathologizing sexual activities disapproved of by society. This tendency has meant that changing social values about sexual activity have often caught them off guard, making some at least seem old fashioned or even bigoted. For this reason, I have argued elsewhere (Denman 2003) that the psychotherapeutic notion of perversion or paraphilia is unhelpful since it picks out not sexual pathology but instead the moral or social acceptability of sexual practices. Instead, I have suggested that sexual activities that are outside the mainstream of a culture can be thought of as transgressive sex. Some transgressive sexual acts are harmless – for example, a rubber fetish or, in some cultures, masturbation. Other transgressive acts are harmful, either to the self or, more worryingly, to others. Where sexual acts harm others, I have suggested that they be classified as *coercive*. Such a classification system focuses on cultural attitudes and moral questions in relation to sex and remains silent on putative psychological mechanisms that may underlie non-standard sexual wishes. Depathologizing even very aesthetically disgusting or morally reprehensible sex is a necessary preliminary to understanding it.

One particularly interesting form of transgressive sexual preference can immediately be discerned. This is a preference for sex that is transgressive purely on that basis. The eroticization of the transgressive is found, for example (among much else), in the work of Battaille (1987) and Marquis de Sade (1966) but equally in the transgressive erotic celibate choices of

Christian mystics such as Theresa of Avila (Du Boulay 2004). The importance of this sexual preference is that it is a political act. Certain sexual activities are chosen because they are proscribed. This notion opens up the intriguing reciprocity that while sexual activities clearly have political ramifications, political activities may have erotic potential. Hunter Thompson, the maverick American political commentator, has, I think, tumbled to this in the title of one of his collected books of political writing, *Better than Sex* (Thompson 1995).

> Stuart was a lifelong animal rights activist. He consulted complaining of anxieties over loneliness and a failure to maintain any sexual relationships. During therapy it became clear that he was exceedingly anxious about his sexual wishes towards women and worried that these were not politically acceptable. It was also clear that in many ways his major love affair was with his organization in which he struggled and fought, at times rising to positions of power but at other times rebelling and threatening to leave. He described the thrill of political manoeuvring and intrigue in almost erotic terms and ultimately admitted that sometimes when he was particularly excited he would masturbate secretly during political meetings. Stuart used his time in therapy to explore his erotic wishes and his politics. Ultimately, he met a woman who had little interest in his political life but supported his rather neglected artistic and musical side. He married her but commented that erotically he felt he was settling for less than the best. His therapist commented that perhaps, for him, nothing much could compete with the erotic potential of political power and domination.

Sex in the consulting room

One area where sex has come to be proscribed is the consulting room of therapists themselves and patients who have been sexually exploited by their therapists have been harmed by this, even if there was apparent 'consent' at the time. However, one difficulty with evaluating the degree of harm is that it must be very likely that sexual contact between therapists and patients is substantially underreported and probable that where underreporting occurs the patient involved may be protecting the therapist from professional censure and may feel unharmed by the sex that occurred. So even though it is clear that the outcome of sexual contact is poor for patients and potentially detrimental in every case, it remains unclear that the results of sexual encounters between patient and therapist are more seriously damaging than other less investigated negative events in therapy, including financial misconduct by the therapist, breaches of confidentiality or technical errors. Furthermore, it is often the transgressive nature of the sex that both excites and upsets the patient, who becomes complicit in the transgression of a social taboo and is therefore to an extent damaged by sex in the consulting room simply because it *is* taboo. Thus current political interest in, even panic over, sexual boundary violations may have roots other than a purely rational concern for patient well-being.

Samuels (1999b) takes up some of these issues. He notices the harmful effects of sex panic on psychoanalytic psychotherapy, arguing that the effect is to promote the analysis of all erotic feeling as rooted in early mother–baby dynamics and thereby to do 'safe analysis', but even he returns to a safe zone by arguing for an eroticism that is experienced but not enacted in therapy. His work exemplifies a tendency in modern therapists to argue paradoxically for the value of felt but not enacted eroticism in psychotherapy (see, for example, many of the authors collected in Mann 1999). If the ban on sexuality in the consulting room is seen as, at least in part, the enforcement of a taboo rather than a purely rational prohibition, then its political value becomes clearer. Battaille (1987) suggests that the threat fought off by a taboo is of the contamination of the world of work by a sexuality that is too dangerous, and related to death, to be contained. Battaille's analysis of taboo provokes the thought that a necessary prohibition on sexual exploitation in the consulting room may also serve the political function of civilizing psychotherapy, fitting it and helping it to fit others for work and drawing them away from the dark excitements of the underworld.

The taboo on sex in the consulting room is therefore not as a necessary good that, if managed right, may be productive for the patient. Instead, it is probably a necessary evil that protects the patient from coercion and exploitation while chaining aspects of the erotic imaginations of both parties. Seeing the restraints on sexual expression in therapy as a politically necessary evil rather than as a personally difficult good has implications for therapy. It means that the restraint on the freedom of the erotic imagination in therapy can be genuinely mourned because it is genuinely being acknowledged as a loss.

Given the tendency of humans to have sex whenever possible and the potential for the eroticization of the transgressive, it is unlikely that any form of regulation will eliminate sexual contact between patient and therapist. It is important that patients who disclose and are troubled by sexual contact between themselves and a therapist are treated with sensitivity and care. Recognizing the taboo aspects of the disclosed contact may help guard against scapegoating the patient, as has sometimes occurred.

Conclusion

This chapter has tried to show how political struggles in the areas of gender, sexual orientation and sexual behaviour can touch on and complicate the lives of patients. Since therapists concern themselves centrally with the struggles, emotional and practical, of their patients, knowledge of the politics of these areas is invaluable. For this reason therapists should inform themselves about a wide range of such issues and should strive for a position that, because it is as non-judgemental as possible, allows the maximum room for the lived complexity of their patients' lives.

A second theme that has been illustrated in this chapter is the way in which struggles over gender, sexual orientation and sexual behaviour can also be found in the politics of the organization of psychotherapy. In relation to issues of sexuality, there are often considerable moral, political and practical complexities to negotiate. Therapists therefore owe it to their profession as well as their patients to think hard about these issues.

Annotated bibliography

Bancroft, J. (1989) *Human Sexuality and its Problems*. Edinburgh: Churchill Livingstone.
The basic primer for doctors and sexologists on the biology and psychology of sexual difficulty viewed from a medical perspective.
Butler, J. (1990) *Gender Trouble: Feminism and the Subversion of Identity*. New York: Routledge.
A complex post modern book which seeks to unsettle received notions of the natural categories of gender and argue that these are socially constructed entities.
Chodorow, N. (1978) *The Reproduction of Mothering; Psychoanalysis and the Sociology Of Gender*. Berkeley CA: U niversity of California Press.
An influential feminist psychoanalytic text showing how gender asymmetry in childrearing practice serves to reproduce stereotyped male and female roles in each successive generation.
Califia, P. (1997) *Sex Changes; The Politics of Transgenderism*. San Francisco: Cleis Press.
A sensitive and well-informed history of transgendered people and their struggles. Partly included here to entice the reader to explore the radical writings of Pat Califia further.
Denman, C. (2003) *Sexuality: A Biopsychosocial Approach*. London: Palgrave Macmillan.
A general book on sexuality aimed at informing psychotherapists and counsellors. It covers a wide range of topics in the field of sexuality and therapy. The book advocates a sex positive approach, and the importance and transformative potential of the erotic imagination.

Isay, R. (1996) *Becoming Gay: The Journey to Self Acceptance.* New York: Pantheon Books.

An important and well-written book by an out gay psychoanalyst. It argues that homosexual orientation is a biological given but that gay identity an acquired state of self-acceptance. It contains a good range of sensitive case discussions.

Mohr, R. (1992) *Gay Ideas; Outing and Other Controversies.* Boston: Beacon Press.

A powerful collection of political essays centering on homosexuality by an engaging and radical thinker.

O'Connor, N. and Ryan, J. (1993) *Wild Desires and Mistaken Identities: Lesbianism and Psychoanalysis.* London: Virago.

Discusses the theory of female homosexuality as outlined by psychoanalysts and exposes the homophobia, prejudice and misguided assumptions inherent in their work.

Samuels, A. (1993) *The Political Psyche.* London: Routledge.

An important book arguing for therapists to consider politics much more seriously. It covers issues of sexuality and gender extensively.

Stoller, R.J. (1991) *Pain and Passion: A Psychoanalyst Explores the Word of S & M.* New York: Plenum.

An open-minded exploration of one kind of transgressive sexuality by an analyst turned anthropologist. Stoller's other books in this area also repay study.

6 Working with difference: the political context of psychotherapy with an intersubjective dialogue
Judy Ryde

Introduction

There has been a tendency within the field to see psychotherapy as being primarily about the inner world of individuals and not about understanding them as they exist within a cultural context (Kareem and Littlewood 1992: xi; Ryde 1997). In fact, Hillman and Ventura (1992) pointed out the failure of psychotherapy to address societal issues. In this chapter, I want to explore the way in which difference in culture can be addressed within the psychotherapy relationship and show how, if we understand it within an intersubjective context, we do not have to desert the personal to address cultural and societal issues.

If we understand psychotherapy as an intersubjective endeavour, then our subjectivity has to be acknowledged as part of the field. My own research (Ryde 2004) has shown how white people need most importantly to understand themselves as having a racial identity within the racialized context of our society and how this is an important part of the intersubjective field of the therapy. While acknowledging that culture can be defined more widely and include issues of sexuality, gender, class etc., I am concentrating on issues regarding race in this chapter. The main thrust of what I describe does hold true, however, in these different areas. For instance, within the intersubjective space of a therapy in which there is a gay client and a straight therapist, the straight therapist needs to know their own sexuality, rather than see themselves as representing a 'normality' from which the gay person deviates. In the same way, a white therapist will know themselves as racially white and not merely representing normality from which black people deviate.

My focus here, then, is on therapy in a western context in which there are differences in 'race' between therapist and client. (I understand 'race' to be socially constructed and not biologically 'real' and racism to be different from xenophobia, where no difference in power relationships is implied. For the purposes of this chapter, I understand racism to exist where there is cultural difference plus a difference in the institutionalized power relationship; and, importantly, to include people from the Islamic world such as the Middle East.)

As psychotherapy originated in and has grown out of the western world, it tends to focus on the *individual* psyche. In doing so it reflects a society that has become more and more individualistically oriented in the last few centuries (Elias 1994). It follows from that very individualism that notions such as 'personal growth' seem perfectly natural and self-evidently a 'good thing'. For those for whom the natural unit of society is the family or tribe, this desire for self-improvement can be seen as selfish or self-centred. Sue and Sue point out that:

> When an Asian client states to a counselor or therapist, 'I can't make that decision on my own; I need to consult with my parents or family' he or she is seen as being quite immature. After all, therapy is aimed at helping individuals to 'make decisions on their own' in a 'mature' and 'responsible ' manner.
>
> (Sue and Sue 1990: 36)

Many authors (Bateson 1982; Bohm 1980) are questioning the turn that western society took in understanding the individual as a unit that is a separate subject in a world of objects. In theorizing psychotherapy, the intersubjectivists of the Institute for Contemporary Psychoanalysis (Orange 1995; Stolorow and Atwood 1987, 1992; Stolorow *et al.* 2002) take a similar approach. They understand the 'self' to be co-created in the relationship, so that the 'self' I co-create with one person is not the same 'self' I am with another. This position naturally leads to an understanding of human beings inhabiting a complex web of interrelationship that becomes the cultural context in which we live.

Psychotherapists are sometimes criticized for focusing on the needs of individuals when it is society that needs attention. For me, however, inter-subjectivity theory resolves this dilemma as the two are understood to be completely interrelated. It also therefore starts to address the dilemma posed by some cultures being individualistic while others see the individual as more importantly part of a group. In fact, intersubjectivity theory provides more of a challenge to individualistic ways of thinking than to group ways as intersubjectivists regard the idea that we are 'isolate minds' as a 'myth' (Stolorow and Atwood 1992: 7). They propose that this myth has led humankind to be alienated from nature, from social life and from subjectivity, which they regard as the most important since the myth perpetuates the idea that the mind is reified – 'a thing among things' (Stolorow and Atwood 1992: 11). Cultures that do not stress individuality are typically less likely to be alienated in this sense. For instance, Lago and Thompson (1996: 86) say that Asian culture 'emphasizes an ontology of cosmic unity, with the highest value (axiology) on the cohesiveness of the group', and that

African culture 'emphasizes both a spiritual and material ontology with the highest value (axiology) on interpersonal relationships between women and men'.

For those who live in these cultures, the 'mind' is not isolated but part of a greater whole. For people who originate from cultures with these sorts of value, intersubjective psychotherapy may, in some respects, have epistemologies in common. I will return to the ways in which intersubjectivity theory is useful in this context later.

Inevitably, if there is a meeting between those from non-western countries and a western therapist, political issues are also present, including the power imbalance caused by the privilege of those from western countries. These are necessarily part of the field of the psychotherapy inquiry and so need to be addressed within the therapy.

For example, a gay, Muslim, African client was extremely distressed about having lost his family, country and religion, all of which are of the utmost importance to him, because of his homosexuality. His loss of family and religion, which occurred because of cultural and religious attitudes and political policies, are incalculable losses that are very hard for him to bear. He impresses on me the circumstances that have led him to experience these losses and finds that prejudice about homosexuality is rife in this country as well. When he gained refugee status in this country he became even more acutely aware of his sense of loss and this led to his feeling more rather than less depressed. Having this loss received and understood and the pain of it borne by another brings some relief and the possibility of re-finding a fulfilling life (Fox 2002: 103).

Understanding clients' difficulties as purely internal, personal manifestations can be reductive and disrespectful. This attitude ignores the emotional effect of racism and often, in the case of refugees and asylum seekers, extreme persecution and trauma caused by political decisions and actions both in Britain and in their country of origin (Dalal 2002: 76; Tuckwell 2002).

Unconscious Processes and Institutional Racism

While it is important for the political/societal to be acknowledged within psychotherapy, maybe it is also possible for psychotherapy to bring some insight into the political world. Furthering an understanding of unconscious processes working within society could be an example. Ideas concerning institutional racism and 'politically correct' behaviour seem to me to be good examples of this.

Institutional racism is a term that describes the way in which racist attitudes can run through the fabric of society in an endemic and largely unconscious way and seems to be much more intractable than personal racism. Institutional racism was famously brought to public attention in the Macpherson Report (Macpherson 1999) on the murder of Stephen Lawrence. In it Macpherson writes about 'unwitting racism' and seems to make this interchangeable with 'unconscious racism'. The latter implies that there is no consciousness of the racism where the former only implies that it is accidental.

If racism is 'unconscious' rather than 'unwitting' it implies a different and much more difficult path to bringing about change. In fact, for me, the term 'institutional racism' implies that the racism is embedded in the 'organizing principles' (Stolorow and Atwood 1992) of society in an endemic way. While individuals may be horrified to think that they are racist, by their unconsciously held assumptions and complicit involvement in society, they partake in racism.

There is a similar confusion in the area of 'politically correct' behaviour. This code of behaviour has grown up more or less informally but has had a powerful effect on racist attitudes in western society as well as on attitudes to other minority groups. It is implied that if you follow the code 'correctly' you will not be seen to behave in a prejudiced way. What you really think consciously or unconsciously may be different or, at least, more ambivalent than that which you apparently espouse, of course. Feelings towards those one regards as having a different 'race' may be very complex and not readily dealt with by prescribing a simple formula. The reception of 'politically correct' behaviour in society has been mixed and is often derided as being absurd, for instance in its embargo on the use of the word 'black' in any circumstances.

Nevertheless, 'politically correct' ideas have certainly been successful in changing many behaviours and attitudes that are racist or sexist, etc. It is almost unheard of now to refer to black people as 'coloured' or 'negro', for instance, or, indeed, use the word 'chairman' rather than 'chairperson' or 'chair'. It provides a simple code of behaviour that is relatively easily followed and can be taught in a straightforward way. Although change is not as easy as this implies, I do also think that changing our habits of speech can effect a change in attitude as well.

The difficulty with this approach to racism is that it can encourage racist thoughts and feelings to go underground. I am not suggesting that the hiding of racist attitudes is necessarily unconscious. An individual may make a conscious effort not to use offensive language when in certain situations (such as at work where it is required that they do not show racist attitudes) while knowing quite consciously that they actually do not think in that way. This was clearly shown on a BBC programme and reported in the *Guardian* (Wednesday November 5 2003) in which a reporter joined the police force under cover in order to show the real racism that is found there. Although the police in this case were conscious of their racism, it is my contention that the reason for their racism is, at least in part, unconscious, much of it being held within the organizing principles (Stolorow and Atwood 1992: 33) of individuals and groups.

Provision of psychotherapy for non-white, western clients

However well psychotherapy is able to provide some insight into these kinds of unconscious process in society, it does not mean that psychotherapy as a profession is immune to these same processes. It seems, from the small numbers of black trainers, therapists and students, that racism is institutionalized within the psychotherapy profession as well.

Nevertheless various authors have responded to the needs of those from black and minority ethnic groups to receive culturally sensitive counselling and psychotherapy and feel strongly that equality of access to these services is deeply important for the well-being of all communities (Kareem and Littlewood 1992; Lago and Thompson 1996; Sue and Sue 1990). Akinsete (2002), whose research explored why black men typically do not take up counselling, found that the black men he interviewed would only be prepared to see a counsellor who was black, if they saw one at all. However, most authors who write in the area of culture and psychotherapy tend to focus on encouraging sensitization to cultural difference (Lago and Thompson 1996; Sue and Sue 1990). I am nevertheless very aware, as someone who used to be director of a counselling service, that most black people do ask to see a counsellor who is black just as gay people and lesbians often want to have gay or lesbian therapists.

Although it is often good policy to have the facility of a diverse group of psychotherapists available to meet this need wherever possible, I consider it, as a catch-all solution, to be problematic on three counts:

- If cultural matching is thought of as a complete solution, it may not seem as necessary to try to ensure intercultural sensitivity in the training and ongoing development of psychotherapists.
- In our society, any individual's cultural mix is hard to match, often making it impossible to carry out even when it seems to have been attended to (both parties are not white, for instance).
- Psychotherapy itself is a western phenomenon so, to some extent, the psychotherapist has been enculturated in western attitudes, thus ensuring that cultural matching may not, in itself, guard against prejudiced views.

In the light of these considerations, I do not advocate that people from any or all cultures would or should find psychotherapy acceptable. I do, however, think that it should be openly available to all comers and sensitive to people of any or all cultures should they want to engage in it. My experience in working with refugees and asylum seekers shows that those who come from non-individualistic cultures welcome a chance to explore their own experiences and value a relationship in which this inquiry becomes possible. My own approach, as I earlier explained, is inquiring and does not reduce all to personal pathology, which helps me to find a 'meeting place' with such clients.

I have several Muslim clients who describe their own culture to me as one in which the family and 'tribe' is very 'close' so that dishonour to the family implies dishonour to the self. Conflicts within the family must not therefore be shown to strangers and to do so itself dishonours the family. Normally, speaking in this way to a non-family member would be unthinkable. Nevertheless, I find that clients who have few supports, particularly as they come in extreme distress, will often be prepared to explore their own difficulties in psychotherapy. Their desperate need seems to lead them to understand that not having anyone to talk to increases their sense of isolation and interferes with their ability to cope with life in England. I have the sense that they also think 'this is how things are done round here' and are more prepared to do things differently than they would at home, particularly in private in a professional context.

Impact of power differences on the psychotherapeutic relationship

We can see then that differences of race or culture have significant ramifications for the psychotherapy relationship. As I have shown already, this is partly because difference in culture leads to difference in basic assumptions about life. On top of these differences, there is an often unspoken power difference in the relationship between people from white, western and non-western backgrounds. In psychotherapy, this power difference is compounded if the therapist is western and the client is non-western (Lago and Thompson 1996: 16-27; Ryde 1997, 2000). The white therapist may be considered by the client and, indeed, by herself and society at large as the one who is mentally healthy and who defines what 'mental health' is, as well as having the power to be 'helpful' (Sue and Sue 1990).

Hofstede (1980, quoted in Lago and Thompson 1996: 45) discusses how different cultures regard small and large power distance. Power distance concerns how power is distributed within the culture. In some cultures, rigid hierachies of power are accepted as desirable while others prefer relatively flattened hierachies. This means that the power between psychotherapist and client may have a particular meaning that may not be understood between them (Ryde 2000; Thomas 1992: 136). For instance, a western therapist may consider a client to be unusually submissive when, from the client's point of view, it would be unthinkably impolite not to give way to the opinion of a professional.

If the power imbalance implicit between those whose cultural roots are in the predominant global culture of the white western world and those outside this culture is to be addressed, it needs to be acknowledged and responded to within the therapy. Thoughtfulness rather than reactivity about these power dynamics can be encouraged in supervision. It is important therefore that supervisors understand the way in which power differences may affect both the therapeutic and the supervision relationship.

Brown and Bourne have addressed this by exploring what happens in the supervision triad when there are cultural differences in at least one of the parties. They point out (1996: 39) all the different possible combinations that can arise when someone from a minority group is in each of the possible roles and the complex power dynamics that result. Inskipp and Proctor (1995) have also pointed to the dynamics in relationships between black and white in a series of eight triangles showing all the possible combinations of supervisor, client and counsellor with each being black or white. Each triangle has its own dynamic that is influenced by the different power dynamics inherent in the roles and the ethnic grouping.

To draw this out further I have devised another triangle (Figure 6.1): one that demonstrates the complex power dynamics inevitably present in cross-cultural supervision (Ryde 2000). At each corner there are three different types of power: role power, cultural power and individual power.

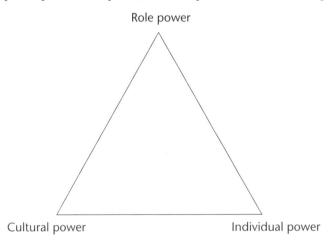

Figure 6.1

Role power identifies the power inherent in the role of supervisor, and *cultural power* the power of the dominant ethnic grouping, usually someone who was born within the white, western majority. This power is emphasized if that person is male, middle class, heterosexual and able bodied. *Individual power* points to the particular power of the individual's personality, which may be over and above that given to the person through role or culture.

Intersubjectivity and working across cultural difference

The complexity of the way in which power is held within the relationship is important to recognize within the intersubjective field of the therapy. As I hope can be seen by my responses so far, my starting point is not so much to try to understand other people's culture but to understand my own within my political and social context including my racial identity as a white person. From there I hope to open a dialogue across any difference in culture.

The intersubjectivists suggest that, in a therapeutic encounter, there is a meeting within an intersubjective field of two *differently organized* subjectivities (Atwood and Stolorow 1984: 65). Because of that, we need to take into account our own 'organizing principles' (Atwood and Stolorow 1984: 36), which are formed within our own cultural context when we attempt to meet our clients. Orange *et al.* (1997) suggest that we need to:

> strive ... in [our] self reflective efforts [for] awareness of our own personal organizing principles – including those enshrined in [our] theories – and of how these principles are unconsciously shaping [our] understandings and interpretations.

I have found that when I do not reflect on myself in this way, my clients are likely to feel that I am not present for them. Sometimes they tell me this, but more often I sense it in their withdrawal. If I do sense this, I might ask them if they experience it too, if I feel that our relationship is ready for this sort of exploration. This is particularly important because it is not being *immediately* understood that matters but the *genuine and sustained desire* to try to understand on the part of the therapist that is so vitally important (Orange 1995: 129). Casement is referring to something of this nature when he says that it is important as a psychoanalyst to 'survive, but only just' (1990: 88). He is referring to the attacks that clients make on us when they feel us to misunderstand them and the importance of not only surviving these attacks but also of *only just* surviving. If we survive easily we will not have really experienced the attack and understood its ferocity. In referring to the importance of a 'sustained empathic inquiry' (Orange 1995; Stolorow and Atwood 1992: 93; Stolorow *et al.* 1994: 45), intersubjectivists also emphasize the importance of showing a continuing desire to understand. Orange (1995) has devoted a book to this subject. In it she says something that I find useful in working across culture:

> Misunderstanding often seems to be the normal state of the psychoanalytic triad – the two subjectivities and the intersubjective field that includes them. If some fundamental emotional safety exists, however, analyst and patient together can attain understanding by continually working through in a fallibilistic spirit, the small and the large misunderstandings.
>
> (Orange 1995: 158)

Listening in this way is not always easy even when the therapist thinks her intention is good. Stolorow and Atwood (1992) explore this by pointing to the way intersubjective conjunctions and disjunctions occur in the therapy. Intersubjective conjunctions refer to a situation in which the organizing principles of the therapist and the client are closely aligned and disjunctions to the way in which they are dissimilar. Both may lead to difficulties in the therapy as conjunctions may lead to collusion with the client and disjunctions may lead to a lack of attunement. A psychotherapist who is working intersubjectively looks out for this phenomenon both in their private reflection on the work and in supervision. Stolorow and Atwood say: 'Whether these intersubjective situations facilitate or obstruct the progress of the therapy depends in large part on the extent of the therapist's ability to become reflectively aware of the organizing principles of their own subjective world' (1992: 103).

Crucially, it is the recognition of these conjunctions and disjunctions and the way in which they are understood within the therapy that makes the difference. I have found that owning to a lack of attunement can feel deeply significant to the client and helps to move the therapy on. These are particularly useful concepts when working across cultures as the organizing principles of the therapist may well be very different to those of the client, leading to serious lack of attunement. The recognition of this when it happens can make all the difference, although this recognition is not always straightforward. A Middle Eastern client often rejects my attempts to show an understanding of her but does seem to appreciate that I try to understand what is not correct about it. She acknowledges that the sessions are an important part of her week and has only missed once, in spite of being quite seriously ill. Thinking through what she has told me after the session and in supervision helps me to 'stay with' the difficult and painful material.

In understanding racism in an intersubjective way it seems to me to come as part and parcel of seeing human beings as not having completely separate watertight identities, but all intrinsically connected through culture as I will show later. I have an image of a web or network of invisible lines that runs through society, joining and connecting us. At places this web is thicker and more complex where culture is shared but maybe we would have to go to another universe to find someone to whom this web did not connect us at all.

The threesome of me, an interpreter and an Arabic client comes to mind in illustration. The web connects the interpreter with the client. They belong to the same national culture so share many of the same basic assumptions and ways of approaching life. They are both Muslim and deeply religious and they both have had to flee their country, so share something of what that means to them. The interpreter and I are both pro-fessional women and work within a primary care trust together. The threads of professionalism and care and respect for clients join us also with a certain professional cultural norm. The client and I are both women in our 50s who have married and had children and know the depth of feeling and contact that that brings us. The web joins us in this profound knowledge. We are all joined by our human experience and cultural knowledge, though the web may be thicker in some places than others.

Since working more intensively with people who are not white or western I have never found myself working with someone who is a com-plete mystery to me. Some point of connection can be found and often this feels a deep and significant connection. Sometimes the other's reality is harder for me to understand. My interpreter, maybe because of having dif-ferent organizing principles, finds it hard to say certain things to my client. She cannot, for instance, refer to my client's husband as a 'husband'. She must refer to him as the 'father of your children'. I find that I am not quite clear why this is, even though I have asked her. The subtleties of this are hard for me to understand. She also cannot refer to my client's body. I find this easier as it accords with some of my own organizing principles. My mother could never refer to 'bodies', as they were intimate and embarrass-ing. Maybe I overlay my own situation on hers here so that I thought the feeling was like my own in what Stolorow and Atwood (1992: 103) would call an intersubjective conjunction and the thread is broken at this point. Although I think I understand this, maybe I have *assumed* something from my own experience.

Nevertheless, I feel my client's bodily experience is important to talk about and ask the interpreter if she would mind making an exception. I am aware that we are both taking a big risk but I weigh it up and think it is worth it. I remind myself that this client is not living in ordinary times so that extraordinary measures have to be taken. My interpreter agrees to interpret. I refer to the arthritis she has had since her daughter was murdered. I say: 'I think the death of your daughter has entered your body and gives you pain in every cell of it.' The client cries and nods. My sense is that we have had a breakthrough in our understanding of one another. I feel that the interpreter and I also reach a greater intimacy as we all participate in moments that feel painful but connecting. The client does not appear to notice that something has been infringed. Maybe this is because my understanding of her deep sorrow has been heard and that is more important. Another human being can approach something of what she feels.

Conclusion

It is clear that understanding those who have different cultural assumptions is vitally important within the therapeutic encounter. The greater the difference in culture, the more important it is. What makes it most important is that, unless we are aware of the impact of cultural difference, we make our own assumptions and think that we are able to understand based on those assumptions. Maiello shows this very clearly in her paper 'Encounter with an African healer' (1999). In it she struggles to understand the basis of the healer's approach, which, it seems to her, is built on an understanding of the power of the ancestors and involves very little verbal communication with the 'client'. She makes some attempt to understand the process in her own terms and to describe her own work in the healer's terms. However, when the healer suggests that they exchange medicines – a herbal remedy for a 'word' – Maiello is at a loss. There is a sense in the paper of respect but also of mystification. She points out that there is a psychoanalytical anthropology but not an anthropological psychoanalysis and concludes:

> The first step that can be made towards finding an answer to the question of the depth at which cultural factors influence the intersubjective and intrapsychic dimension of mental life is the openness to the intercultural exploration and debate.
>
> (Maiello 1999: 237)

As a psychotherapist and supervisor of psychotherapists, I am constantly amazed at how complex the intricacies of relationships are when they are thoroughly explored and reflected upon in psychotherapy. Cultural differences are always present in some guise, however small. As I intimated at the start of this chapter, these 'differences in culture' can be those brought about by differences in sexuality, gender, class etc. There is a similar power difference within the majority culture from which powerful cultural assumptions arise. It is interesting to me that in America, the branch of sociology known as 'white studies' is often taken up by feminists who recognize the dynamics involved through the way they have addressed issues of gender (Frye 1983; McIntosh 1988).

Maybe developing an ability to stay open to the painful and confusing feelings that arise in these situations while being able to articulate something about them is a way forward. In that way we keep open an inquiry and a dialogue that provide a foundation on which a psychotherapeutic encounter may be based.

Perhaps psychotherapy that recognizes the intersubjective field provides a way forward for the provision of psychotherapy where there is a difference in culture. An intersubjective understanding allows for both psychotherapist and client to exist within the intersubjective field in which the encounter occurs. An intersubjectivist understands the self to be structured around a set of organizing principles that are arrived at within a cultural context. The work is grounded in the knowledge that this is true for both psychotherapist and client.

7 Power in the therapeutic relationship
Nick Totton

Can anyone do effective therapy without becoming an instrument of social control, without participating and contributing, often unknowingly, to the construction or the maintenance of a dominant discourse of oppression?

(Cecchin 1993: ix)

Psychotherapy is the only profession where the practitioner can be insensitive, evasive, patronising, arrogant, discourteous, self-righteous or just plain wrong and where clients' observations of this can be taken to be an expression of their *problems, evidence that what they really need is more of the same therapy.*

(Sands 2003: 15)

Introduction

The psychotherapy relationship is vulnerable to the abuse of power, from hard-to-define but nonetheless damaging emotional manipulation to very concrete behaviours such as financial and sexual exploitation. These abuses are fairly common; but how far are they part of the *structure* of the psychotherapy relationship and the feelings it fosters – exaggerated versions, perhaps, of something underlying every therapeutic encounter? I will focus on how the structure of psychotherapy builds in stubborn problems of power and control, irrespective of the good intentions or otherwise of the practitioner.

Like the fact of abuse itself, these structural issues have often been pointed out – often, understandably, as part of an argument against therapy per se. My own position is much more optimistic than this. I believe that *by making the struggle over power a central focus of the therapeutic encounter*, we can do as Freud did with transference: turn a structural problem into a creative aspect of therapy. In fact, this is what many therapists and their clients are already doing. It may actually be a necessary condition for a positive therapeutic outcome.

Abuse of power

Outright therapeutic abuse is serious and widespread. According to the UK charity POPAN (2004), 50 per cent of calls to their phone helpline are alleging abuse within the talking treatments; this amounts to around 300 people each year and – since many clients have never heard of POPAN – must represent only a small proportion of what actually occurs. Several different forms of abuse have been documented, including such things as clients being unable to tell their counsellor that the counselling is not being helpful or being afraid to quit therapy because of the anticipated response of the counsellor (Dale *et al.* 1998); gay users of counselling reporting that their therapists advised them to change their sexual orientation (Garnets *et al.* 1991; several psychoanalysts freely admit to this, e.g. Socarides 1996); and – far more researched than any other abuse – sexual activity between therapists and their clients.

Many different figures are quoted for sexual abuse, probably the highest being a finding that 9 per cent of male psychotherapists anonymously admitted to having had sexual involvement with clients (Pope *et al.* 1986). According to Prozan's (1993: 354–6) collation of American research on sexual abuse in therapy, around 5 per cent to 7 per cent of therapists admit anonymously to sexual contact with clients, while 65 per cent to 70 per cent of therapists report hearing from a client that a previous therapist has had sexual contact with them. Pope's recent survey (2001) indicates 4.4 per cent of therapists admitting to sexual abuse and argues that the incidence may be declining; it is also possible that the tightening of accepted standards means that, even anonymously, fewer practitioners will admit to sexual abuse (i.e. more self-deception is being practised). Sexual abuse happens at the top of the therapeutic hierarchy at least as often as lower down (for instance, Noel and Watterson 1992).

Sex in therapy is a difficult subject to address soberly, being subject to the 'moral panic' effect (Pearson 1983). Denman (Chapter 5, this volume) offers a valuable reconceptualization of therapist–client sex that, without condoning it, positions it as one of a *range* of harmful activities in therapy and suggests that its prohibition is 'a politically necessary evil rather than ... a personally difficult good'. One might also suggest that, like child or adult rape, sex between therapist and client is symptomatic of an inability to perceive or imagine the other person's experience and needs and that this inability is unacceptable in a psychotherapist at work.

Structural problems of the therapy relationship

Critics often argue that the sorts of abuse just outlined are related to how therapy is structured and how this makes clients feel. Many focus specifically on the power imbalance that accrues around transference (see, for example, Sands 2000). Generally speaking, clients arrive at therapy hoping and expecting that the therapist will be able to help, through their wisdom, understanding and expertise: in a very natural way, they tend to give power to the therapist. In Krause's words: 'There is always the possibility of conflict in communication. There is therefore also always the possibility that the most powerful will persuade, command, or even terrorize the less powerful' (1998: 153).

Many familiar therapy techniques intensify the transferential power imbalance: not only do clients give power to the therapist, the therapist acts so as to grab power with both hands. As Sands points out, the rules of conversation are strikingly different within therapy from outside it: 'for example, they do not follow the conventions which cover "turn-taking" … in normal speech' (2000: 39). The client has to learn what sort of communication is expected and accepted. In this and many other ways (for example, therapists' obsession with precise punctuality and their apparent belief that clients can control the traffic), the unfamiliar situation throws the client off balance, in fact infantilizes them – in David Smail's phrase, it creates 'social dislocation' (Smail 2003: 22). I recently watched a video of an assessment interview conducted by a psychoanalytic therapist, which started approximately as follows: after a long pause, the clearly uncomfortable client asked the very reasonable question, 'So should I just tell you about why I'm here?' The therapist's response was, 'Is there something else that you feel should happen?' – a familiar and comprehensible move from an 'insider's' viewpoint, but from the prospective client's perspective, a humiliating and mystifying one.

It is this sort of interaction that leads Mearns and Thorne to say that, at the start, 'the counsellor holds nearly all the cards in a game of which the client does not even know the rules' (1988: 98). As Hinshelwood argues (1997: 101–2), no genuinely informed consent to undertake psychotherapy is possible: no one can appreciate in advance what it will be like, however much it is explained. And even when the client learns the rules, they are not her rules, but those of the therapist, or of the therapy 'game' itself.

> It is always the analyst … who establishes the rules that govern behaviour in this primal space. However much these rules may be constructed to enable the patient's cure, the analyst is their maker and enforcer.
>
> (Kurtz 1989: 27–8)

This situation is open to massive exploitation, as Claude Steiner confesses:

> As a successful psychotherapist ... I used my power to the hilt – and not always to my client's advantage ... I interrupted, overrode, ignored, judged, evaluated, insulted, attacked, patronized, discounted and lied to the people I worked for ... assuming that they needed my gentle, authoritative, sometimes devious, parental attitude, in order to get better.
>
> (Steiner 1981: 214)

Steiner is not confessing to malice or bad faith, but simply to compulsive helping combined with belief in his own expert knowledge.

> The profession of psychotherapy unfortunately does include those who believe that they know what other people really think and feel. We all make this mistake, of course, we do it all the time, but it becomes particularly dangerous when it is given the benediction of the status of expert.
>
> (Sands 2000: 190)

This uncannily echoes a criticism put to Freud by his friend Fliess in the earliest days of psychoanalysis: 'The reader of thoughts merely reads his own thoughts into other people' (Masson 1985: 447). Clearly, the more unresolved issues the therapist has (and only psychopaths believe themselves free of unresolved issues) the more danger there is that these 'thoughts' will be positively misleading – that, as Cecchin puts it in the context of family therapy, the therapist will try 'to instruct the family in his own pattern' of neurosis (1987: 411).

And if the client protests, the therapist has a number of finely honed tools for putting them back in their place. The greatest of these is interpretation. I remember once hearing a presentation (similar things are said every day) where a therapist described a difficult relationship with a client who argued against many of his interpretations of her words and behaviour. One day she came in and told him she had bought a new bath, which turned out not to fit properly, so that she had to bash it around to get it into the available space. His immediate interpretation was that this represented her distortion of her own material in order to accommodate her version of its meaning. But might it not have been the therapist himself who was portrayed as bashing the client's material into his own preferred shape?

Readers who are psychotherapists or counsellors may be starting to feel anxious and defensive. Me too. After all, we know we are (fairly) good people! We know that we are (consciously) well intentioned. Yet therapy can often feel to the client like a 'no win' situation, where someone else always holds the better cards. (For an extended analysis along these lines of a case history of Patrick Casement's, see Totton 2000: 144–6.) Sometimes this is recognizably a matter of 'bad' therapy, where the practitioner is unskilful, arrogant or in bad faith. But is there such a thing as 'good' therapy, free from problems of uneven power? Jeffrey Masson believes that there is not:

> Psychotherapy cannot be reformed in its parts, because the activity, by its nature, is harmful. Recognizing the lies, the flaws, the harm, the potential for harm, the imbalance in power, the arrogance, the condescension, the pretensions may be the first step to the eventual abolition of psychotherapy that I believe is, one day in the future, inevitable and desirable.
>
> (Masson 1990: 297)

As I will explain later, I disagree with Masson that psychotherapy should be abolished. But I think he is right to suggest that it is not only the 'bad' therapist who imposes her own judgements and understandings on her clients. Masson's discussion (1990: 229ff) of Carl Rogers – by general agreement a highly skilled, empathic and conscientious practitioner, whom Masson nonetheless shows exercising a 'benevolent despotism' over his clients – must lead us to ask whether *something about the practice itself*, rather than about particular practitioners, creates problems around power.

This goes beyond the issue of the individual power relationship between client and therapist and raises questions about how therapy works to support and enforce the power relations of society as a whole. Ian Parker draws attention to 'the power of the therapist as a … part of the regime of truth that defines what subjectivity must be like' (Parker 1996: 459); a 'regime of truth' being a discourse that 'is effective in organizing and regulating relations of power' (Foucault 1980: 131; cf. Rose 1990). Therapy that positions the client as powerless in the face of socially sanctioned expertise clearly supports the uneven distribution of power.

Thus Felix Guattari argues that even a radical analyst is repressive through the nature of his work:

> His [sic] whole way of working reproduces the essence of bourgeois subjectivity. A man who sits on his chair listening to what you say, but systematically distances himself from what it is all about, does not even have to try to impose his ideas on you: he is creating a relationship of power which leads you to concentrate your desiring energy outside the social territory.
>
> (Guattari 1984: 69)

(That is, it leads you to alienate your subjectivity.)

In one way or another, I suggest, all therapists are carrying out a political programme in their work with clients. Therapists have their own, often highly developed, beliefs about how people should be and live. These beliefs are essentially political in nature; they are also often unconscious and implicit. For us to hold such beliefs is an inevitable part both of our lives as citizens and of our whole approach to interacting with our clients. This is very obvious with therapy styles that think explicitly in terms of cure and adjustment: people *should* be healthy, *should* be well adjusted – and, of course, each school and each practitioner has their own set of small print about what 'healthy' or 'well adjusted' actually means. 'Well adjusted' to what? Each practitioner believes their clients should adjust to whatever aspects of life they themselves see as natural or acceptable.

This programmatic aspect, although more obvious with approaches that explicitly seek cure or adjustment, does not only apply to them. We can see this clearly in relation to sexuality: each therapist has their own ideas about what constitutes normal sexual behaviour and inevitably applies these to their work with clients. It is actually not at all easy even to make our ideas about sex available for conscious consideration. We can spend years in therapy achieving this. Consciously or unconsciously, we listen to our clients talk about sex through the filter of our own sense of what is OK or not OK; and consciously or unconsciously, our clients pick this up – pick up our sexual politics. Consciously or unconsciously, we seek to move our clients towards a view and a practice of sex that is closer to our own. One position we may take, of course, is that we accept, or try to accept, any sexual behaviour that makes our clients happy. (We may or may not agree unconsciously with this conscious position.) And that itself is a political judgement, a liberal one, that any sexual behaviour is acceptable as long as its participants are happy.

Ideas about how people should be are equally present in more process-oriented approaches, which try to follow and support whatever arises, whether or not this matches the practitioner's expectations. Personally, I see this as a splendid intention, which I try to apply in my own work; but even if we succeed in this quite difficult project, it is still based on a set of beliefs about how people should be. For a process-oriented practitioner, people *should* be spontaneous, *should* follow their unconscious wisdom rather than try to control it, things *should* be left to sort themselves out in their own way – again, an entire political programme.

Many people want to draw a line between a programme for individuals and a programme for society – as if it was possible to have one without the other. But like it or not, our position on how individuals should be necessarily entails a position on how society should be organized. If individuals should be this way, then obviously society should be organized so as to permit and support this way of being – which may or may not already be the case. If our position about individuals is a conservative one, our position on society will also be conservative: that everything should stay more or less as it is or perhaps go back to how it was when we were a bit younger. In that case, our programme can stay more or less invisible: everything is all right as it is. But this is no less a programme than one that wants people and society to change.

In other words, there is no political neutrality, since politics permeates our social experience. Psychotherapy that advocates 'adjustment', 'realism' or dealing with 'the world as it is' arguably damages the client's capacity to tolerate a *difference* between their desire and reality – and to do something about it. As Joel Kovel points out, 'many anxieties can be stilled by fostering acceptance of the established order of things' (1978: 316); equally, anxiety can often be lessened by pointing out to a client that their problem is not simply a personal one, but something set up *by* the established order of things (for example, society's arrangements around gender and sexuality).

Let me emphasize that I am not saying there is anything wrong with therapists having beliefs. We are human beings, we have views about how things should be, how people should be. Some of those views, in *my* view, are more compatible with the working of psychotherapy than others; but operating from a set of beliefs is in no way wrong, in fact it is inevitable. What I *do* think is bad practice is to pretend that we are *not* operating from a set of beliefs or that those beliefs are different from what they really are. Then we confuse both our clients and ourselves.

I suggest that it is also bad practice to claim that we are not influencing the client in the direction of our own beliefs or even that we are not *trying* to do so. We do not have to give a lecture in order to communicate our views to our client quite effectively. Our choice of topics and vocabulary, our slightest intonation, pause or silence, the way that we respond enthusiastically to certain remarks and lackadaisically to others – all of these responses tell our client what we believe and their transference, in all probability, tells them that they should be convinced by us if they want to get better.

What is more, we *want* them to be convinced. This is a bitter pill to swallow, but I think we must do so. The closer an issue is to our own hearts, the more we genuinely feel that one viewpoint is the creative, humane and *correct* one, the more we hope that everyone we care about, including our clients, will agree with us. Take the example of a woman client who tells us a tale of many years' mistreatment and abuse by men. She clearly has very low self-esteem and seems to feel that women are nothing without the validation and protection of men. We are likely to harbour a burning wish that she will discover feminism in some shape or form; and if she does – through our subtle and tactful guidance – this will certainly (in my view) be very good for her.

We have to accept, however, that this is no less controlling of the client than the 1950s' American analyst who believes this woman is suffering from a lack of adjustment to appropriate sex roles and tries to help her become 'better adjusted'. The difference is that we, of course, are right, and he is wrong! But so far as power is concerned, we are trying just as much as the 1950s' analyst to impose our view of the world on our client. For her own good (*cf.* Lees and Freshwater, this volume)

I am simplifying wildly here and most therapeutic situations are much more subtle and complicated than this. The values towards which we are trying to steer our clients may be a lot harder to define. But if we accept that such steering is always in some fashion going on, then I do not see how it can make a difference to our judgement of the therapeutic power relationship *which* position the therapist is inculcating in their client. And this means that therapy is faced with a fundamental political problem at its heart.

Attempted solutions

There have been many attempts to deal with this fundamental problem. One of the most radical happened very early on: Sandor Ferenczi's experiments with 'mutual analysis', where he tried to address certain patients' suspicion about his motivations by splitting the session into two halves, one in which he analysed the patient and one in which they analysed him (Fortune 1993). These patients were survivors of massive abuse, who would now no doubt be called 'borderline personalities'. Probably everyone who has worked with such people can see the point of Ferenczi's experiment but also its pitfalls: for the therapist to stick their arm in the fire like the Roman soldier in order to 'prove' their genuineness does not ultimately help the client to bear and explore their mistrust.

Communicative psychoanalysis (Langs 1982; Smith 1999) is a more recent approach that takes seriously the client's sense of mistreatment. For the communicative analyst, the core task is to hear and interpret the analysand's unconscious messages about breaches of the analytic frame: only if they experience the analyst's capacity to acknowledge such breaches undefensively can the analysand go deeper into the work. Otherwise, 'we can identify which person is introducing the most confusion, conflict and defensiveness ... the designated therapist ... is the functional patient and the designated patient ... is the functional analyst' (Smith 1999: 117). Two problems arise here: the first is that there is no clear account of what constitutes the analytic work beyond the interpretation of boundary violations. More seriously, the specific, historically contingent details of Freud's clinical parameters – couch, 50-minute hour and all – are somehow hypostasized into the necessary conditions of psychotherapy (Smith 1999: 174ff).

Many other innovative methods have been inspired by the desire to resolve stubborn issues of power: for example co-counselling, which dispenses entirely with the expert role of therapist and uses a set of simple techniques to let two people swap sessions (Kauffman 2004); and any number of experiments with leaderless groups (Ernst and Goodison 1981). Rogerian person-centred therapy had as a founding motivation addressing power issues in the therapeutic relationship; as already mentioned, there are reasons to think it has not wholly succeeded (Masson 1990). Perhaps, in fact, it *could not* succeed: the core situation of two people in a room, each with their own view of what is real and what is not and one of them being paid to meet the other, inevitably make issues of power central to what is going on. The idea that the purpose of therapy is basically to correct the client's understanding, much as an optician might aim to correct their vision, is still pervasive. But all methods of attempting this amount, ultimately, to coercion.

Working with power issues in therapy

The only way to tackle this adequately, I suggest, is that instead of trying hopelessly to eliminate power struggle from the therapeutic relationship, we place it dead centre, highlighting the battle between therapist and client over the definition of reality, baring it to the naked gaze and making it a core theme of our work.

In a dyad where each member has exactly one vote on what constitutes 'reality' – and can use a wide range of techniques to influence how the other person uses their vote – very early hurts around power, autonomy and validation can be re-experienced and transformed; if mishandled, they can also be reinforced. The most obvious way, it seems to me, that as therapists we can mishandle the situation, is to claim that because we are therapists we have more than one vote on the reality of the situation: that my expertise, my specialist knowledge, my insight into the human heart and its foibles, entitles me to an extra vote. Unfortunately, irritatingly, this is no more true of the therapy relationship than it is of a parliamentary election.

In order to move forward from this impasse, we need to acknowledge that the therapeutic situation is nearly as hard for us as it is for our clients. No one likes to be in a struggle over reality; and for us there are even certain things at stake (our status, our income) that are not at stake for the client. Hence the temptations to cheat are enormous; especially when, as we have said, a large part of the client wants us to cheat, to assert our authority as expert healer.

To resist the seductions of expertise is not, however, to claim a different sort of immunity from challenge, as some sort of ego-free guru. It is, instead, to come back to Bion's famous picture (1990: 5) of 'two frightened people in the room': two people both experiencing a threat to the beliefs on which their identity rests. What our training then hopefully allows us to do is to bring awareness, the magic ingredient, to the situation. Then client and therapist can start to explore all the ways in which we are competing to define reality, through assertion, manipulation, seduction and deception. And, ultimately, we do what is best done in every such situation: we negotiate. This negotiation of realities (where 'negotiation' also has the meaning of crossing tricky and dangerous terrain), I would argue, constitutes an authentic and viable psycho-political practice. And as we start to unknot the reality and fantasy of power relations in the room, so we discover threads leading back to power relations in the client's wider world. This does not propose any radical change in psychotherapy practice, but a reconceptualization, bringing out the political aspect of transference and countertransference that is always already present.

As an analogy for a successful therapeutic interaction, consider two language groups encountering each other (see, for example, Hymes 1977; McWhorter 2000). If the members of one language group are considerably more powerful than the other – for example, if they have guns and the others don't – then the second group simply learns the first group's language. But if they are roughly equal in power or if each wants something the other can provide, a new form of communication develops between them: what is known as a *pidgin*, an artificial medium using a simple syntax and a vocabulary drawn from both languages. A pidgin is not a natural language: it cannot develop, generate new words and concepts, become a medium for poetry. However, once children are born who grow up speaking it, a pidgin is transformed in an extraordinary way: it becomes what is called a *creole*, a new natural language, as creative and infinite in potential as any other language on earth.

This, it seems to me, is what happens in successful therapy. First, the client and practitioner create a pidgin, assembled from elements of the language that each person brings with them. But from a fertile exchange between therapist and client, a creative intercourse, a new language is born, a creole, a vessel for new thoughts and feelings that did not preexist in either original tongue.

What much more often happens, however, is that the therapist overawes the client – who may well want to be overawed – into *learning the therapist's language*. And, of course, speaking the therapist's language, the client will only tell us what we know already: as Fliess told Freud, the reader of thoughts will always find only their own thoughts in other people. After the passage about 'two rather frightened people in the room', Bion continues: 'If they are not one wonders why they are bothering to find out what everyone knows' (1990: 5).

Getting the client to speak our language is one of many ways in which, as therapists, we can re-enact clients' early trauma. Children grow up forced to speak their parents' language, both literally and symbolically. Most children have painful experiences of being misunderstood or not listened to in the first place. In this and also in other ways, at some point we will almost certainly repeat our clients' early painful experience; this can be minimized, but not avoided. And it is how we negotiate this painful and difficult situation – our ability, simply put, to identify, acknowledge and apologize for our mistake – that decides whether the therapeutic encounter will be a reinforcement of early experiences of powerlessness or a site where new experiences of empowerment can occur.

Conclusion

I have argued recently in several contexts that therapy is centrally a *practice of truth*. This has not been a very popular line to take. I think people have sometimes misunderstood me to be saying that therapy is a search for *absolute* truth, which is very different. But what therapy does and must do is to examine everything we can know about the truth of a situation – very much including emotional truth – precisely to establish experientially that *there is no absolute truth*, that truth is not singular but plural and contingent and, therefore, subject to negotiation. This is perhaps the greatest realization of modernity and of immeasurable political importance: it is the gradual spreading of this realization that has caused fundamentalism to stir in such destructive ways. Many people are coming to psychotherapy in search of help for anxieties that are ultimately produced by the clash between relativism and fundamentalism, as it affects their own deepest subjectivity. For psychotherapy to respond helpfully, on a clinical and on a social level, it needs to think seriously about the power politics of its own practice.

Part III
Psychotherapy, the state and institutions

8 Values, ethics and the law: a story with some morals
Petruska Clarkson

Dedicated, with appreciation, to Vincent Keter

> *The willingness to monitor and correct unethical and incompetent behaviour by colleagues is difficult to instil or to encourage. Yet without such willingness the entire structure collapses.*
>
> (Thompson 1990: 133)

> *In the corrupted currents of this world*
> *Offence's gilded hand may shove by justice,*
> *And oft 'tis seen the wicked prize itself*
> *Buys out the law.*
>
> (King Claudius's prayer in *Hamlet*)

Introduction

A young law student, Vincent Keter, and I have the dubious historical honour of having established in the High Court on February 18 1999 that the United Kingdom Council for Psychotherapy (UKCP) is indeed a *professional* body. This judicial finding was against the express wishes and intentions of the Governing Board of the UKCP. The UKCP had argued that it was not a professional body, but 'a club'. This was the legal defence that the UKCP used in order to avoid – for 10 years – hearing serious ethics complaints against two of its members.

The UKCP is the only comparable body that I know of in the world whose members cannot be expelled for ethical misconduct. This is because the UKCP only has *organizations* as members – not individuals. Thus, the unethical conduct of member organizations – for example, if they refuse to hear ethics complaints against some favoured individual registrants – is completely protected and covered up while the complainant can be persecuted with impunity.

I have also spent hundreds of hours participating in the development of ethics codes, publishing papers and books on ethics and moral issues and serving on the boards of numerous ethics hearings in several different professional organizations. With Geoff Lindsay, I am probably the only person to have actually researched ethical dilemmas in UK *psychotherapy* organizations – particularly the UKCP and the British Association for Counselling and Psychotherapy (BACP).

Ethics research findings about collegial ethical misconduct

In researching what ethical dilemmas were most troubling to UKCP psychotherapists, after dilemmas to do with confidentiality, the largest category was dilemmas to do with colleagues' unethical conduct. In other words, confidentiality was the only issue that was more troubling to UKCP therapists than unresolved concerns about the unethical conduct of their own colleagues (Lindsay and Clarkson 1996):

> The effectiveness of these [professional ethic codes] depends on four main factors: (1) the benefit that members perceive in retaining their membership; (2) the effectiveness of the association in communicating the code and a sense of its importance to its members; (3) the willingness of members to monitor the behaviour of fellow members and to apply the sanctions when appropriate; and (4) the efforts by the profession to educate the public as to what constitutes competent and ethical behaviour by its members and to support any legitimate complaints about such behaviour by members.
>
> (Thompson 1990: 130)

The injunction to do no harm (non-maleficence) can be construed to include the mandate not to remain passively acquiescent when fellow professionals are violating ethical principles and standards of practice (Pope *et al.* 1986: 78).

Several of our research respondents specifically mentioned not filing ethics complaints, some feeling that 'somebody else' (such as a boss) 'should have done something'. The largest proportion of our respondents considered taking action but did not. This is compared with one-quarter of respondents in a North American study who have actually filed an ethics complaint against a colleague.

> If only some 10% of colleagues are willing to act on information about other colleagues' violation of ethics codes, that means that 90% of ethical violations against clients' colleagues and members of the public are continuing unreported and unchecked.
>
> (Clarkson and Lindsay 2001: 133)

'Moral problem: Where does my responsibility lie? With him [colleague] – or my patient so as not to be provoked into being the expected punishing father – or to the world who will probably meet an angry therapist with deeply unreached power issues?':

> North American studies also found respondents who were worried about 'diploma mills' (termed 'a crisis' by one UK respondent) but many reported ethical concerns about programs accepting students 'with marginal ethics and competence who were so identified in graduate school and no one did anything about it'.
>
> (Pope and Vetter 1991: 52)

The American Psychological Association (APA) has a rule stating: 'Psychologists do not file or encourage the filing of ethics complaints that are frivolous and are intended to harm the respondent rather than to protect the public' (APA 1992: code 8.07). With only one possible exception, our research evidenced no indication that the serious action of laying a complaint against a colleague for their unethical behaviour towards clients or trainees was ever considered lightly.

To the contrary, UKCP psychotherapists often thought that they could not do it, were confused about how to do it or evidenced the fact that they did not even if it was an item in their 'ethics codes'. As Friedson wrote in 1970:

> A code of ethics has no necessary relationship to the actual behaviour of members of the occupation ... In this sense a code of ethics may be seen as one of many methods an occupation may use to induce general belief in the ethicality of its members without necessary bearing directly on individual ethicality.
>
> (1970: 187)

The kinds of ethical dilemma about collegial behaviour that emerged from our research were:

- serious concerns about colleagues' competence
- sexual misconduct with clients or students
- attacks by colleagues on professional reputation
- boundary breaks
- issues to do with moral competence including publishing lies about qualifications
- issues to do with discrimination of various kinds including racial discrimination

- issues to do with the abuse of power over clients or students or members
- mismanagement of a colleague's death – effect on clients.

Bernard and Jara wrote in 1995 that all kinds of 'unwritten protection laws' have proliferated as result of psychotherapists' fears of the destructive organizational retaliation when reporting or pursuing complaints about the unethical conduct of their colleagues. Several of our research respondents had themselves experienced or witnessed such punitive actions against complainants.

'The organization was furious when we made the complaint … a colleague lost her job without due notice' (quoted in Clarkson 2000: 129). Another person wrote: 'Some other practitioner is working with what I see as an incompetence that is culpable and damaging. I may understand well why, but since I'm not being approached by them for supervision I feel uncomfortably powerless. But when it's close to home I feel obliged to act then ultimately it is about recognizing abuse and not tolerating it' (*ibid*: 131).

It is thus our moral and ethical responsibility to each other and to our clients, students and members of the public to take action with proper confidentiality preserved, after appropriate and timely consultation and without malice, yet the complainant may be wrong, deliberately or accidentally false informed, misled or simply making a mistake. These additional concerns may prevent professionals from acting appropriately by laying complaints against the unethical conduct of colleagues in relation to clients and trainees.

The code items usually specify words like 'where there is reason to suspect', 'where there are grounds to believe', etc. The codes do not require that the complaint be proved true or valid before it is formally made. It does imply a requirement to make an informed professional judgement about the seriousness of the charge and the urgency of confronting the colleague or calling for an investigation into organizational cover-up of ethics process abuses.

It is important for colleagues seeking such redress of harm to clients or other colleagues, for example, to be aware that even if they have taken proper consultation to avoid malice or breaches of confidentiality, they may still be wrong about such assessment of probabilities without incurring the risk of being sued for defamation. (This is, of course, after confrontation and attempts at mediation have failed – Clarkson 2000: 136–7.)

The interface between values, ethics and the law

Now let us look at these issues from a technical and philosophical standpoint. In this field we have at play values, ethics, morals and the law in a complex dynamic human system. Such complex systems are fractal. *Fractality* means that there is a distinct recognizable mathematical pattern that is self-similar across scale (Clarkson and Nicolopoulou 2003).

This complex system potentially affects:

- every individual client or practitioner/registrant (micro scale);
- every training institution/member organization (meso scale);
- the UKCP as involved in national statutory registration (macro-macro scale).

Another characteristic of complex human systems is *connectivity*. This means that each of these fractals of the whole WHOLE is in *relationship* with itself and the others, at all scales.

All relationships show a fractal pattern comprising the following five aspects:

1 contractual
2 distorted
3 needed
4 existential
5 transpersonal.

These are the five minimum categories of human *process* into which all forms of all of the relationships in this complex system can be exhaustively sorted. An impressionistic sorting of all the human issues involved reveals that the three categories that comprehend all the human issues involved are: secrets, money and sex – not necessarily in that order. Perhaps the third and last characteristic of complex human systems – *cyclicity* – is that secrets, money and sex move in cycles.

Of course, in terms of *content*, each of these three issues co-exists both ontologically *and* epistemologically at seven levels or domains: Physiological level 1, Emotional level 2, Nominative level 3 (words and images), Normative level 4, Rational level 5, Narrative level 6 (theory, story) and Transpersonal level 7 (Clarkson 2004).

Every epistemological domain of discourse appears to have its own well-established, but quite different, truth criteria. Logical category errors are committed, as they constantly are in most of what passes for human verbal and written communication, through ignorance or intent. Such category errors are dangerous and harmful – as Heraclitus and philosopher Gilbert Ryle (1984) both agree.

The best level 5 truth criterion for so-called empirical scientific objective 'facts' – the best gold standard human beings have found for themselves so far – can only be agreed to be 'true' by the sane people of any particular time and place. At one time the earth was flat. Now it is a 'fact' that the earth is round. In the next century it might be a fact that the earth is triangular. 'True' knowledge, then, even the best we have now, always remains corrigible. In the meantime what we have got is an assortment of current 'certainties' and various statistical probabilities for the reoccurrence of certain kinds of phenomena under certain kinds of conditions.

Juries and judges have the unenviable task of having to make important decisions based only on the facts known at the time and the *probable* weight of available evidence in their more-or-less expert legal opinion – a task that we know they may do well, badly or indifferently. But even the judges' judgements can (in principle) be overturned. Juries and judges can only do their job as well as the facts and probabilities presented to them in the prescribed legal formats allow them to act. If a complainant cannot afford an expensive lawyer to put their case as best they can in opposing a rich complained-against, the judge cannot be held responsible for an unfair decision. His or her hands are literally tied.

Let us consider the question of getting consensual agreement on what the terms 'values', 'ethics', 'morals' and 'the law' actually mean to the communicating parties – even if they are 'not speaking to each other'. How can we even begin to talk intelligibly to each other if we can't mutually agree on the meaning of commonly used English words? Here are my own working definitions as a special contribution to the conversations in this book:

> **Values** *are inferences of perceptual preferences based on a person's consensually observable behaviour.* Whatever you do or do not do, observable by others, embodies your values to others. Values that are only 'avowed', but not proven in observable conduct, may be ignored in this discussion – or the *deception* may be confronted. (Deception of self or others, in or out of awareness, involuntary or choice-full.)

> **Ethics** *is that branch of philosophy devoted to the study of good and bad. Also used to describe a set of rules that a group of people have between them agreed on about what is better or worse about how to behave.* The only sense in which the term 'personal ethics' can be used correctly is to indicate which normative group/collective an individual has chosen to continue to belong to.

> **Moral** *means whatever you believe is good in your opinion.* **Immoral** means whatever you believe is bad in your opinion. Often used as a rough synonym for what you believe is ethical – in your opinion.

And note that ***power*** *simply means the ability to make things happen*, to be used for good or ill. Nobody from the planet Chiron would ever guess that from the way that the word 'power' is so often inaccurately and promiscuously thrown around in psychotherapy discourse as a derogatory term!

The law *is the body of rules that a state implements on its subjects through its courts and provides for those subjects as a means of conflict resolution.*

My ethics and morals training manual (Clarkson 2000) addresses these issues extensively and intensively along with their interface with the law (see also Jenkins *et al.* 2004).

Points of energy concentration on different scales

I will now examine three selected scales of fractal intersections between ethics, values and the law. I am basing my sample on what, from my research, seem to be the points of most intense energy at all seven levels in this complex human system at the scales of the individual, the organization and a larger organization of organizations – the UKCP. I make no secret of my own profoundly critical attitude towards UKCP and its processes, based on my personal experience of conflict with that organization. However, in what follows, I aim to make general points about the psychotherapy profession as a whole.

Currently, at the micro scale, the biggest concern for most individual psycho-practitioners appears to be being sued and/or complained against. At the meso scale – the training organizations as members of the UKCP – the greatest significant concern is how to survive financially. At the macro-macro level the intersecting point of government statutory registration of psychotherapists seems to be where the most intense energy is concentrated at this time.

The individual practitioner (micro scale)

It is highly *unlikely* – but not impossible – that you as an individual practitioner could successfully be sued by a client or trainee unless:

- The other person can prove that a crime, e.g. gross negligence, had been committed (in such a rare case, the plaintiff might get legal aid, which is rarely granted unless lives, limbs or property have been lost).

- The plaintiff has otherwise access to the necessary financial resources to engage in a most protracted distressing and extremely expensive court case.
- The practitioner has not paid up their professional insurance.
- Finally, unless you are yourself well off, it won't be worth any plaintiff bothering to go after you for a lot of money – their legal advisers won't let them. So don't worry too much.

It is highly *likely*, however, that an individual psycho-practitioner will be complained about. Pursue scrupulously competent practice by keeping up to date with how the ethics codes keep changing and keep your working alliance as clear as possible. I reckon in 95 per cent of ethics cases where clients or trainees did succeed in their complaints, it could all have been resolved earlier and better if the practitioner or training organization sincerely listened to the complainant, tried to understand how s/he came to feel so offended and quickly ameliorated the distress by full empathic apology and shared responsibility for the relationship breakdown.

Never blame a complainant for being 'borderline' or 'narcissistic' or any other abusive label. If you did not spot it at initial assessment, you are admitting that your clinical skills were inadequate! If you took them on, they have a right to be *healed* by you, not abusively labelled should they be unhappy with your services.

Often, the more innovative a practitioner is, the more they are likely to be complained about, because such individuals usually diverge in their practice from the conventionally accepted ethical norms at level 4; so the more conservative your practice, the safer you will be on this count. Clients or patients, like other human beings, have a known tendency to attack their rescuers. So learn as much as you can about this distorting transference/countertransference dynamic and always keep at least one good supervisory eye on its workings.

Psycho-practitioners sometimes do the most terribly *bad* things to clients and trainees and should be complained about and fairly, justly and impartially sanctioned – for their own sake as well as for the sake of other people. However, I have personally come across very few bad psychotherapists in my life, notwithstanding the fact that I have personally been sexually abused by at least one and experienced the destructive consequences on whole communities of trainer/trainee sexual misconduct. Usually such practitioners are tripped up ethically, legally or morally through ignorance and carelessness or are completely misguided by their own unmet personal needs – commonly for secrets, sex and money equivalents, for example, referrals or jobs.

Your immediate collegial normative group (meso scale)

At the meso scale of the training organizations, a common concern is how to survive financially in what has been aptly described as a 'glutted market'. In order for organizations to survive financially, each member of each organization has to weigh up ethical, legal and moral decisions in the light of this overarching survival value. If a register is based on individual registration like the BACP, then individuals remain individually responsible for how they support, collude or confront ethically abusive colleagues, given the financial imperatives, in their own membership organizations.

As the UKCP is still currently organized, its 'members' consist of dozens of different training organizations all competing for a share of a limited consumer market. When they are also competing for money/customers with other professional bodies, the chance of fairness in their ethics processes becomes increasingly remote.

National statutory registration (macro-macro scale)

At the macro-macro level, the intersecting point of government statutory registration of psychotherapists seems to be where the most intense energy in our field is concentrated at this time. The many arguments against statutory registration have been well rehearsed by Independent Practitioners Network (IPN) participants such as Richard House, Denis Postle and Nick Totton (e.g. House 2003; House and Totton 1997; Postle 1998; Totton 1999). Historically I have held out for all practitioners having available a maximum number of 'good-enough' choices of normative ethical allegiance to the UKCP and/or the BACP and/or a campaigning organization such as IPN – or entirely outside these systems as coaches, educators, facilitators, traditional or New Age healers, philosophers, teachers, trainers or whatever else they want to call themselves in order to 'help the people'.

We all know that laws and codes of ethics do *not* prevent abuses by 'registered' psycho-practitioners. Laws do not prevent crime, they merely give us ways in which to work with those who break them. The scale of global human emotional distress is so vast and pressing that I am not personally willing to exclude from my own professional recognition almost every psychological healer on this earth who is not European, not middle class and not white (i.e. poor).

These are the practitioners who usually do not earn much and serve consumers who often cannot pay much either, that is, those who won't be seen by your average private practice therapist. And they also see the people who are mostly considered 'not suitable' for psychotherapy on the NHS. Then there are a few master psychotherapists at work in our ethically challenged postmodern cultural world who earn vast amounts of money. And in my opinion they deserve every cent of it. For me these are the best 'good guys': they help thousands of ordinary people and give moral psycho-education to millions across the world. They are doing good work; they are accountable; they work in public, for the public – without being registered psychotherapists.

I am, of course, talking about Oprah, Tricia and Dr Phil. Would that their videos were routinely studied on psychotherapy training courses! They are observably and demonstrably helping people – their customers say so (unless they are all lying). And we can all see when it works and when it does not. Dr Phil's communications are virtually category-error free – perhaps he was a logician in a previous life.

These master psychotherapists are rich and therefore most vulnerable to being sued by very disturbed people for very large amounts of money. Look ma – no theoretical orientation or schoolist allegiance – *just helping the people*. Right in the public eye. How? Through the contractual intentional use of relationship to alleviate human suffering and encourage the development of human potential.

Notice how many working-class and black people turn up for this particularly 21st-century form of therapeutic psycho- *and* socio-drama. Compare that racial distribution with any gathering of psycho-people in the UK. You'd be lucky to see one non-Caucasian face. If you want to learn how to do effective time-conscious and culture-conscious psychotherapy, you could not have better living examples.

Of course, each person's individual choice has its own unique moral, ethical and legal costs. Nothing is for free and certainly not our allegiance to our level 4 normative groups. *Enacted values.* As Humpty Dumpty said about level 3 nominations: 'The question is who is to be master. That is all.'

It mostly depends on who *you* believe the good guys and the bad guys are, in your level 4 opinion. Each one of us wants to be one of 'the good guys' and our opponents to be the 'bad guys'. But, then, please notice that that's the bad guys' moral motivation too. From *their* perspective.

Conclusion

Good and bad from a natural ethics perspective

Let us meditate finally on the everlasting dynamic tension between good and evil from a transpersonal level 7 perspective. This is just what happens in nature (*physis*) all the time. It is simply creaturely to hang out with 'creatures like us' or other creatures who like us or who serve our normative groups' interests. So here's a picture to meditate upon (see Figure 8.1).

It has been ever thus: 'It is weariness always to toil at the same tasks and always be beginning' (Heraclitus).

9 The institutions of psychotherapy
Nick Totton

Intelligence succumbs to coercion; hierarchical pyramids, far from being flattened, grow even higher; affiliative communication gives way to hierarchical blocking; leadership of ideas and trends gives way to the pressure of personalities in authority and 'leaders'; obfuscation rules the day.

(De Mare 1975: 153)

Where qualification is not based on a real body of knowledge, disintegration products abound, leaving the way open for the rule of power plays, anointment, cultism, personality, psychopathology and politics. Power plus mystification gives rise to irrational authority in the form of anointment.

(McDougall 1995: 234)

Introduction

What is striking about psychotherapy's institutions is their remarkable unwillingness to apply to themselves what psychotherapy knows about group dynamics. The first passage just quoted is by a group analyst discussing what happens in the large groups with which they work. As we shall see, everything in it applies to the typical organization of therapists – including therapists who spend every day trying to improve the functioning of groups! Why do psychotherapists leave their theoretical understanding at the door when entering their own institutions? And why are these institutions so noted for their fragmentation, dishonesty, authoritarianism and rivalry?

The problem

Before we try to answer these questions, we need to look at some of the evidence of malfunctioning. Most of the available information comes, one-sidedly, from psychoanalytic institutions; but it is unlikely that they are any worse than other institutions. In fact, plenty of word of mouth, and many deeply wounded practitioners, indicate otherwise (for one humanistic example, which has partly appeared in print, that of Marianne Fry, see

Clarkson 2000: x–xii); analysts may simply have been more open and honest about institutional failings.

This disclaimer actually introduces another striking feature of the therapy world: its propensity for competition, rivalry and dominance games – for example, between psychoanalysis and (other forms of) psychotherapy; between psychotherapy and counselling (where Dryden famously defined the real difference as 'about £8000 a year' – 1996: 15); between psychotherapy and psychiatry; between the humanistic and psychodynamic branches of psychotherapy and counselling; and, in fact, between every group and subgroup of the entire field.

> One of the most striking features of the profession is its fragmented state, in which rivalrous groups claim allegiance to different theoretical orientations and protect themselves by arcane terminologies that restrict the possibility of interchange. Each group prizes its own orientation above all others.
>
> (Hinshelwood 1985: 16)

And, we can add, each group tries to place itself higher up some pecking order than its rivals – refusing to admit, in fact, that they are rivals, but trying to label them as junior partners or inferior imitations. Robert M. Young has written at length (1996; 1999) about how, in the UK, psychoanalysts trained by the Institute of Psychoanalysis try to assert hegemonic dominance over psychotherapists (not allowed to call themselves analysts) who have done entirely similar trainings elsewhere – and then, in descending degrees of inferiority, over all other practitioners of psychotherapy.

> The pecking order goes: Institute pecks BCP [British Confederation of Psychotherapists] which pecks UKCP [UK Council for Psychotherapy], whose psychoanalytic and psychodynamic section uses up most of the oxygen and doesn't even bother to peck the rest of the psychotherapists, much less the counsellors. Beyond the pale are those who believe that all of this stuff betrays what is essential in therapy.
>
> (Young 1999: 455)

We shall return to the specifics later; but similar processes seem to control the institutions of many competing brands of therapy. Kirsner gives thorough documentation of how this has worked within American analytic organizations. As he summarizes his own conclusions, 'psychoanalytic institutes have always been troubled everywhere' (Kirsner 2000: Introduction). He demonstrates, for example, how the prestigious New York Psychoanalytic Institute was for decades run by a more or less secret cabal, which 'acted as though it possessed special power and magic' and maintained its position through control over training. Only once the demand for psychoanalysis went into drastic decline in the 1990s were democratizing changes forced on the Institute.

The New York Institute is only one example of a widespread malaise in psychoanalytic organizations, up to and including the International Psychoanalytic Association, documented in a number of papers, particularly those by the eminent analysts Leo Rangell (1962, 1982) and Joseph Arlow (1972, 1982) and two papers by Otto Kernberg that describe 'the paranoid atmosphere that often pervades psychoanalytic institutes and its devastating effect on the "quality of life" in psychoanalytic education' (1986: 803–4). In a satirical paper, 'Thirty methods to destroy the creativity of analytic candidates' (Kernberg 1996), he 'proposes' measures, by implication already in place, that combine bureaucracy, intimidation, authoritarianism and indoctrination. Young is even more direct:

> I also have the impression that those who rise to power in training institutions, whether psychoanalysts or psychotherapists, often suffer from a need for power ... They will do anything at anyone's expense to have and retain power.
>
> (Young 1999: 440)

Like psychotherapy in general, psychoanalytic institutions have been subject to endemic splits and exclusions. The history of this goes right back to the early days of psychoanalysis, when Adler, Jung, Rank and Stekel each split away from Freud to form his own school (for one account, see Gay 1995). This could be a healthy process of growth and competition, except for the level of vituperation and mutual contempt that generally accompanied the separations (cf. Leitner 1999). Other important exclusions include Wilhelm Reich in the 1930s (Sharaf 1984: 186–91) and Jacques Lacan in the 1950s (Lacanianism itself has subsequently experienced endless splits and sub-splits: Nobus 1998; Roudinesco 1990); while the unpleasant story of the internal exile and subsequent airbrushing from history of Sandor Ferenczi has been retold several times in recent years (Gay 1995: 578–85; Rachman 1997). It is all unpleasantly reminiscent of Stalinism.

As Jacob Arlow points out (cf. Kirsner 2000), psychoanalysis is also prone to:

> recurring splits of institutes. There have been about half a dozen such in the American Psychoanalytic Association, with almost as many splits threatened but fortunately averted ... During the past eight years alone the [IPA] Central Executive Committee ... has had to deal with identical problems in France, Spain, Brazil, Venezuela, Columbia and Australia.
>
> (Arlow 1972: 558–9)

Again, non-analytic therapies are at least equally prone to division and rivalry – I know of three humanistic training organizations that have even split with their own founders.

Why?

It is clear that this situation is both absurd and unacceptable. I want to look at four interlocking factors that seem to be important in creating and maintaining the problem. These are:

1 the positioning of psychotherapy as a profession, with all the consequences that follow
2 the particular stresses of the occupation of psychotherapy, as they affect its institutions
3 training and transmission issues, in particular as regards transference
4 the particular functions that psychotherapy has for society as a whole.

Therapy as a profession

Determined to bring psychoanalysis into the cultural mainstream, Freud set up a traditional European professional society with a hierarchical and bureaucratic structure – president, secretary, committees. Ever since, psychotherapy has tended to represent itself and seek acceptance as one of the *professions*, of which medicine is the quintessential example (Parsons 1951: Chapter 10). The current tendency in our society to regulate and formalize every sort of occupation has created a partially defensive intensification of therapy's wish to be a profession, driven by concerns about income and status as well as by a belief – partly healthy, perhaps partly not – in the social importance of our function.

It may not be obvious what else psychotherapy could aspire to being other than a profession. But it is rather an odd beast to find alongside medicine, law, architecture and accountancy. I have argued (Totton 1997a) that psychotherapy in many of its forms is more like a spiritual and/or political practice than a profession. Others have suggested that it would be better organized as a craft guild or as an academy (for instance, Kernberg 1986). The choice to identify as a profession has had a powerful effect on what therapy does and how it organizes itself.

A profession is defined partly by its claim to unique, expert knowledge in its field (Abbott 1988). Professional societies organize to establish and enforce a monopoly on this knowledge, by setting up training, licensing practitioners and often by lobbying the state to formally recognize and guarantee their legitimacy while banning their competitors as quacks and impostors. Psychotherapy has had some difficulties around its claim to expert knowledge, since there is no general agreement as to how it should be either practised or theoretically conceived; as already indicated, any two psychotherapists will have three conflicting views of good practice and in line with Borch-Jacobsen's concept of 'mimetic rivalry' (1988) or Freud's 'narcissism of minor differences' (Freud 1930: 305), the closer their views, the more furiously they are likely to struggle to distinguish themselves.

Despite these difficulties, psychotherapy has risen to the challenge by creating a body of expert knowledge more or less out of whole cloth. What was previously conceived as an art or craft is now portrayed as a science, outcome oriented and research based: psychotherapy submits to a regime of truth (Foucault 1980) appropriate to its positioning as a profession of expert knowledge (Totton 1999). Many have objected to this process, but have failed to hold back the sea (what one might call, reversing Freud, the black tide of scientism).

Another defining factor for a profession is self-regulation (Figlio 2000). In recognition of its practitioners' ethical solidity and discipline, society and the state allow the profession an exceptional degree of autonomy in its procedures of surveillance and regulation. The implicit contract is that it will be motivated not by self-interest, but by a wider sense of what is right and desirable. In practice, however, professionalization means a shift in focus away from broader issues of the common good and toward strategies for supporting the interests of the profession; this seems to have accelerated over the 20th century (Brint and Levy 1995). Professionalization also intensifies competition: in a field like psychotherapy, where available models are both infinite and varied, there is always a fear that one school will lose out and end up in the cold, like homeopathy in relation to allopathic medicine. The sharks circle constantly, assessing the potential for gain and loss of status (Young 1999).

Society *wants* psychotherapy to be expert; so do many psychotherapists. But if this expertise is spurious – if, as Douglas Kirsner writes, 'qualification is not based on a real body of knowledge' – then 'disintegration products abound' (Kirsner 2000: Conclusion, III). The problem is that the knowledge of psychotherapy, albeit real and powerful, is mostly not the sort of thing it is pretending to be. The great bulk of it is encoded inextricably in the embodied practice of psychotherapists, unavailable for examination or testing (Totton 1999). Hence the professional institutions of therapy are in a state of permanent masquerade.

Occupational stresses

Hinshelwood (1985: 16) describes as 'maladaptive collective defences' the fragmentation, 'siege mentality' and 'often very painful' 'internal competitive culture' that are all intensified by the drive to professionalization. As he says, 'like other professions, psychotherapy no doubt displays its neurotic heart on its sleeve' (1985: 15) – for instance, in specific features of clinical practice, notably the need to restrain and suppress our natural, occasional angry and anxious responses to clients, which are then redirected onto colleagues and professional organizations (1985: 17). Hinshelwood also suggests that many clients' perception of us as magical healers, their positive transference onto us, supports our own omnipotence fantasies and encourages us to manage lurking feelings of inadequacy by attacking other groups of therapists as useless and unhelpful.

This seems very sensible, especially when combined with other stressful aspects of our work situation – the slow pace at which therapy develops, the uncertainty of outcome and the client's own despair (Hinshelwood 1985: 17). All these factors, of course, are increasingly being disputed by the 'expert knowledge' wing of psychotherapy, which argues that therapy can be fast and certain and overcome the client's despair. One could suggest that this whole approach amounts to a manic defence against practitioners' experience.

Roger Kennedy echoes and extends Hinshelwood's first point:

> One may wonder whether the general need for restraint [during sessions] accounts for the way that analysts at times can be so unrestrained in their institutional behaviour, when they come together in group settings … Also analysts are notoriously prone to particular sorts of character problems which limit their capacity to be ordinarily human and sociable.
>
> (Kennedy 1998: 121)

These 'character problems' are the shadow side of the very qualities that enable people to carry out this peculiar job – self-motivation, reserve, inner-directedness, sensitivity. Perhaps the kinds of people who make good therapists are not the kinds of people to run good organizations.

Training and transmission

One of the primary functions of institutions, of course, is to organize the training of new therapists. This is where many people locate the central problem. For most psychotherapies, training is not simply acquiring knowledge and skills; it is a process of personal transformation, primarily through work with a therapist, which closely parallels the work one will then try to do with clients. The efficacy and central role of this personal work has been questioned (Mcaskill 1999), but to the great majority of therapists, it is both obvious and essential that it should be undertaken. At the same time, however, trainees' therapists will obviously usually be trained in the same style of work they are learning; often they will be members of the institution running the training. So there is a close and difficult linking between the intense and emotional therapeutic relationship and matters of institutional politics – which, one might suggest, is asking for trouble.

This reaches its apogee in the institutional role of the training psychoanalyst. Only certain analysts – defined as particularly sound, skilled and experienced – are entitled to analyse trainees, eventually reporting on their suitability or otherwise to become analysts. Clearly those who decide who can be training analysts have tremendous power within organizations and Kirsner (2000) sees this as the key issue in his account of the New York Institute. As well as guaranteed income and status, training analysts have huge influence over their trainees:

> The position of training analyst is endowed with charismatic implications. The training analyst is regarded as possessing the psychoanalytic equivalent of omniscience. It is from the training analyst that candidates claim their descent. In many places the professional career of an individual may be determined by who his training analyst was.
>
> (Arlow 1972: 559)

Arlow derives the constant splits within analytic institutions from conflicts over 'who shall have the right to train' (1972: 559). Splits are also encouraged by the factionalism that accompanies discipleship, as trainees follow the theoretical orientation of their own analysts and supervisors:

> The experience of personal analysis and case supervision, as well as the close teacher–pupil relationship that characterizes the transmission of psychoanalytic knowledge, are all marked by strong positive and negative transference affects. These, if not recognized, may readily be used in near-perverse ways. They certainly contribute to the violence that usually accompanies our theoretical and clinical divergences. The sanctification of concepts and the worship (or denigration) of their authors appear to me to be sequels to unresolved transference ties.
>
> (McDougall 1995: 234)

These problems are by no means restricted to psychoanalysis, although perhaps are most obvious there. Most psychotherapies operate in broadly similar ways, with a convergence of therapeutic and institutional relationships in a training context that very easily sets up situations of undue influence – conscious and unconscious – and factionalism. Chris Robertson, a transpersonal therapy trainer, makes an analogy with cults, identifying eight possible parallels: a closed system; group conformity; idealization of leaders; scapegoating; charismatic mission; denial of the shadow; group narcissism; and secrets. Many people who have experienced therapy training will recognize these:

> Whatever the explicit skills, awareness and practices the students learn, they inevitably pick up many implicit ones. Unfortunately it is often the worst habits that students imitate and then unconsciously perpetuate in their own work. Where they themselves have been the victims of abusive trainers or of abusive training systems, the students may unconsciously act out this abuse with their clients. Just as dysfunctional families tend to produce abusive parents for the next generation, dysfunctional training organizations tend to produce abusive therapists.
>
> (Robertson 1993)

Charisma is a hugely problematic factor, in clinical work as much as in training. No one just *has* charisma in a neutral, objective way; it is always produced by a complex cooperation between the 'charismatic' person, their devotees and the entire sociopolitical context. The practitioner who encourages, or even silently allows, a charismatic, idealizing response from clients or trainees is being profoundly untherapeutic – transference, whether positive or negative, needs interpreting, not acting into. Charisma is thus in itself a form of the abuse Robertson refers to. However, it is also enormously seductive and corrupting for the person given the opportunity to 'be charismatic'; and this is perhaps the biggest scourge and the weakest aspect of psychotherapy. Perhaps therapists are additionally prone to the attractions of charisma through our constant exposure to negative transference and disappointed expectations.

Steltzer, who left analytic training convinced that 'the training process could be described as a kind of narcissistic illness, both of the candidates and of the institution' (1986: 59), makes the interesting point that training produces a 'decathexis of external reality' (1986: 67) – everything is ascribed to internal factors – and 'the loss of the dream experience and the transitional space' (1986: 69), as the trainee analyses rather than *experiences* her own psychic life. In Steltzer's view, trainees and analysts become 'a special kind of schizoid-alexithymic population' (1986: 72), losing touch with their feelings and fantasies through too much intellectual processing. But those feelings and fantasies are still there, still resonating powerfully through institutional processes – even more so if therapists are unable to own them.

Reflecting societal issues

We have already touched on how the wider social context reinforces and amplifies some of the weaknesses of therapy institutions. Like certain other occupations, psychotherapy has a public existence, a representation of itself to and by the surrounding culture, which is full of contradictions. It frequently finds itself playing an important role on behalf of society. These roles can be ambiguous, however, sites where some of society's deep tensions and splits express themselves – sometimes mirrored in the splits and tensions of psychotherapy itself. Hence there develops a destructive synergy between what society wants of psychotherapy and what psychotherapy wants of society.

A central example is the ambiguous role of 'cure'. Although most psychotherapists would disclaim any wish or capacity to cure psychological distress – in fact, the word 'cure' is deeply unfashionable in this context – cure is nonetheless what most of our clients come for. As I have already argued, the stress of evading and psychically processing this demand is a significant element in psychotherapy's institutional problems. And on a macro level, society tends to look to psychotherapy for cures to problems that it is unable or unwilling to work through – the most obvious being child sexual abuse. Just as we often find individual clients demanding to be made better without having to change, so we are expected to resolve deep social problems without addressing their causes.

Alongside this burdensome, ambivalent demand on therapy, we encounter a simultaneous mistrust of therapy's insight, complex interpretation, acceptance of regression and highlighting of sexuality. Therapists still get called 'shrinks', 'quacks' and 'trick cyclists'; jokes are constantly made about their rate of pay and about making a living from other people's distress. The general view is that therapy may at times be necessary, but should be completed as fast as possible and above all without becoming 'dependent' on it. As a further twist, public and private providers – health service, managed care, voluntary sector – all find the expense and long timescale of 'traditional' therapies hard to stomach.

Combining these positive and negative transferences, society's injunction to therapists could be summed up as: Make us 'better', without rocking the boat, without us depending on you, without costing too much and – above all – quickly! It is scarcely surprising, then, that psychotherapy has come up with the many versions of brief therapy – a respectable approach, but one that would surely not have gained its current sway without the influence of this injunction.

Society's deep suspicion of therapists' power to do harm emerges most clearly in the repeated moral panics (Pearson 1983) about psychotherapists as abusers, whether by general incompetence, by creating false memory syndrome or by having sex with their clients. As we saw at the beginning of the chapter, this latter at least is a very real issue; all three are called into play as justifications for the statutory regulation of psychotherapy.

Several factors come together around this: the suspicion of therapists as uncanny and manipulative; the powerful universal trend in our society, particularly under New Labour, towards the regulation of every activity and occupation; and, of course, the push towards professionalization by many psychotherapists themselves. This push has many sources, including, certainly, money and status, but also, I am sure, an unconscious or semi-conscious concern about our own motives and attitudes towards our clients, a cloudy guilt that demands strict treatment. What gets left out of all of this is the mass of good evidence and argument that state regulation contributes neither to the safety of clients nor to the effectiveness of therapy (Hogan 1979; House and Totton 1997; Mowbray 1995).

Challenging the institutions of psychotherapy

Over the last century many practitioners have argued, from a wide range of perspectives, that the institutions of psychotherapy need a radical overhaul (for more detail, see Totton 2000). Within the space available, I will consider just two aspects of this: a series of challenges to the monopoly role of the International Psychoanalytic Association (IPA) and an alternative to hierarchical models of therapist accreditation.

The Platform movement and other challenges to psychoanalysis

The Platform movement began at the 1969 IPA World Congress in Rome, which tried to digest the stirring revolutionary events of 1968; according to Marie Langer, however, its attempts were 'totally disappointing' (1989: 111). A notice in the lobby invited delegates to a 'Para-congress' in a nearby bar, set up by a group of candidate analysts from Austria, Italy and Switzerland, 'young, attractive people in hippie clothing … carrying on the climate of 1968 in Paris' (Langer 1989: 112), who had a set of complaints, a 'platform' about the cost of training, enrolment criteria, required texts and other issues.

From this emerged four 'Platform' groups, in Argentina, Austria, Italy and Switzerland; at least one, the 'Zurich Psychoanalytic Seminar' (Modena 1986), is still flourishing. The Argentinian 'Plataforma' group (Langer 1989) helped create a training that combined Marxism and psychoanalysis, lasted from 1971 until the growth of right-wing terror in Argentina in 1974 and had a major influence on the development of radical analytic groupings in Latin America. Several veterans of the Platform movement were involved in the 'Estates General of Psychoanalysis', a large gathering of radical analysts in Paris in 2001. Many papers from the Estates General are available on the internet; a major concern was the discovery that a Brazilian analyst had been part of a death squad during the period of right-wing repression and that they were not only protected by the IPA, which seemed to want to ignore the whole issue, but might also be part of a crypto-Nazi grouping within Brazilian psychoanalytic institutions (see, for example, Villela 2001).

The issue of 'Who owns psychoanalysis?' (Casement 2004) is particularly hot in the UK at present, where a major challenge is being mounted to IPA monopoly control of this title. This monopoly has no legal status and has always been cheerfully ignored by Lacanians worldwide; but in the UK, the British Psychoanalytical Society (BPAS) has been the only body to issue the title of 'psychoanalyst', while many practitioners with an equivalent claim through training and experience have had to settle for names such as 'psychoanalytic psychotherapist'. This was exacerbated by analysts' attempt to assert a pre-eminent position within the UK Council for Psychotherapy; the failure of this bid led them to withdraw from UKCP into a separate organization – and force the analytic therapists to join them (Young 1999).

In 2004 a number of dissident groupings came together in a new College of Psychoanalysts, open to 'all practitioners who have undergone a psychoanalytic training which has been recognized by The College', as its website announces. It is perhaps hard for outsiders to appreciate the seismic effect of this initiative, levelling as it does distinctions that have been seen as essential in every sense of the word; it was met with thundering denunciation from the BPAS.

All these initiatives, different as they are, seem very welcome; but how radical are they – and how radical should they be? What do they really challenge and what needs to resist challenge? Many questions arise. The College of Psychoanalysts reserves to itself the right to approve or reject analytic trainings, on whatever basis it chooses. The Zurich Seminar holds – or held in 1989 – that 'everybody is an analyst-in-training by self-declaration' (Modena 1986: 10): every analysis can be a training analysis – no distinction is made between this and an ordinary analysis and one can change one's mind partway through about which one is engaged in.

But does this *solve* the problem of training analysis or simply *deny* it? Since analysts and analysands coexist as peers within the seminar, many situations of dual relationship arise. Modena is rather sanguine about the effects of this on analytic work or vice versa: 'In most cases negative consequences are easily avoided; indeed these "disturbances" can even enrich the analytic process ... One way or the other a reasonable resolution can usually be found by two adult people who have complementary interests in the continuation of their common work' (1986: 21). This notion of adulthood seems a remarkably un-analytic one.

Independent Practitioners' Network

The UK Independent Practitioners' Network (IPN) originated in response to the pressure for compulsory registration of therapists referred to earlier (see Postle *et al.* 2004; Totton 1997b). It has developed from a union of practitioners defending their right to practise into a proactive initiative for a new model of accountability and organization. Formed in 1994, the Network consists of groups of between five and ten practitioners who agree to 'stand by each others' work', a much debated phrase that essentially means they take responsibility for processing together any problems that arise – for example, conflict with a dissatisfied client. A full member group must circulate an ethical statement and form links with at least two other groups, satisfying themselves that the other groups are genuinely monitoring and challenging their members' practice and being available to help with this process.

Thus the Network is rooted in face-to-face relationship, in direct contrast to the formal, top-down qualification basis of accreditation with the two mass British organizations, UKCP and BACP. IPN is much smaller in membership than either of these – not directly because of its face-to-face structure, which being cellular could accommodate any number of participants, but probably more because of the demands of time, commitment and emotional depth this structure entails. However, all its members are necessarily active participants, whereas the great majority of UKCP- or BACP-accredited practitioners have an essentially passive and impersonal involvement.

This structure means that clients can take a grievance to any of 14 or more people – ultimately, to anyone in the Network; if their practitioner's group fails to resolve the conflict to the satisfaction of its link groups, those links will be withdrawn and the group will lapse from membership. (The group withdrawing its link would itself no longer be a full member until it found a new link. The structure encourages groups to test each other's integrity, but not to fall out over details.)

Participation in the Network is open to anyone. There is no monolithic position on therapeutic methods, theory or training: IPN supports diversity and plurality, recognizing that there are many ways of becoming an effective practitioner. There is also no single shared ethical code; each member group publishes its guidelines to the whole Network. IPN's central goal is defined in the constitution as 'furthering and supporting good practice'; the question of what 'good practice' is does not have a simple answer, but openness about practice allows a wide and ongoing debate, including criticism and challenge. The Network's whole ethos is that there is no centre to give authoritative judgement; individuals must take responsibility for their own version of good practice and share this publicly.

Over the last decade IPN has suffered many vicissitudes: it has found itself by no means immune to splitting and the process of coming to stand by each other's work and forming links has proved much more difficult and time consuming than was originally hoped. Most seriously, resolving practitioner–client conflict and maintaining 'sharp edges' against bad practice has been very challenging. IPN has found that it has no magic solution –

indeed, that there are even perhaps certain advantages to formal structures. However, a great deal has been learnt; and the Network continues to flourish and evolve, offering an accreditation process at least as rigorous, as and perhaps more appropriate to the practice of therapy than that of the mainstream organizations.

Conclusion

Standing back from the institutional state of psychotherapy and taking a good look, there is something genuinely scandalous about the prevalence of authoritarianism, bureaucracy, manipulation, rivalry and mutual contempt. It is hard to see how the stables can be cleansed as long as therapists are not willing to take that look; and certainly, as things stand, we are hardly in a position to tell the rest of society about its shortcomings. Thinking about psychotherapy and politics must surely entail thinking about the politics of psychotherapy itself.

10 Politics and psychotherapy in the context of healthcare
John Lees and Dawn Freshwater

Introduction

The problem of how to respond to the mental health of the population is a very real one. The World Health Organization (WHO) warns that by 2020 death from mental health disorders will be the second most common cause of morbidity (Freshwater 2003, 2005). Various rationales exist for the increase in prevalence of mental illness, with writers such as Tod Sloan (1996) pointing out that contentedness seems to be scarce, arguing along with Mirowsky (1989) that this is a price we pay for the lifestyle we call modern.

In contemporary society, most people experience some degree of emotional dissonance, ranging from vague anxiety, inability to concentrate, manic work habits, desire to drug oneself, alienation, estrangement and fantasies of a radical change of lifestyle (Freshwater 2003). Thus, it is not surprising to learn that, in the year 2000, there were counsellors and psychotherapists working in at least half of all general practices, with the government setting out clear guidelines on treatment choices including counselling and psychological therapies. Psychotherapy and indeed counselling, does, of course, have an established history within the NHS and other healthcare agencies. It is interesting to track its development, funding and availability within a political and societal context, particularly in the light of the National Service Framework (NHS) for Mental Health (DoH 1999) and more recently the implementation of the National Institute for Mental Health in England (NIMHE).

It is fair to say that the huge amount of research conducted into areas such as the value and effectiveness of psychological therapy over the past 40 years has, to a large extent, failed to influence the design of either services or treatments (Parry 1996). And yet, in spite of this, the medical model builds on such research, incorporates such notions as diagnosis and evidence-based practice and continues to dominate and, indeed, drive healthcare systems. Such notions can be seen to underpin guidance originating from the National Institute for Clinical Excellence (NICE), whose expert panel members have generated clinical protocols relating to the best treatment for such conditions as depression, early intervention psychosis, family intervention therapies and schizophrenia, among others, based in the main on the meta-synthesis of randomized control trials. Naturally, funding for such organizations is provided by the government and is predicated on some wide-scale evidence of *management* of the mentally distressed. However, in our view, there is little doubt that such organizations and systems have a political as well as a healing intent and that management, containment and control has a higher priority than healing.

In some countries, the political aspects of healthcare are quite explicit. Almost three decades ago, Illich (1976: 173) noted that mental illness in Maoist China was viewed as a political problem and so politicians were placed in charge of the mentally ill. Conversely, perfectly healthy dissidents in Soviet Russia were locked in hospitals and treated as though they were mentally ill. In both cases 'political re-education' and 'self-criticism' was seen as the solution to the state-decreed politicization of mental illness and the medicalization of political dissent.

While contemporary western societies do not use such overt methods of oppression, many people have argued that such oppressive political practices exist in western societies in a less perceptible form than in the examples just given. Indeed there have been a stream of critiques relating to the politics of mental illness in the west in recent years, which imply that mental healthcare is equally politically motivated, albeit in a less obvious way. Critiques have ranged from the anti-psychiatry movement to the work of Illich and such humanistic psychotherapists as Carl Rogers and other practitioners who have challenged the practices dominating our mental health systems today, such as the use of efficacy measurement tools (on the grounds that they are more about 'prediction' and 'control' in a political sense than healthcare). Writers such as Foucault (1987) have done much to raise awareness of some of the hidden hierarchies and agendas put forward under the guise of liberalism, not least within the mental health field.

The *Diagnostic and Statistical Manual* (DSM) of the American Psychiatric Association has also been challenged on the grounds that it discriminates against some sectors of society. For instance, feminist psychologists objected to the category of 'masochistic personality disorder', which the authors tried to introduce in the 1987 revision, on the grounds that the category could include women who stayed with husbands who beat them up as opposed to seeing them as victims of abuse. Indeed, the critique of DSM has been extended to all aspects of the manual and the whole enterprise is 'perceived by some critics to be a way for society to allow mental health professionals to become the social control agents of various irritating deviant members in society' (Todd and Bohart 1994: 77). The same questions can be, and have been, applied to the process of psychotherapy (see, for example, Boadella 1999; Wehowsky 2000; Wilkinson 1999).

In the light of such critiques, we would assert that it is important to be aware of the political nature of the mental health system. Further, as responsible and politically aware practitioners, we are ethically obliged to keep an open mind about our *collusion* in the process. At the very least, practitioners need to be aware of how their own personal political positions with regard to mental illness and public/private healthcare impact on the therapeutic relationship for, as Totton (2000) contends, all practitioners have a view on what *should* inform their everyday practice. In addition, it could be argued that individual practitioners and, indeed, psychotherapy as a profession, need to be prepared to interrogate and deconstruct the cultural politics associated with their practice. Practitioners embedded within a healthcare system are especially under the influence of social institutions and their own particular and universal cultural politics (Coyne and Woods 2002).

Our collusion in this process arises out of the fact that the healthcare system's politicization is based on a way of viewing people that is so pervasive as to be almost imperceptible. For instance, it focuses on 'parts' and 'bits' of the human being (or, in healthcare terms, specific symptoms) rather than attempting to look at the whole human being. It also judges health and illness in terms of what is considered to be normal by the medical or psychotherapeutic expert and, in so doing, does not always take into account the individual characteristics, or cultural context, of the client or patient. As Todres (2003: 196) has said:

> ... [C]ontemporary culture and science enable us to have a view of human identity that focuses on our 'parts' and the compartmentalization of our lives into specialized 'bits' ... As such it may unconsciously collude with a cultural trend to view humans as objects, like other objects and thus fit 'normatively' into the emerging world of specialized and efficient systems.

The net result, from the point of view of psychotherapy and counselling (henceforth therapy), is an approach to mental healthcare that fails to recognize the uniqueness of each individual human being and that, in terms of its diagnostic and assessment techniques, has power to influence that person's view of themselves. It also undermines the individual's creative potential, including the potential for self-healing, reducing his/her capacity to actively participate in the healing process. Finally, it impacts on the therapeutic relationship. This is important since therapy practitioners work with the relationship and many of them assert that the quality of the relationship is the most salient factor in therapeutic change (Clarkson 1995; Paul and Pelham 2000). Yet a system that privileges the opinion of the practitioner expert to such a high degree has a profound impact on the relationship. It creates a power imbalance within it based on the principle of I–It that is a 'relation of person to thing, of subject to object, involving some form of utilization, domination or control, even if it is only so-called "objective" knowing' (Herberg 1961: 14). Guggenbuhl-Craig (1978) examined the effects of the inherent asymmetry in the helping relationship, relating this to political issues such as power, oppression and organizational culture.

In the rest of this chapter we will look further at the political aspects of the mental healthcare system. This is especially current for therapists in view of the fact that our profession is increasingly coming into contact with the broader healthcare system. Yet therapists have specialist skills that enable them to understand the psychological impact of these developments and to find a way forward arising out of these specialist skills. So, having examined the broader aspects, we will then proceed to look at the psychological implications of a politicized healthcare system and conclude by pointing out a way forward.

The broader context and psychotherapy

The World Health Organization's (WHO) observation that (in Europe at least) depressive illness ranks alongside ischaemic heart disease and cerebrovascular disease as one of the three leading contributors to the overall burden of disease is a welcome one (Freshwater 2005; Murray and Lopez 1997). Freshwater observes that it is important that mental illness should not be perceived as the (stigmatized) behaviour of an apparent minority when, in reality, it is a common occurrence and arguably merges seamlessly into what we regard as normality. While this may not avoid the application of the DSM or International Classification of Diseases (ICD), it becomes much harder to regard people with such labels as fundamentally different and thereby exert (political) power, as is often the case with vulnerable groups. Further, once recognized and accepted as a major health problem within the population, campaigns and policy initiatives begin to be taken seriously and importantly *challenged* at all levels (Freshwater 2005). For example, the profile of mental health has been raised by campaigns such as those of the Royal College of Psychiatrists, 'Changing minds' (1998) and 'Defeat depression' (1992).

In order to manage this enormous shift in the increase of mental illness and distress there have been a number of policy initiatives. In 2003/4 funding was made available in the United Kingdom for 1000 new primary care mental health workers. There has been some controversy over the role, training and responsibilities and how the workers will fit into existing practices. Initial government guidelines indicate that the role of such workers will be in three broad areas:

- liaising with other statutory and non-statutory services (such as welfare and benefits, housing, charities and voluntary organizations)

- practice teamwork, providing support for audit, registers, routine measurements, implementation of referral protocols and advocacy
- client work including assessment and screening and onward referral and providing CBT for common mental disorders (mental health policy implementation).

While on the surface it might appear that the primary care/mental health worker will have little contact or relationship with therapists in private practice, once the role boundaries are unpacked, it is clear that not only will the workers work closely with therapists in both private practice and in the public sector, but also that many of these workers will, in fact, be trained in basic psychotherapeutic skills themselves, albeit in one chosen theoretical model, deemed to be more cost effective both in terms of time and finance.

Such initiatives in particular, and the healthcare system in general tend to be based on the orthodox scientific experimental model with its emphasis on objectivity and truth. However, this is not the only way of viewing healthcare. In recent years constructionist dialogues have replaced such traditional views about objectivity and truth with concerns related to discourse and practice (Freshwater 2005; Gergen and Gergen 2003). Such dialogues are made possible by the idea that we live in worlds of meaning making and language, which are used to 'do things'. In other words, meaning and language are inextricably linked to our actions and our practice. Mental health professionals attempt to explain, predict and control mental illness through their privileged knowledge. As such, *expertise* lies in making the diagnosis, in prescribing treatment and in reorienting patients to live in the 'real' world in order to restore them to 'normal' functioning.

From a constructionist perspective, notions about what is 'real' and 'normal' in a society, or indeed within a profession, are not determined through the application of a universal standard, but are social constructions driven by relations of power and control. To illustrate this point, Fernando (2002) suggests that the social construction of mental illness was brought into sharp relief by the aforementioned political abuses of psychiatry in the former Soviet Union and in the decision of the American Psychiatric Association in 1973 that homosexuality should no longer be seen as a pathological condition. What these actions show is that rather than mental illness being defined against some absolute yardstick, the process of labelling is generated through and by powerful societal institutions that have the authority to both constrain and liberate individuals. Freshwater (2005) opines that:

> The social constructionist perspective challenges the notion of mental illness as the result of biological, genetic, psychological

malfunctioning. Rather, it sees psychiatric pathology as the labels given to the damaging effect of disadvantage and discrimination such as racism or homophobia for example on the identity of individuals. These in turn are likely to lead to experiences of alienation arising from a socio-political system that denies those individuals the opportunity to express themselves, to be heard and understood, or to live in a particular way.

These considerations form the broad context in which the relatively new therapy profession (and indeed the mental health profession) had been developing in recent years. Indeed, as a result of this rapid growth, therapy is becoming increasingly embedded within the dominant healthcare system driven by requests for statutory registration under the aegis of the Health Professions Council. As the Chief Executive of the BACP has said: 'The Government has made it clear that the Health Professions Council (HPC) is the only mechanism' and furthermore 'the way things stand at the moment I really don't think that there is an alternative for the psychological therapies other than statutory registration and regulation' (L. Clarke 2003: 7). If this prediction is borne out, therapists will join a system having its own discourses that serve to construct and label not only what is health and ill health from a psychological perspective, but also construct and define the notion of what constitutes a profession. Such a system favours 'appropriate assessment techniques'. In order to become registered and able to practice, practitioners need to demonstrate their ability to do such things as 'conduct evidence-based practice, evaluate practice systematically and participate in audit procedures', 'formulate specific and appropriate management plans including the setting of timescales' and 'conduct appropriate diagnostic or monitoring procedures, treatment, therapy or other actions safely and skilfully' (Health Professions Council 2004). Freshwater and Rolfe (2004) note that such universal discourses or meta-narratives serve to maintain a sense of authority (and power) based on the notion of expertise, which in itself is both defined and constructed from within that dominant discourse.

We are thus faced with a dilemma. On the one hand, the therapy profession is becoming more and more a part of the healthcare system, with its possibilities for increasing the power factor in the therapeutic relationship. On the other, it is a particular discipline that, as previously discussed, places the quality of the therapeutic relationship at the centre of its work. On the face of it, we could take the view that the entry of therapy into the healthcare system presents a crisis for the profession – that it threatens the therapeutic relationship and can alienate both the therapist and client. So we will examine this further in the next section. However, we also view these developments as an opportunity for developing the profession further – a matter we will return to at the end of this chapter.

The healthcare system and psychotherapy

The notion of alienation, which we introduced in the previous section, begs the question: alienated from what? Marx referred to alienation as arising out of the dissociation of the worker from the products of his/her labour: 'the object which labour produces – labour's product – confronts it as *something alien*, as a *power independent* of the producer ... In the conditions dealt by political economy this realization of labour appears as *loss of reality* for the workers ... as *alienation*' (Marx 1844: 58). In other words, the fact that the workers have no control over the products of their labour leads to their alienation from these products. However, our usage of the term alienation is psychological rather than economic. We view it as alienation from our experience (including our experience of our illness) and, ultimately, ourselves. Just as the capitalist profits from utilizing the products of the workers' labour for his own ends, so in contemporary healthcare systems healthcare workers (doctors, therapists and so on) profit from labelling and pathologizing the patient/client/service user/person. We mean this literally – less pathology, fewer consultant psychiatrists; less emphasis on madness, fewer lengthy therapy contracts. For the individual, this form of alienation is well expressed by the following:

> The concepts of 'myself' and 'I' that underlie our ordinary actions are simple ones, *closely linked to actual experiences* and thus to our reality. Science constructs its own, *different version of reality* that is extremely useful for its own purposes. However, when it starts to create explanatory models that purport to account for our experiences but do not fully fit with the totality of those experiences one may not unreasonably suggest that if the models are to be taken seriously then they should be adjusted to conform better to the latter.
>
> (Josephson 2001: 55, emphasis added)

Interestingly, there are echoes of similar disenchantment and alienation in the works of Eric Fromm (1995) who writes of human alienation afforded through market economy and Cohen and Taylor (1992) who notably describe the individual's attempts to escape from everyday life. We might urge the reader to reflect on both the healthcare system and the profession of psychotherapy as market economies themselves; this is certainly true of the former. The alienation epidemic that forces people to seek all manner of escape routes could indeed be lining the pocket of more than a few psychotherapists!

In terms of the discussion so far, the process of alienation can be seen as consisting of at least three stages arising out of the gradual accretion of medicalized thinking within therapy practice. First, the imposition of 'part' and 'norm'-oriented thinking based on diagnostic, assessment, treatment and evaluation techniques that have been constructed by medical and psychotherapeutic experts who have, in Josephson's terms, constructed their 'own, different version of reality', which they perceive to be the best way 'to account for our experiences'. Second and arising out of this, the imposition of an I–It therapeutic relationship in which the client is an unequal partner in power terms and is viewed in the light of expert viewpoints. Third, as a result of these features, the promulgation of a client view of themselves that, in person centred terms, is based on an external locus of evaluation in which the medical/psychotherapeutic system's version of illness (or rather its version of the existential–phenomenological state that, at that moment in their lives, both the therapist and client are experiencing) influences the way in which we think about our direct lived experience; in short, we become alienated from it.

Such views echo the work of Rogers. He was deeply concerned about therapists' use of diagnosis and assessment and its consequent effect on the therapeutic relationship and our clients. He asserted that it placed 'the locus of evaluation so definitely in the expert [*that is to say in therapists themselves*] that it may increase any dependent tendencies in the client and cause him to feel that the responsibility for understanding and improving his situation lies in the hands of another' (Rogers 1951: 223, emphasis added). Indeed, he asserted that 'when the locus of evaluation is seen as residing in the expert, it would appear that the long-range social implications are in the direction of the social control of the many by the few' (1951: 224). So, he was concerned with what therapists are purported to be *doing to* their clients. Freshwater (2005) similarly observes that:

> For the client, the process of diagnosis or classification, using what are potentially concrete criteria (and subsequently stigmatizing labels), may be seen as placing the locus of evaluation in the 'expert'. There is an inherent risk in this process of diagnosis and classification insofar as the client may expect the responsibility for understanding and 'curing' the problem to lie with the counsellor, rather than himself or herself.

In her discussion on the politics of labelling, she goes on to say that: 'Other dangers include the potential for feelings of *alienation* and resistance, or of growing dependency on the counsellor in whom the client may invest the power to "cure" their emotional distress.'

McKenzie (2002: 26) extends the notion of alienation further: 'In surrounding ourselves with increasingly sophisticated theories and models we create the illusion of progress. In denying the primacy of experience by its reframing within the counselling culture to match the theories and models, there is a very real or serious danger of alienating our patients.' By implication, he introduces the notion that therapists do not just alienate their clients from their experience but also themselves from others by giving too much importance to theory and conceptualization. This mutual cycle of alienation results in devaluing the direct experience of clients and under-rating their capacity to see experience as it is. The therapist is unable to connect with his/her direct lived experience because of the theories and concepts that tell him/her what to see and the client is unable to connect with his/her experience because s/he is viewed by the therapist in the light of these theories and concepts. Everyone is an unwitting victim.

If the thinking of both therapists and clients is thus taken over by the medical/psychotherapeutic system's version of the 'illness/existential–phenomenological state of the client at that moment in time', then it will be dominated by the 'version of reality' constructed by science and psychotherapy. We become overawed by the authority invested in the scientific expert's view of our experience and, even though the thinking that now dominates our perception of it does 'not fully fit with the totality of those experiences', we will meekly succumb to it. Privileging the opin-ions of the expert in our field, abstract and distorted as it often is, above our own understanding leads to a sense of alienation from self (and, interest-ingly, this is what we foster through our practice, almost the complete opposite of the rhetoric!), by allowing the medical expert and theoretician to determine our thinking to such a degree that we become alienated from our own experience. We are overcome by a theorized or medicalized view of ourselves. Yet we are unable to see this because of the pervasiveness of the dominant discourse, which, as already discussed, structures the way we view things. Indeed, this principle extends, as McKenzie has suggested, to our psychotherapeutic theorizing. As Parker (1997) has noted, psycho-analytic ideas have permeated us so much that they influence our capacity to think about ourselves: 'psychoanalysis can be used to illuminate cultural phenomena, but this is because psychoanalytic discourse already *structures* those phenomena' (*ibid*: vii). Our alienation is driven by the multiple dis-courses that separate us from our experience.

In psychotherapeutic terms, the dominance of the experts' view under-mines both therapists' and clients' connection with their experience but also undermines our capacity to think and act for ourselves out of an inter-nal locus of evaluation. It thus destroys our self-actualizing capacity – our need to be ourselves (Maslow 1970). Instead of being ourselves we succumb to authority *no matter what it says* – a phenomenon that has been recog-nized for some time:

> In the field of medicine, in the law, but also in other fields, people
> are declaring themselves incapable of acquiring their own knowl-
> edge and are instead accepting whatever science tells them ...
> People are growing ever more helpless in the face of authority.
>
> (Steiner 1916: 131)

It may well be the case that, as therapists, we are indifferent to the
alienation from our experience and from our capacity to think for ourselves
and are prepared to subject ourselves to others' theories and concepts.
However, it is one thing to subject ourselves to this and quite another to
work out of such principles in our client work. We would contend that
health professionals can usefully, as already discussed, develop an awareness of such tendencies and that this is an ethical and moral issue: the principle of 'autonomy: respect for the client's right to be self-governing' (BACP
2002: 3). So, once again, the question is how to act and inform our actions
with our psychotherapeutic understanding.

Conclusion

Current developments, as we have discussed in this chapter, delineate what
constitutes health and deviations from health; that is, they participate in a
series of existing discourses, thereby colluding directly with such decisions
about who and what can be represented in society. This goes back to the
earlier comments about the DSMIV and the way in which the healthcare
system relies on such models of categorization. However, Gergen (1994)
goes even further. He argues that any system that explicitly engages in a
deficit model of individual functioning contributes to a cycle of progressive
infirmity. It may be the case that therapy is somehow legitimized within
society when placed within institutions such as the NHS under the auspices
of such regulatory bodies as the HPC and yet those very institutions rely
heavily on structured models of categorization that bear no resemblance to
reality and furthermore they are politically driven and rely on government
funding.

Having outlined the dangers, we also view crisis as an opportunity (a
notion that arises out of our therapy training inasmuch as we have been
taught that therapeutic crisis, while posing a danger, can also be an opportunity for transformation and, indeed, in many cases might be *necessary* for
transformation). Moreover, wherever there is energy, there is also the
potential for empowerment and emancipation, what might be seen as the
bedrock of psychotherapeutic work.

This can be understood from the point of view of the transformatory
nature of research and therapeutic work (Freshwater and Rolfe 2001; Lees
2001). Freshwater and Rolfe describe three types of reflexive research that

can also be viewed as three significant stages in the research *process* (Lees 2001). The model involves reflecting on our reflections about a phenomenon; that is to say, turning 'thought or reflection back on itself' (Freshwater and Rolfe 2001: 529). In this chapter, we have attempted to do this in relation to the topic. We have also moved on to the second stage of raising awareness about the social and political context of our work. Indeed, much of the chapter has been concerned with doing this. Finally and crucially, we are concerned with building on such reflection and consciousness raising as a basis for change and transformation. We have been concerned with disseminating a point of view that encourages practitioners to turn the political nature of healthcare systems (which will continue to have an increasingly profound effect on our work) back on themselves. We are thus concerned with 'politically-informed action or "praxis"' (*ibid*: 530) as a result of self-empowerment and the empowerment of others. Just as class consciousness, in Marxist terms, aims for 'revolution', so our response to our current concerns about healthcare from the point of view of therapy is to use it as an opportunity for change and transformation. At the very least we can attempt to do this within our own practice and within ourselves.

Part IV
Working at the interface: psychotherapy in political action

11 Transforming conflict into community: post-war reconciliation in Croatia
Arlene Audergon and Lane Arye

The personal and the political

Heading to Osijek: introduction

Heading to Osijek, Croatia, in a UN van, the landscape was dotted with charred houses. In Osijek, every building was pockmarked from gunfire and shelling. That evening, we took a walk along the river that had been the dividing line between Serb and Croat sides during the war.

It was 1996, a year after the war had ended. One of the women who had invited us said it was the first time that Croats, Serbs and Muslims were meeting together to talk about the war and their future. They gathered from different parts of Croatia and from Bosnia. We (Lane and Arlene) and the participants were heading onto a steep learning curve. How do you open a discussion about the war, about reconciliation and moving forward? We learned that even asking people to introduce themselves publicly was charged. Saying their names could identify them as Croat, Serb or Muslim. If they also said where they lived, people could assume an entire story about what someone had done during the war.

The project

This was to be the first of many visits to Croatia, between 1996 and 2001. The first forum was sponsored by the International Rescue Committee (IRC). This seed grew into a project called 'Building Sustainable Community in the Aftermath of War'.[1] It was organized by Udruga Mi, a Croatian NGO (nongovernmental organization), and was funded by the UN High Commission for Refugees.[2] The project included four-day forums twice a year, regional meetings, a training group and a journal. The forums were

---

[1]   Tanja Radocaj and Mirela Miharija invited us to Croatia after meeting us at a Worldwork seminar in Slovakia in 1994. Tanja had a vision and, together with Nives Ivelja, Edi Zitnik and others from Udruga Mi, developed and implemented the project.

[2]   Other funders included OSCE, USAID, the Threshold Foundation and the Open Society Institute, as well as the British, US and Norwegian embassies.

made up of 60–90 participants from all war-affected regions of Croatia. They were Croat, Serb, Muslim and from other ethnic backgrounds such as Hungarian and Roma. They represented many NGOs, governmental organizations and international organizations. Participants were active in their communities as social workers, doctors, nurses, teachers, counsellors, mayors, city administrators and lawyers.

The purpose of this project was to support the work of key players involved with reconciliation and community building throughout Croatia. The idea was that if they worked among themselves on the painful and complex post-war issues, they could in turn better meet these problems in their communities and organizations. Each forum was a temporary, diverse community; a microcosm in which the region's difficulties would naturally arise, so we could learn together how to work with them.

Approach to facilitation: process work, deep democracy and hot spots

Our facilitation approach is based on our training in and practice of Process-Oriented Psychology or Process Work, developed by Dr Arnold Mindell. The facilitator's task is to bring awareness to what is actually happening in an individual or group. The method recognizes patterns for change that first appear as a disturbance (Mindell 1986). A teleological approach, Process Work looks not just for the cause of a problem or how to eradicate it; rather when a problem is unfolded with accuracy and heart, a new way forward is discovered that is often surprising, creative and transformative.

A main concept in this approach is 'deep democracy' (Mindell 1992). Democracy usually means that different points of view are represented but, ultimately, the majority rules. In most groups and societies, however, some voices are pushed to the margins. They are considered irrelevant, irrational or too extreme.

Mindell's idea of deep democracy means supporting both mainstream and marginalized voices. It also sees the emotional experiences at the margins of group life as potentially transformative. It is through the expression, and especially the interaction of all the parts, that the wisdom and creativity of a community can emerge. Deep democracy also includes facilitation of the different dimensions of a group's experience: the outer themes and issues, the background emotions and polarizations and the underlying shared human experience.

In Process Work, we use the term 'hot spot' to refer to those moments in our interactions where conflict cycles and escalates (Mindell 1995: 81). They are spots we tend to back off from, or where we can be rapidly polarized in dramatic and potentially violent ways. Yet the hot spot is also a doorway to potential change and deepening of community relationships. Careful facilitation is needed, so that points of inflammation can lead to transformation, rather than a repeat of suffering.

In a mixed group of Serbs, Croats and Muslims in 1996, the very idea of talking about the war was terrifying, threatening and ran the risk of re-traumatizing. As facilitators, we tried at all times to discover and support the group's innate wisdom, timing and direction. We attempted to welcome the group, including its fears and its reasons to not touch on the issues at all.

We also worked with the atmosphere that was so terrifying, to not leave it threatening from the background, where it was more dangerous. The issue of 'differences' was charged. The atrocities in the former Yugoslavia were a direct result of the political manipulation of differences. It was therefore important as facilitators that we did not fall unconsciously into the role of pressing to speak about their divisions.

A bomb in the bakery: a friendship between a Croat and Serb

During that first forum in Osijek, a participant came into the room after a coffee break, saying she had just heard that a bomb had exploded at a bakery. A woman rushed out to call her husband who worked near there. No one had been hurt. We asked about the level of danger in town. A man who later described himself as a frontline fighter during the war said in a casual and relaxed way: 'It's nothing to worry about – it's just the local mafia.' We were a bit shaken, but the group was ready to move on.

So we did. We offered to work with two people in relationship. Two old friends, one Serb and one Croat, wanted the opportunity. We recall how we then felt relaxed – working with people in relationships is something we might do anywhere – and we enjoyed facilitating them. They discussed what had until then been a taboo subject between them: what they had actually experienced during the war and how it made them feel about each other as Serb and Croat. They had not had a 'real conversation' since the war. Each wanted the other to understand her experience, not only friend to friend, but as Croat and Serb.

We looked around and people were riveted. In the break, the same man who had spoken so casually about the bomb at the bakery came to us now in a great state of excitement and agitation. He thought their work was tremendous and wanted to know how it was possible. He had never seen Croats and Serbs speaking together so personally and politically since the war. He said it was potentially life changing, yet also life threatening. A woman said that if some people in her town knew that she was in a room where this kind of conversation was taking place, her physical safety could be endangered.

Here, as was often the case in future forums, personal interactions were highly charged and political. And the 'political' was always deeply personal.

Don't talk politics

When any issue about the war was touched, a silence came over the group like a low, chilling fog. We learned quickly not to try to forge ahead in this fog, but also not to be swallowed in it. Moving too quickly could be dangerous, re-triggering acute symptoms of trauma. Just sitting in it was as dangerous, furthering distress and hopelessness.

We decided to explore the dynamics creating this silence and fog. Rather than trying to overcome this silence by getting people to speak, we represented what we imagined was an as yet unspoken voice that said: 'Don't talk about the war.' It threatened, 'Don't speak to people from the other side, or else.' Participants joined in to give expression to this voice. 'Don't talk about what divides you. It's far too dangerous.' Others added, 'Don't open up old wounds. It could inflame the conflict all over again.' 'It will open up too much pain.'

Several people said that anything 'political' must be avoided and that it is important that we discuss only humanitarian issues of rebuilding society. The predominant attitude with which the group identified was: 'We are all humanitarians here. We like each other. We are not the intolerant ones who created the conflict.'

As facilitators, we respected their fears and their urge for unity after the devastation of their lives in the name of ethnic/national difference. At the same time, we noticed a thick tension in the room that no one was talking about. And during breaks, the Serbs went with Serbs, Croats with Croats, Muslims with Muslims.

A useful Process Work method is to observe how a group identifies itself (the 'we'), as well as what goes against or disturbs this identity (the 'not we') (Mindell 1995: 42–3). Facilitation involves supporting the interaction of all parts of the group's experience, including both that which is closer to the group's identity and whatever disturbs that identity. This group identified with 'humanitarian aims'. They were *not* the 'intolerant ones'. They were disturbed by the underlying conflicts that they feared could escalate, which were already apparent in their signals (separating into ethnic groups during breaks) and in the tense atmosphere between them. The tension in our group was a small mirror of the tension in people's communities, which appeared both in a generalized depression and in occasional violent outbreaks. To begin a process of reconciliation and rebuilding within communities, there needed to be a way to talk about what happened at an individual and community level, without inflaming further violence.

The stories pour out

One morning something happened that was apparently small, yet extraordinary. A woman courageously and shyly said: 'I feel a *little* more comfortable with people from my own ethnic group.' With this small admission, she opened a floodgate and people's upset poured out. 'I knew I couldn't trust you!' We asked why? Participants spoke emotionally about what people from another ethnic/national group had done to their sisters, families, communities; what it was like when faced with terror, or when standing in long refugee columns with screaming kids and no water.

As people began speaking for the first time in the group about their experiences, others couldn't listen. Personal stories about the brutality committed by the other side were felt to be (and sometimes were) accusations toward the other side's whole group. After a terrible story, someone would want to tell a different story about the good things that had been done by their side – or about the brutality that had been done by members of the other group.

The group was at a new stage of interaction. The participants were now speaking personally and emotionally about the war. Their stories and accusations led to a temporary escalation that brought the conflict out into the open. As their distrust and the experiences that divided them came to the foreground, there was a need for the group to find ways to respond to both the accusations and the pain of their traumatic experiences.

Trauma and bridging the distance

Museum pieces and watching TV

A small group from Sarajevo hung out together in the forum, becoming friends. Many of the participants felt this subgroup as a kind of clique. But, that afternoon, an opposite picture emerged. A woman from Sarajevo said that the large group was holding the participants from Sarajevo at a distance. Although everyone had suffered loss during the war and many had traumatic experiences, Sarajevo had been through a recent hell. She said: 'You keep us at a distance. You look at us like museum pieces. You look but don't touch.'

A woman from Croatia went across the room and faced her. She said: 'It's true. I remember keeping you at a distance when I watched Sarajevo on TV. At that point the war in Croatia had stopped and, though I lived only 200 kilometers from Sarajevo, I watched it on TV and it seemed so far away. I couldn't feel anything. I remember thinking I was glad it was there and not here.' Tears filled each woman's eyes. At the moment the Croatian woman acknowledged that she had been keeping them at a distance, the distance was bridged. Looking around the room, every participant in the group of 60 was now crying. While continuing to facilitate, we also had tears rolling down our faces. The professional translator began to cry and was very upset that she wasn't able to keep a professional distance, as she had been trained to do. When we assured her it was okay, she dropped to the floor and wept, others pitching in to keep translating. It was an extraordinary and intimate experience; several people went on to speak personally about how they had distanced themselves from their own and others' pain, and had also isolated themselves from one another.

A deeper unity

Perhaps everyone knew the experience of watching television, frozen, unable to feel, and even being glad it was there and not here. The experience touched the core of the tragedy, beyond the participants and beyond the Balkans. The world had stood by, watching TV.

Traumatic war experience often results in feeling cut off or distant from memories and one's own emotions. A natural response to traumatic experience is to split it off, because it is too much to witness, too much to bear. There is a need to focus on survival and moving forward. The more the traumatic experience is split off from consciousness, however, the more the experience may reoccur and intrude in debilitating symptoms, and the person may feel overrun by emotion and flashbacks (Hermann 1997: 1–4). Similarly, the more a communal trauma is split off and not talked about on a community level, the more likely the experience can reoccur and intrude in the form of community-wide hopelessness and depression, community violence and even war (Audergon 2004, Audergon 2005: 173–207).

We've seen how the group at first wanted to avoid politics and the divisiveness that had torn apart their hearts and community. At the same time, the 'divisive politics' that they feared was already palpable. When someone said the unspeakable in the most subtle way imaginable – 'I'm a little more comfortable with my own group' – the stories and mistrust that divided them spilled out.

The 'divisiveness' appeared also in their emotional distance from their own traumatic experience and from each other. This was expressed in the accusation: 'You keep us at a distance.' Admitting the truth of an accusation can be transformative. When the Croatian woman admitted that she had been keeping both Sarajevo and her feelings about what was happening there at a distance, the group got in touch with the pain of being cut off. When the distance was acknowledged, a space opened in people's hearts to share the enormous pain; with that came a sense of relief from isolation. The compassion and momentary unity the group now shared was miles from the forced feeling of togetherness and 'tolerance' from earlier in the week.

That evening, there was a spontaneous party. Local wine and a guitar seemed to appear from nowhere. Until early morning people sang together, everyone singing songs from all parts of the former Yugoslavia. The atmosphere was wild, festive, intimate, joyous. We remember one moment when we felt goose bumps but didn't know why. Someone whispered that that they were all singing a song from a beloved Serbian singer who had been outlawed during the war.

Accountability and responsibility

In 15 minutes, we were in the 14th century

Throughout the six years of our work in Croatia, participants frequently spoke of the need for accountability. We have come to believe that grappling with matters of accountability and responsibility at a personal and community level is essential for reconciliation in post-conflict zones and as a method of conflict prevention.

Six months after our experience in Osijek, we returned to Croatia for a forum in the ancient town of Split, on the Adriatic Sea. One morning, some Croatian Serbs (ethnic Serbs whose families had lived in Croatia for generations and who held Croatian citizenship) accused the Croats of poor treatment of Serb returnees, who had fled during the war in 1995 and were now returning to Croatia. They also wanted someone to stand accountable for the atrocities committed against them in 1995. Croats were outraged that they were being blamed for not being open armed to returning Serbs, after the Serbs had committed such atrocities in 1991 against *them*, while occupying regions of Croatia. Serbs responded that Croats had committed grave atrocities against *them* during World War II, when Croatia was allied with the Nazis. Within 15 minutes we were back in the 14th century! Each side wanted the other to take responsibility for the problems of the country and the region.

Symmetrical blaming leads to escalation and cycling of conflict, but it can also be an important step on the way toward conflict resolution.

The 'killer'

As we listened, we realized that each side was talking about the same 'ghost role'. A ghost role is a part of the process that is being referred to or implied, but no one is representing it directly or identifying with it (Mindell 1995: 89). Whether Serb or Croat, each side accused the other of being a killer.

That afternoon, we told people that although it might be difficult to watch and listen, we felt it could be useful to represent 'the killer' whom everyone was suffering from. After getting the group's permission, we entered the role, representing the glory of killing and power. One woman, looking shell shocked, stood up and said that she knows this man; he was in her kitchen. She proceeded to tell the story of when a warlord forced his way into her house and threatened her and her family. Then she played this man, swaggering and strutting around the room, making threats and spitting venom.

At first the participants looked on in stunned silence. Then one by one they started reacting to this role, arguing with it, expressing their fury, their terror, their loss and pain. The woman left the role and joined the chorus of outrage. For a long moment, the whole group was united against the killer, united in their common story, no longer blaming one another, able for now to see each other's humanity, anger and grief. Some of the shock and numbness of the past few years began to lift as their reactions that would have been dangerous or even fatal to express during the war now rang out and were echoed and welcomed by the community.

This process suggested that the group needed – and perhaps the larger community needs – to express its shock and outrage against the 'killer'. This is important in two ways: first, this expression unlocks frozen reactions within traumatic experience, beginning a process of individual and collective healing. Second, it is an important step toward accountability, because people cannot begin to think about taking responsibility for the violence in their communities unless they have had a chance to process their shock and pain about it. These parallel processes of working with trauma and accountability are essential for reconciliation and for preventing the replay of conflict and war (Audergon 2005: 38–40, 200–2).

Personal and collective accountability and responsibility

Over several years, essential discussions arose, differentiating personal and collective responsibility.

A national debate was raging in the media and the government about sending those accused of war crimes to the Tribunal in The Hague. Many people in society and some in our group were against sending any Croats to The Hague. Some Croatian nationalists felt that individuals now considered war criminals had valiantly defended Croatia and should not be prosecuted. They felt it would destroy the morale of soldiers who had fought to defend their country. Some felt that Croat war criminals should not be sent to The Hague until Serb war criminals had first been sent. Others feared the international community would withhold aid if Croatia did not cooperate and some felt that this would be a form of unfair collective punishment. Still others felt that war criminals on all sides needed to be held accountable by the Tribunal, so that society could move forward. They supported the principles behind the Tribunal: that accountability is an essential component of reconciliation and conflict prevention; and that it is important to hold responsible those individuals who are most guilty of crimes against humanity in order to make sure that collective guilt and retribution is avoided.

These far-reaching issues about individual and collective responsibility played out within the microcosm of our forums. Some people thought we should not talk about accountability within our group, because that was only a matter for war criminals. Others insisted that even those individuals who were not directly responsible, or who had even opposed the war, needed to assume some accountability for what their group or nation had done. Still others resisted the idea of anyone assuming responsibility for what they had not personally done. They firmly believed that each person should be seen only as an individual, accountable only for his or her own actions, and not as a member of an ethnic/national group.

Taking responsibility and community leadership

In most conflicts, whether it is at home or in a situation of war, people have a need for accountability. This is connected to an urge for justice and closure. It includes someone admitting what happened (versus denying what happened or making counter-accusations), filling in the holes of missing information and expressing remorse for what happened.

During one forum, amidst calls for accountability, an older Croat woman stood up and did something unheard of at that time. She spoke about a Croat soldier who had entered a Muslim home and killed a woman and child. Then she said: 'I was a person who wanted military action to liberate Knin (a region of Croatia that had been held by the Serbs). That was war. But I did not want Savka and Jovan to be thrown into the well.' (These are Serb names.)

Then a Serb woman stood up, on the verge of tears. She said: 'No one can tell me that an 87-year-old Croat man should be made to suffer at the hands of Serbs. I graduated from the best university. But I still can't explain to a Croat mother why her 4-year-old had to die. Why did they beat up an 87-year-old man? How can I learn to forget this?'

It was so painful to listen to these specific horrors. But, as each woman spoke about atrocities committed by *her own group*, it transformed the feeling of the whole group.

It was potentially dangerous, and therefore very courageous, for these women to speak in this way, due to an implicit code of loyalty. But each of these women had credibility within her own ethnic/national group, having suffered deeply during the war at the hands of the other side.

The Serb woman went on to say: 'It's not that I'm personally guilty, because I'm not. But if I were silent, I would not be taking responsibility. By speaking I take responsibility.'

With this shift in the notion of responsibility, the forum changed direction. An older Muslim man pleaded with the participants to turn together with him toward the future. First in small groups and then in the large group, participants discussed what they would do if they could identify with a sense of responsibility and leadership in their own communities.

Several people commented that the discussions on personal and collective responsibility had led to a new understanding of their experiences during the war and in the present time. One man said: 'It never occurred to me until now that I had any responsibility for what happened in this region. Now I see that if something similar happens again, I can make a conscious choice about whether I will do something about it.' Enlivened, he said: 'This feeling of responsibility does not make me feel guilty; it gives me hope for the future.' A woman agreed, saying that she had been a teenager when the war started and so she could not do anything. 'But now I see that my feelings then – my hatred – contributed to the atmosphere that led to war and that has led to wars throughout history.'

The ripple effect

Six months later, we convened the next forum. A young woman who had been quiet during the last forum told the group that the process about responsibility had influenced her in profound ways. She told the following story:

> I came to the last forum with a problem on my soul. The state had decided to build a nuclear waste dump in my town and I felt helpless to do anything about it. But after listening to the others talk about responsibility and then talking in my small group about what it would be like if I could take responsibility and leadership, I returned home and started to act step by step. I drafted a petition and gave it to the local municipal board. They convinced the neighbouring town to also gather signatures. But they only gathered 700 signatures. So I organized volunteers and gathered 4000 more. Now there is a halt on construction. In the midst of this, I met with the mayor. He told me that he is too small to make a difference. I told him that he is not small. Imagine me, a young woman, telling the mayor that he is not small! Now I feel much more powerful and free, because in spite of all odds, I have changed something in my community and in my head.

This woman's personal transformation made her a political force to be reckoned with and an inspiration to others.

This was part of the ripple effect of these forums. Participants had life-changing experiences and witnessed others having such experiences. Sometimes people unlocked emotions and expression that had been frozen by trauma. Or they saw people from opposing sides talking with each other, fighting with each other, crying with each other and loving one another.

They were shocked and thrilled to realize that conflict need not lead to war, but rather can be a doorway to intimacy and community. Then they went back to their local communities, changed. Participants often told us that when they now met a conflict in their community, where they would have normally been afraid or at a loss, they realized they could approach the situation with a new orientation. They felt not only that it was possible to work with conflict, but that doing so could strengthen their communities. As they brought these new patterns home with them, the ripples of change widened and others saw new possibilities of living together, talking openly with one another and taking responsibility for their common future.

Conclusion

The project in Croatia can be seen as one model that might be useful in other post-conflict and conflict prevention efforts. Reconciliation and conflict prevention requires political and humanitarian intervention, at local, national and international levels, to deal with criminal accountability, build civil society, provide basic services for those displaced during war and support human rights. These efforts are more likely to be sustainable if the post-war issues are processed in depth at the community level.

Working deeply at the community level also builds relationships. In this project, lasting friendships grew across ethnic/national lines. Professional collaboration was also fostered, essential to the joint effort needed to rebuild society. Relationships also spanned organizational boundaries. Organizations that had been at odds with one another, competed with one another, or had even worked at cross-purposes, were able to work on their differences and increase their cooperation.

The very notion of working with conflict at a community level requires a shift in how we look at conflict itself. It means looking at our own responsibility and recognizing how our own feelings and attitudes influence our communities and world. It means not only aiming for peace, but being willing to have conflicts together, inviting all voices and facilitating the whole interaction – even or especially when it seems most difficult. And it means looking at how the problem 'out there' may also be playing out inside us.

This is both a psychological and political process. In Croatia, we saw individuals and groups transform when they intentionally and consciously stepped into the complex issues and painful emotions surrounding the war and post-war period, rather than feeling only at the mercy of these dynamics. Many people said that their participation in these forums was of life-and-death importance to them on their personal journey. They spoke of finding hope for humanity that they had been convinced they would never feel again. At the same time, they did not just hope for peace, but recognized that they are active and essential players in shaping their society.

We honour the participants who were willing to go to the extremes and depths of their outrage and suffering. Sometimes the conflict seemed intractable; sometimes what the group heard was too terrible, unspeakable. Yet, there was a sense of the whole group working through it together, as if we all were one body. The most intimate personal things, spoken in the community, were not only personal, but also belonged to everyone. And as the group moved together through accusation, traumatic experience, hatred, terror and hopelessness, there was a sense that the group itself belonged to something that transcended it, something that could hold and transform its conflict and pain. When we reflect on our experiences in Croatia, we feel a sense of awe – that what is transformative is ultimately beyond the individuals and group, beyond a method and beyond words.

12 Israeli psychotherapists and the Israeli–Palestinian conflict
Emanuel Berman

Introduction

The deterioration of the Israeli–Palestinian conflict has been of enormous concern to mental health professionals in Israel. Over 200 of us published a petition in the Israeli press in 2002, calling attention to the enormous and potentially irreversible post-traumatic emotional damage caused on both sides and calling for an immediate return to the negotiating table, in order to stop the vicious cycle of mutual violence and bloodshed. At the same time, many Israeli analysts and therapists – joining academic colleagues in other disciplines – expressed outrage at the call by some European professors to boycott the Israeli academic world, which has been for many years the location of thoughtful attempts to challenge narrow Israeli nationalism and to search for an Israeli–Arab dialogue aimed at putting an end to the occupation and resolving the tragedy of the Palestinian people. Some Israeli protesters described a feeling of being backstabbed by their foreign colleagues, while being engaged in a painful frontal struggle with the Israeli government, which is being criticized by a vast majority of the professional and academic community in Israel as narrow minded, militaristic and unwilling to offer any viable perspective for the resolution of the conflict.

Earlier on, in 2001, numerous Israeli analysts and therapists joined an international call formulated by Israelis (notably the late Rafael Moses), Palestinians (notably Eyad el Sarraj from Gaza) and others (notably Theo de Graaf and Vamik Volkan), parts of which said:

> In our view, the Israeli–Palestinian conflict has now reached *a deadly stalemate where neither side can win*. Apparent gains, whether achieved by military strength or by spiritual dedication to overthrowing the conqueror, are short-lived and illusory in the light of the devastating effects of the violence on all parties involved. We are profoundly concerned over the immediate and the long-term injurious impact of the protracted conflict. The deleterious consequences of this situation include:
>
> > t*he cycle of recurring traumatization involving violence, humiliation, retaliation and revenge;*

> *the protracted exposure to conditions of uncertainty, anxiety and stress;*
> *the personal and national impact of loss of family members and friends;*
> *the dehumanization of the other side viewed as enemy;*
> *the dehumanizing effects on young people of being involved in violence and killing and of participating in, or being a party to, oppression;*
> *the distorted picture of the other side inculcated from a young age into future generations, perpetuating the conflict.*

We therefore invite the Israeli government to announce its genuine intention to end the occupation of the West Bank and Gaza and to dismantle the settlements in these areas within an agreed upon time-frame. We similarly invite the Palestinian Authority to officially announce its intention to achieve independence only by peaceful means and to explicitly declare its wish to find a permanent and peaceful resolution of the Palestinian–Israeli conflict. Such declarations should be made concurrently. It is our conviction that breaking the present vicious cycle of trauma and successive violence is absolutely essential and we will continue to work in this direction.

These initiatives are part of a long tradition, which I will attempt to outline here.

The question of political involvement

This question has baffled analysts – as clinicians and as intellectuals – for many decades.

A well-known example is the Third Reich. The reaction of the international psychoanalytic community to the rise of Hitler was, from our present viewpoint, cowardly. It is amazing, when looking in the old volumes of the *International Journal of Psycho-Analysis*, to find the brief factual announcement informing the readers that the German Psychoanalytic Society was disbanded, without one word of commentary, not to mention protest. Ernest Jones was apparently determined not to provoke the new German authorities and so were some German analysts who stayed in Berlin and worked in the Goering Institute (Cocks 1997).

In retrospect, we may say that a belief in 'neutrality' allowed these analysts to collaborate with a most destructive fanatical force, to disregard the danger that such collaboration will allow its toxic effects to penetrate them and to give up even the slim chance of reducing its murderous impact through its honest critical examination. In their illusory 'neutrality', in their avoidance, they actually helped Hitler in gaining legitimacy, in creating a semblance of 'normal life' in Nazi Germany.

These issues are far from being limited to Nazi Germany. *International Psychoanalysis*, the bulletin of the International Psychoanalytic Association, had become, in 1998–99, the arena of a stormy debate regarding Chile under Pinochet. In preparation for the international psychoanalytic congress held in Santiago, the bulletin published a note by a Chilean analyst (Arrue 1998a) about the recent history of Chile. This note treated the Pinochet years in a very cavalier way, avoiding terms such as dictatorship, assassination, torture, disappearance or the like. Several analysts from around the world (Gampel *et al.* 1998) protested angrily; Arrue (1998b) did not seem to genuinely grasp the outrage of his critics. At the beginning of the 21st century many individuals around the world see the issues of assassination, torture, abduction and brutal political persecution as problems involving all of humanity, so that no country has a mandate to 'forgive and forget' such phenomena.

As psychoanalysts, we have our own unique reasons to object to such 'forgetfulness'. Our work with trauma, both individual and collective, has taught us the crucial role of bringing the pain – and the rage – into full consciousness and of their honest verbalization, if a recovery is to be eventually reached. Denial, affective isolation, rationalization and identification with the aggressor are major obstacles to insight and to recovery.

The lessons from Germany under (and after) Hitler and from Chile under (and after) Pinochet are not limited to dictatorships. They point, I believe, to the need for analysts in all countries to confront openly major issues in their country's history, when these issues have unavoidable psychological implications for their analysands and for their society.

An analytic session and its historical context

Some time ago, the Israeli daily *Ha'aretz* published an interview with a woman dedicated to teaching about the Holocaust in Israeli schools. Among other points, she protested the fact that the memory of Holocaust victims is commemorated in ways resembling those of soldiers who died in battle. As an example, she used the Holocaust memorial sculpture in Jerusalem by Rapaport: 'Those Tarzan-like figures bear no resemblance to actual Holocaust victims.'

I was upset about the comment and wrote a letter to the editor. The sculpture in Jerusalem, I pointed out, is but a replica. The original sculpture was erected on the ruins of the Warsaw Ghetto, in the late 1940s. It was planned by the Central Committee of the Jews in Poland, chaired by my late father, before the state of Israel was established. Therefore it represented, besides the sculptor's personal style, the aesthetic values of European Holocaust survivors of that generation and not Israeli images.

The day after my letter was published, one of my analysands lay on the couch and started talking about it. He was particularly intrigued by the figure of my father and by my identification with him. He noticed I refer to my father as 'Dr Abraham Berman' (that was the way my father presented himself) and asked me what was the doctorate in. I told him it was in psychology, although since the war years my father abandoned psychology in favour of political activity. My patient made the comment that this explains a lot about me, as a politically involved psychologist.

His subsequent associations turned to his own father. His father's family left Europe shortly before the Holocaust and only recently he found out about some of his uncles who were killed by the Nazis, a topic his father avoided. He thought about his impression that while the rupture caused by the Third Reich apparently made my father expand, it made his own father constrict himself, limit his ambitions and goals. One expression of that constriction was a disinclination to influence his children in vocational or ideological matters. At the time of elections he used to ask father for what party he voted and father would answer that the ballot is secret. He also recalled his aging father's recent suggestion that he could take a beautiful antique secretaire the father owns and with it all the old family documents stored in it for decades. This possibility intrigued the patient, but also scared him. How will he decipher those documents, in a language he only barely reads?

In my subsequent interpretation, I referred to a recent trip my patient made to Europe, in which he discovered his grandfather's grave and other milestones in his family's history. Father declined his invitation to join him, but was helpful in planning the trip. I pointed out that the analysand built a bridge to the family past, a bridge that was also constructed on his father's behalf.

There were two additional levels to our dialogue. While our fathers indeed responded very differently to the rupture in their lives caused by the Nazi regime and by their immigration from Europe, the two of us responded similarly *vis-à-vis* our fathers: my letter to the editor and my analysand's trip to Europe were acts of filial loyalty, of seeking links, of trying to restore the rupture and to create intergenerational continuity.

Moreover, our own transferential–countertransferential relationship differs from the patient's relationship with his father. While his father emphasized that the ballot was secret, my 'ballot' was never secret to the analysand. My left-wing views are well known in Israel and so are my critical opinions about psychology, psychoanalysis, training and related topics (Berman 2004). Moreover, one of our first contacts before analysis was in the context of an initiative to organize a conference on psychological aspects of the Israeli–Arab conflict. He actually chose me as an analyst on the background of this known affinity. And in the session I described, I chose to answer in a brief factual manner his question about my father, on the basis of an intuitive feeling that my willingness will serve the intrinsic goals of analysis (goals such as free association, open exploration, direct emotional expression) better than silence or a stereotypical 'turning the question back'.

The session described is a very Israeli session, because the issues it raises – issues of the Holocaust, of immigration, of rupture, of intergenerational transmission, of war and peace, of political activism – are central preoccupations of Israeli culture, typical of a society in which history and politics have visibly affected the life of so many individuals and in which analytic and therapeutic involvement often activates questions of national, ethnic, religious and ideological identity. We cannot understand our patients, I suggest, if we are not attentive to the way history and politics shape their destiny, in subtle and complex interaction with intrapsychic factors. We cannot understand ourselves without similar self-scrutiny and this has implications for countertransference and for being clinically effective.

Political and historical reality

Among other things, the Israeli–Arab conflict forms an omnipresent layer in the mind of any Israeli. Doing apolitical, ahistorical analysis in such a society implies a degree of denial. Naturally, the particular form and intensity in which this 'external' reality is represented differ enormously from individual to individual.

I do not share the opinion that psychoanalysis deals exclusively with inner, psychic reality. Freud paid attention all along to the impact of 'civilization and its discontents' and his theories often gave rise to ideas about potential social change (Berman 1993). In my view, '[t]he capacity to explore "external" reality undefensively may be conceived as facilitating a greater acceptance of psychic reality, rather than as competing with and taking away from, the importance of psychic reality' (Berman 2004). I fully agree with Winnicott (1945: 153) when he states: 'Fantasy is only tolerable at full blast when objective reality is appreciated well.' In discussing Winnicott's notion of transitional space, Phillips (1988: 119) suggests: 'Transitional space breaks down when either inner or outer reality begins to dominate the scene, just as conversation stops if one of the participants takes over.'

The history of psychoanalysis in Israel (starting before the state of Israel was established: Rolnik 2002) is characterized by two opposing trends: mobilizing psychoanalysis for societal goals, while at times sacrificing some of its radical, critical nature; and at the other extreme, an attempt to keep its universal intrapsychic purity, at the risk of turning a deaf ear to the historical and social context. The first trend appears more dominant from the 1920s to the 1950s and is expressed in the idealistic (but at times naive) involvement of psychoanalysts in moulding educational systems, in the kibbutz movement and elsewhere, in the Bernfeld tradition (Berman 1988a). The second trend is more dominant now, as part of the shift of Israeli society away from idealistic pioneering concerns. Most Israeli analysts and psychotherapists work nowadays mostly in private practice and avoid the deteriorating mental health system (Berman 1997, 1998) or the problem-ridden school system. Still, they are often forced to realize that private patients are social creatures too and are not exempt from the influence of historical and political forces.

This growing (although conflictual) realization accounts, I believe, for the repeated attempts of Israeli analysts and therapists to express their political concerns; but the conflicts aroused, and possibly the introverted style of many analysts, their greater comfort in the privacy of their consulting rooms and embarrassment about exposure, may account for a certain instability and discontinuity of these attempts.

Overall, the distribution of political opinions among Israeli analysts, therapists, clinical psychologists etc. is consistent. Over 90 per cent identify with democratic values and with the wish to achieve an Israeli–Arab accommodation, including a viable Palestinian state side by side with Israel. Less than 10 per cent side with nationalistic and anti-Arab sentiments. When an extreme right-wing psychologist, Dor-Shav, published a hostile pseudo-diagnostic character assassination of Itzhak Rabin (a prelude to his actual assassination), her article aroused enormous anger among most psychologists, who saw it as unethical (Berman 1996).

But should these views be expressed and if so – how? Can our psychological insights contribute to political understanding, even to political influence?

Overcoming a conspiracy of silence

When Israeli analysts, together with American colleagues, met in the 1960s to discuss the psychological bases of war, their concerns were great. 'At first the Israelis demurred, feeling their views about war were suspect because they themselves are involved in one' (Ostow, in Winnik *et al.* 1973: 9); 'could we be purely objective and our thinking abstract enough, no matter how hard we tried?' (Bental, *ibid*: 17). Eventually the discussions took place and a book was published, but the attempt to keep the exploration apolitical is evident throughout.

Before the elections in 1981 a group of psychologists considered issuing a public statement about Prime Minister Begin's shaky mental condition. Others objected on ethical grounds; and the compromise was to issue instead a statement about the manipulative propaganda of Begin's party, which we feared would lead us towards another war. Although today we have a clear impression that Begin was probably manic-depressive, I am still glad we avoided this particular form of political involvement, which may shift attention from substantial political matters to personality traits of leaders, utilizing amateur diagnosis of non-patients as a political weapon.

Even that petition came under attack from within the profession. You should express your political views as citizens and not tie them to your professional identity, we were told. Rebutting this criticism, we argued that as psychologists we have unique expertise, which is relevant to interpreting political processes as well. An example could be the pioneering theoretical attempt by Moses (1982) to clarify the emotional dynamics of the Israeli–Arab conflict through the notion of the group self and its pathology.

The heavy emotional impact of the Lebanon war led me to present, in 1985, a paper entitled 'From war to war: cumulative trauma'. The Mental Health Division of the Israeli Army did not allow me to use data and case material regarding severe battle reactions of soldiers, so I had to present a fictionalized version. I spoke of three soldiers: Abraham, who went through traumatic experiences in the 1967 and 1973 wars, suppressed his panic and nightmares and collapsed in 1982 when his past reactions were reactivated; Isaac, who went through parallel traumata but was never diagnosed and his agony was only discovered when interviewed as part of a control group in a PTSD study; and Jacob, who was seemingly unharmed, but became cynical and emotionally aloof. I also raised the issue of defence mechanisms developed by Israeli mental health professionals, which led to a conspiracy of silence regarding the impact of cumulative war trauma – on soldiers, on their spouses, on their children – for many Israeli patients.

Similar defence mechanisms may have made it difficult to publish that paper. It was censored when reluctantly first published and only when *Sihot: Israel Journal of Psychotherapy* was started did I manage to have a full version published (Berman 1987). A critic suggested then that I disregard the main source of trauma: 'Our inability to give the traumatic experience of prolonged war a clear, coherent and optimistic meaning' (Shalev and Berman 1988: 147). In my counter-rebuttal I expressed the concern that the belief – on both sides of a national conflict – in the clear and coherent meaning of wars and the illusory optimism as to their outcome prolong wars; maybe only a pessimistic view of wars' meaninglessness could push enemies to seek compromise (Shalev and Berman 1988: 148)?

Sihot also published an intriguing series of papers about the history of battle reactions in Israel, including their initial denial (Witztum *et al.* 1989–91); and empirical studies on PTSD in Israeli soldiers (for instance, Solomon *et al.* 1987).

With the outburst of the first Intifada, the denial of the destructive impact of a continued occupation of Palestinian territories broke down

(Berman 1988b). A group of Israeli mental health workers visited Gaza, meeting with local colleagues. Two petitions of mental health workers about the psychological price of occupation appeared in the press and they gave rise to the foundation of 'Imut [verification]: Mental health workers for the advancement of peace'. This organization had at its peak hundreds of active members. It organized several successful conferences, on topics such as 'The psychology of occupation', 'Psychological obstacles to peace', 'Nationality, nationalism and chauvinism' and 'Imagining peace'. It established ties with Palestinian mental health workers, participated in joint conferences in various countries and initiated fruitful educational programs (Gampel 2002).

In one of the 'Imut' conferences, while rejecting once more the sterility of 'reclusive psychology', I suggested that some of the political discourse of psychologists runs the risk of becoming a 'mobilized psychology'; namely, of seeking psychological rationales for preconceived ideological conclusions. This I contrasted with 'involved psychology', where psychological tools are utilized creatively to rethink political reality and contribute to fresh insights. Such re-examination could be directed towards the Israeli peace movement. One factor in its failure in the 1980s, I suggested, was its rationalistic attitude, its advocacy of principled solutions, while disregarding or even condemning as 'irrational' the emotional obstacles to their acceptance (the deep-rooted national identifications on both sides, the annihilation anxieties of many Israelis and so on). Greater empathy to the emotional experience of the individuals involved in the conflict, rather than a hostile labelling of their motives, can pave the way to detoxifying hostility and fear more effectively, by a new leadership that can more easily be identified with (Berman 1989).

The first Intifada aroused heated debates in the Israeli army, about the impact of military service in the Occupied Territories on the soldiers. I participated in one meeting, which was visibly divided. Most practising mental health officers present described severe post-traumatic stress reactions of soldiers after they participated in violent clashes with demonstrators, shot demonstrators or harshly beat them up and conducted brutal searches in Palestinian homes. Many of their descriptions indicated intense experiences of anxiety, conflict and guilt. In contrast, their superior officers, heads of psychiatry and behavioural sciences in the army made many efforts to trivialize these accounts, dismiss them or rationalize them away and kept warning of risky political influences. (The army prevented empirical PTSD research during the Intifada, unlike in the Lebanon war.) Only those of us who came from outside the army, and participated in the discussion as consultants, kept encouraging the field officers to describe their experiences openly and not to allow them to be silenced.

During the Gulf War of 1991, Israeli cities were attacked by Iraqi missiles; many families left their city homes and moved to the countryside; and citizens were ordered to wear gas masks and enter impermeable rooms when a siren sounds (what does one do if it is mid-session, analysts and therapists debated; what happens to boundaries?). A special meeting of the Israel Psychoanalytic Society was dedicated to discussing the implications of these unusual situations for the practice of analysis; one analyst described the reactions of patients to the destruction of her home and office by a missile.

Sihot urgently published a special issue, with 15 brief papers on these dilemmas. In my own contribution, 'So far only questions', I asked: 'How can we still be attentive to subtle nuances, when the exploding missiles are so noisy? Can we give full credit to the massive influence of this external reality and at the same time keep the door open to the expression of inner reality? How can we take into account the collective experience we all undergo and yet notice its completely individual translations, avoid projecting our own interpretations on our patients and help them reject the banal standardization of experience offered by the mass media?' (Berman 1991; see also Keinan-Kon 1998).

The election of Itzhak Rabin as prime minister and the Oslo process introduced greater optimism into the Israeli peace movement. I felt that Rabin offered the kind of leadership I hoped for a few years before; namely, a leadership that is experienced by many people as close enough to their national identifications, to their resentments and fears, as to allow it the power of detoxifying the darker, more paranoid and violent expressions of these fears and angry affects, transforming them into more pragmatic concerns. His military background was helpful in this respect. When Rabin said his stomach aches when he shakes Arafat's hand, this made the handshake more acceptable to many Israelis, who until then saw the PLO as a demonic arch-enemy and would have rejected a more enthusiastic handshake.

Still, the presence of a vocal minority fighting the budding peace process tooth and nail culminated in Rabin's assassination. In an editorial in *Sihot*, a few days after the assassination, I said: 'It is no coincidence that psychotherapy has developed in a democratic, pluralistic culture. Many of its basic assumptions are close to those of democracy: the complex and paradoxical nature of human reality, which cannot be explained by an overriding single principle; the uniqueness of the experience of different individuals and different groups, which precludes the possibility of absolute truth; the power of words and verbal communication in clarifying reality and solving conflicts; the value of free choice and the difficulty in making it possible; the importance of attempting "to step into the other's shoes" and taking his needs into account; the effort to avoid black-and-white thinking, drastic polarizations of good and evil and paranoid perceptions demonizing the other, individually or collectively' (Berman 1995).

The further political upheavals of recent years in the Israeli–Palestinian arena again left their mark on our lives, including analytic work. The basic tensions of Israeli society, as well as the fundamental difficulties at the core of the Israeli–Arab conflict (including its psychological aspects, such as mutual fear and rage, feelings of victimization and entitlement), will certainly take many decades to resolve.

Broader perspectives on the issue

First, I feel it is quite clear that attention to historical, social and political processes can help Israeli analysts and therapists in better understanding their own lives, the lives of their patients and the juncture in which they and they patients meet, namely the transferential relationship in its broadest sense.

Second, I feel that as concerned citizens, as professional experts and as critical intellectuals, Israeli analysts often find themselves forced to form and express an opinion about central political issues that have a major impact on the emotional life and emotional well-being of many Israelis. Not to do so would be morally reprehensible.

How does such a political involvement of analysts influence their clinical work?

From the point of view of classical theory of technique, such exposure is clearly disastrous. The blank screen is soiled and can no longer serve as a background for the analysand's projections. Anonymity and neutrality are compromised and the analyst becomes present as an actual person, disturbing the development of transference.

The earliest critique of the classical position was offered by Ferenczi (1932), who suggested that the patient often perceives the analyst's emotional reactions in spite of the attempt to maintain anonymity; and that the analyst's denial of such perceptions, while interpreting them as displacements or projections, may become 'professional hypocrisy', mystifying and re-traumatizing the patient (Berman 2004).

Paraphrasing Ferenczi, I would suggest that withholding the analyst's political views and reactions, in a society that experiences political issues with great intensity (especially at times of crisis), may also be experienced by some patients as professional hypocrisy and become destructive for the analytic process.

The growing trend towards relational and intersubjective reformulations of psychoanalysis (Berman 2004) supplies us a new framework for these issues. If we take the personal and subjective nature of the analyst's presence for granted, the political aspects of this presence are not necessarily disruptive. If we come to suspect that 'anonymity for the analyst is impossible', because 'every intervention hides some things about the analyst and reveals others ... [and] *any* way an analyst decides to deal with his or her emotional response is consequential' (Renik 1995: 468), the anxiety and need to be constantly on guard are reduced. A conception that assumes that transference is constantly influenced by countertransference and self-disclosures and enactments naturally happen in most sessions, implies that what is crucial is not the avoidance of contamination (the image of the sterile test tube, which Freud imported from the natural sciences), but the free exploration of this unavoidable reciprocal influence and its utilization for the development of insight and of a deeper and richer analytic relationship.

My open positions on various controversial issues in Israeli psychoanalysis (Berman 2004) allowed my analysands who were analytic trainees to voice their reactions, both approving and disapproving and join in exploring their deeper implications, more – I believe – than would have been possible had I attempted to hide them.

A lot, I believe, depends on the atmosphere. '[A]n analyst who regards his or her own constructions of reality as no more than personal views to be offered for a patient's consideration has no reason to avoid stating them explicitly' (Renik 1995: 478). In this respect, what is destructive is authoritarian certainty, whether in interpreting the patient's unconscious or in interpreting the political situation. If the analyst is not experienced as an omniscient authority, if discourse is free and flowing, a transitional space can evolve, both external and internal reality – and their frequent interaction – may be noticed and contemplated and one can work fruitfully with the analysand's reactions and associations.

Certainly, there can be painful moments in such a process. A realization that one's analyst is 'on the other side of the barricade' can be upsetting (just as being together 'on the same side of the barricade' may lead to defensive solidarity that whitewashes other areas of conflict). But this may happen with personal issues as well, such as when a vocational or romantic choice the analysand is excited about is interpreted by the analyst as destructive. A lot depends on the analyst's tact, on her or his ability to maintain empathic listening in spite of different opinions, without putting down or dismissing the analysand's views, without hurting the analysand's feelings.

The last major issue I want to discuss is the nature of analysts' and therapists' contribution to political discourse. As I mentioned earlier on, this contribution may be at times shallow and limited, when psychological concepts are used in the service of preconceived political opinions. Whether one offers psychiatric diagnoses to a resented leader or derogatory generalized interpretations about resented political groups ('the right wing is prone to projection and splitting', as if such trends never appeared in left-wing movements), these uses of psychology are barren intellectually.

The kind of involvement I believe we should strive for is based on utilizing our expertise in listening for a fresh examination of political reality. To give one example, I would suggest that a major weaknesses of many peace movements is their pacifism; namely, their utopian tendency to deny group loyalties and aggression as basic human realities and to appeal to an idealized peace-loving humanity free of any dividing forces (Berman 1993). Such idealizations, based on a narrative of progress ('from national or religious loyalties towards internationalism'), which postmodern thinking has exposed for its wishful thinking, may become an obstacle to realistic peace making, which in my mind necessitates full awareness of the power of national, ethnic and religious belonging and of the universal tendencies to fear and distrust the other.

For me, fighting chauvinism is aided by fully understanding its emotional dynamics; and only empathy towards national sentiments can facilitate their detoxification from destructive hostilities, so that pragmatic compromises can be reached. This is parallel, to some extent, to the way an analyst can absorb toxic projective identifications and return them to the analysand in a detoxified version, a process Bion and Ogden describe as crucial for achieving change.

A rationalistic, condescending or judgemental attitude, rejecting common human affects as base, primitive and 'irrational', does not allow such healing processes to evolve. Empathic listening, even to a violent patient, may eventually calm down the violence more than moral condemnation.

Listening empathically to the individuals on both sides of a bloody dispute does not imply agreeing with their opinions, which may be extreme and rigid, especially when historical rights are at issue and each side has an experience of victimization based on a frightful memory of past atrocities. It implies, however, a realization that unless the yearnings and anxieties on both sides are not sufficiently attended to, no lasting peace is possible.

Conclusion

In the long run, I personally conclude, social responsibility, leading to an attempt to contribute to the understanding and resolution of crucial political issues and the responsibility to help a particular individual in need of treatment, while they may be in tension and at some moments in conflict, do not necessarily exclude each other.

The analyst's political involvement, if it is thoughtful and non-manipulative and if it is expressed in non-authoritarian terms and remains open for candid critical discussion, can become a stimulus for fruitful intersubjective analytic exploration with each analysand. A straightforward and serious political involvement of analysts may then acquire a positive significance, of broad-minded innovative thinking about our historical destiny, both collective and individual; of willingness to take risks and step out of one's self-centred interests and concerns.

13 The Bridge Project: radical psychotherapy for the 21st century
Jocelyn Chaplin

Introduction

This project in West London shows the change from the theory of 'the personal as political' in the 1970s and 1980s to what it can mean today. It both reflects the demise of left-wing optimism and provides an example of another deeper and more complex revolution. The hope that personal therapy would lead to more feminist and socialist social change has not yet been fully realized, in spite of talk of a post-feminist era. However, in the midst of so much disillusionment, Bridge is one of many projects actually practising ways of working and relating that dissolve the old hierarchical structures at *all* levels of consciousness and behaviour.

The project was set up in 1980 with a left-wing perspective based on class, race and gender as the main and most oppressive hierarchies or structures of domination. These inequalities are still massive and the gap between rich and poor is actually wider now than it was when the project was set up. But in a postmodernist era there has been too much questioning of simplistic narratives to explain everything in these three terms. Yet this very questioning has made possible the victory of consumer capitalism into which psychotherapy has fitted all too comfortably. The search for individual happiness has often become its primary goal. The alternative approach that it is really about transforming the world and increasing equality in it, appears to have been completely lost. Hillman and Ventura (1992) argued this case most convincingly. But has it?

The idea of equality at all levels, political and personal, is often implicit rather than explicit in writings that link psychotherapy and politics. Orbach (1982) talks about the need for 'psychic structural changes at a fundamental and a mass level'. What kind of structural changes are meant? Surely these are from hierarchical structures to more equalizing and fluid ones. Rowan (1976) explicitly writes that: 'More and more research findings have piled up to show that hierarchy does harm to people.' Since then postmodernists and users of the term 'political correctness' tried to demolish the idea of equality along with other enlightenment ideas. Phillips (2002) explicitly writes that we are lost without hierarchy in personal relations;

while Samuels (1993) writes that 'pluralism is intended to be an anti-hierarchical attitude'. Yet without a clearer commitment to equality the strong often still win in a pluralistic world. Derrida (1982) describes our tendency to divide everything into binary opposites with one privileged above the other. This is the structure of hierarchy. But he does not go on to offer solutions.

Perhaps the concept of equality can be rescued. In fact, today it seems to be having a comeback. For example, the word is being mentioned again in government papers (see later).

Perhaps the old, rigid idea of working towards a perfect, totally equal society does need replacing. In a post-postmodern world the paradigm of equalizing as an ongoing process at all levels may be returning in different forms. This paradigm/model fits well with the internal dynamics of the psyche trying to balance itself. In spite of the continuing central importance of class in left and progressive groups everywhere, there is an increasing awareness of all the other hierarchies. These include subtle as well as obvious interpersonal, organizational ones. This change is going on right in the midst of the apparently increasing power of capitalism. Yet what also seems to be happening in the 21st century is a profound paradigm shift from hierarchical ways of being to more complex equalizing processes of change. Bridge is one powerful example.

This mental health project is already working in ways recommended by the government with its theoretical commitments to equality. This project could show the way forward for country-wide provision, using the new paradigm of equalizing and empowering at *all* levels. It is radical, not only in its understandings of social inequality but in its daily working practices and attitudes. It is not only about working with oppressed groups but doing it differently.

The government's (2002) NHS Plan makes the commitment to reduce inequalities. This is quoted in the Department of Health's Strategic Paper on Women's Mental Health (2002) as pointing the way for a study on services for women as a particular unequal population.

The concept of equality is a very complex one. In this chapter, it is not conceived of as a thing to be acquired or some final static state. Neither is it seen as having anything to do with sameness as described and dismissed by Greer (1999) in connection with equality feminism. Difference is vital but still usually still seen in terms of superior and inferior as in Lacan's (1966) sense of women as having a lack. Here the term equality is retained but it is seen as a process: *equalization*.

The model on which this chapter is based is of endless conflict between unequal hierarchical structures in society, institutions and individuals and equalizing, rhythms of change to transform them. This contrast between the rhythm model and hierarchies is explored in *Feminist Counselling in*

Action (Chaplin 1988). The conflict operates in many ways and on many levels, both externally *and* within the psyche.

History

The Bridge Project (Women's Action for Mental Health) was set up by a psychologist called Sue Holland in 1980 on the White City Estate in West London. Its initial aim was to prevent women on the estate from serious depressive breakdown. Its second aim was to put into practice social action psychotherapy and empower women to demand changes in their community. Most of the women were and still are working class, many are single mothers and they come from a variety of ethnic backgrounds. Today many are also refugees.

The project was *and still is* based on a psychological understanding that recognizes the way social and economic structures directly and indirectly influence mental health. In particular, there are the unequal social and economic hierarchies that disempower and create depression among women, working-class people and many other groups. Depression literally means 'being put down, lowered'. As James (1997) points out: 'It is the growing socioeconomic divisions that create depression. Britain is more unequal than it was before the 2nd world war.' Gilbert (1997) argues that our whole psychologies have become focused on winners and losers, superiors and inferiors.

Depression, which is even greater among women, has been linked to their lower social status as well as to practical issues such as relative isolation (Nairn and Smith 1984).

As Sue Holland wrote: 'Prevention must therefore be addressed to both the internalised social structures (object relations) of the human psyche and the external social structures (class, gender, race) of society and state' (Holland 1988: 126). Her theory was that women would start with one-to-one psychotherapy, move on to consciousness-raising group work and then to social action to change their communities. In the early 1980s there was perhaps more optimism about local community action. But there were also more resources available from central and local government to encourage this process.

Bridge in action today

Twenty-three years on, most of the work is focused on the one-to-one stage of individual counselling. There is an ever-increasing demand for this from the local women themselves. But there is also supportive action such as advocacy work, accompanying women to hospitals, courts etc. Wherever the women suffer injustice, the project will help as far as it can. It is deeply committed to redressing inequality, wherever it exists. The *first inequality* that it is concerned with is gender.

Gender

The DoH paper on women's mental health stresses the need for different approaches to women as a particular population. Women often ask for single-sex services. These are seen as more likely to be responsive to their needs. There is statistical evidence from many bodies of research quoted in the paper (DoH 2002) that women have different and particular needs.

Depression, anxiety and eating disorders are more common with women. Two-thirds of adults living in the poorest households are women. They are three times more likely to have been sexually abused with all the ensuing psychological problems. Ninety-five per cent of sexual abuse is carried out by men on both sexes. Social isolation is a major factor in mental illness and women are more affected, have less mobility and more fear of going out at night etc. Lone mothers, who are often particularly isolated and make up a large percentage of Bridge's clients, are three times more likely to be depressed than other women. Between 18 and 30 per cent of women suffer domestic violence at some point in their lives (DoH 2002: 12–15).

Redressing these inequalities in society requires a much deeper social change than has yet taken place. The women's movements of the past have made changes, but we still live in a largely patriarchal world. Indeed, many gains of the recent past, such as greater access to workplaces, give a superficial impression of equality finally achieved. This is clearly not the case. By seeing equalizing as a multilayered complex process we avoid simple conclusions and can look at each context in its particularities.

Bridge is a context in which *many inequalities* interact with each other. They are addressed in a number of different ways. It may be through the psychological empowerment of individual women or by supporting them to achieve justice in their community or from the state. There are the indirect effects of individual therapy/counselling on families and communities. For example, many women have been able to keep their families together and avoid having children taken into care as a result of being counselled at Bridge. It can be argued that the project saves the NHS and social services vast amounts of money on hospitalization, children's homes etc. through its preventative work.

Equalizing practice

Bridge is also involved in dissolving internal hierarchies in women's psyches, in their relationships and even in the counsellors' ways of working. This can be seen in the way the project is run, in the attitude to clients, in the psychotherapeutic methods used as well as in the awareness of the unequal world the clients come from.

Teamworking practices

There is a strong emphasis on mutual respect and a valuing of differences. Equality does not mean sameness. Managers have played their different roles without treating others as 'lower'. This has not always been easy, as women come to work at the project initially with their own internalized hierarchies. But there is a strong culture of equality that women soon learn to be part of. This fits well with the requirements of the government. In the DoH paper there is a recommendation that services have a 'partnership way of working and a reduction in hierarchy'. There should also be 'transparency' and an 'understanding of the dynamics of power and gender' (2002: 30).

The flat that houses Bridge has a warm and welcoming feel. It is a place in which many clients say they feel at home. Some would never have sought help in more conventional surroundings. There is a sense in which the whole team feels responsible for each client, regardless of who their counsellor is. Supervision sessions are conducted in a way that involves everyone, not only the supervisor. There is also much emphasis on the counsellor's own issues in relation to the client, which also encourages a sense of equality.

Relation to clients

Many of the women who come to Bridge have had problems with professionals whom they have seen as 'higher'. The workers at the project do not behave in a superior way, patronizing, dismissing or putting the clients down. While working with strict professional integrity there can be flexibility when it is appropriate. For example, occasionally a mother is forced to bring her baby to a session. The women who come for help are seen as whole people with their physical as well as emotional problems. So at times help with housing or education is given. This is a recognition of the interrelationship between their personal, mental problems and their external conditions of inequality.

But perhaps the most important point is the depth of respect given to the clients whatever they bring to their sessions, whoever they are, whatever situations they are in. In supervision there is often a shared amazement at the courage and determination of so many of the women against all odds. In the DoH report (2002), there is a recommendation that services value women's strengths and abilities for recovery, rather than focus entirely on problems and difficulties. A negative approach perpetuates the very hierarchical attitudes that need dissolving. The report states that women 'want recognition that their psychological vulnerability is not rooted in their biology but in the context of their lives, their sense of pow-erlessness, lack of social status/value and life experiences of violence and abuse that they have survived' (2002: 23).

Although many clients come with a medical diagnosis, this is often put to one side while working with this whole person in front of us. Too much emphasis on labels can at times lead to hierarchical stereotyping. They are often only bringing familiar human issues we all share, only taken to greater extremes. Most of us could be in their shoes. As women we all share some of the abuses of living in a patriarchal society.

Counselling/psychotherapy theory and practice

While the original emphasis was on psychodynamic practice, Bridge has since widened its approach to include humanistic and especially Rogerian ways of thinking and working. There is no sense of a hierarchy in which one approach is intrinsically better than another. Each client is given the kind of counselling or psychotherapy felt to be most helpful. The Rogerian approach fits especially well with the ethos of equality. Most important is really listening to the client, entering her world non-judgementally and valuing her own capacity to change. These are considered the core condi-tions of Rogerian client-centred counselling.

Sometimes the level of distress and practical hardship that women bring make it inappropriate to work mainly with transference issues as they arise in the sessions. They are more likely to need straightforward 're-mothering' (Orbach 1982). Many of the women who come have been too busy looking after others to get their own needs met. It is vital that they have a place where *they* feel mothered.

The same model of equalizing in relation to wider social issues applies to psychotherapy as well. For example, one side of the self may be experi-enced as inferior and suppressed. So the work often includes bringing out those hidden sides. A person who appears in control of everything around her may have unconsciously suppressed the terrified child within. At Bridge the counsellor provides a safe space for clients to express and accept these frightening or unacceptable part of themselves.

Another application of inner equalizing is the raising of low self-esteem, a problem for almost all the women who come to Bridge. Several different techniques are used. Some of these are cognitive, in which clients are encouraged to think differently about themselves. They may be asked to list their strengths or simply brought back to a focus on themselves. Questions like 'What do *you* feel about ... ?' help women to start knowing and trusting their own intuition and judgement. So many want to be told what to do.

There may be other inner opposites that the counselling helps to equal-ize. Gestalt techniques and visualizations may be used to clarify and sepa-rate out opposing sides of the self. The good little girl and the naughty one could be put on two chairs and encouraged to talk to one another to increase acceptance and understanding.

Individual examples

(Names and other details have been changed.)

> **Sylvia** is a 50-year-old, black woman who was born in Jamaica. She was referred by her doctor for serious depression and suicidal tendencies. She arrived at Bridge elegantly dressed, accompanied by an air of superiority. At first the therapist found this hard as she was experiencing the countertransference of feelings of inferiority. Sylvia also talked very disparagingly of black and Asian people. It had to be pointed out that, in this project, we do not talk about other races in that way. But there was also a long process of exploring her own internalized racism. As she felt valued for herself and began to question her cognitive patterns of superiority and inferiority, Sylvia became easier to be with in the room. Slowly she learned to take in the acceptance being offered.
>
> Her parents had been teachers back in Jamaica. There she was, at the top of a class hierarchy. But in London she was living in accommodation for homeless people and had been in mental hospital several times. She only wanted to be re-housed in the perfect home so kept turning down offers from the council. The flat she longed for represented her own perfect unrealistic self. Much of the work was helping her accept her non-perfect real self. She began to express her anger more, finding that this too was accepted. Her self-esteem grew.
>
> During the two years she was being seen at Bridge she was not hospitalized once. She stopped talking about suicide. And although Sylvia continues to be somewhat critical of others, she is less totally dismissive. Her inner hierarchies began to dissolve and eventually she even accepted a flat from the council that was good enough without being perfect.

> **Hana** is 32, a refugee from Iran. She has one child, a little girl of 6. Hana was referred from the women's refuge where they were living after escaping from a violent husband. He had been a good and loving man until he was tortured in Iran and eventually came to Britain a changed person. Hana still loved him, but was afraid for her daughter. She came
>
> *cont.*

to the project in a state of high anxiety. Her family were not supporting Hana's desire to leave her husband. Initially, some of the work was helping her to manage the anxiety. She was taught relaxation methods and given a tape to take home.

Later she was able to talk more about her experiences, although there was a lot guilt for betraying family pride. When she first came she had barely been able to make eye contact with the therapist. But after three months Hana was walking in the room with confidence, head held high. She did have some support from an aunt in London but otherwise the Bridge project played a major role in her survival. Eventually, Hana was able to rebuild her life.

Conclusion

Although the original aim of increasing local social action has not been achieved, other aims have. The project embodies a different paradigm/ model of working, thinking and acting. In this way, it has retained its radical perspective and effected social change in complex and many-layered ways.

Basically, the Bridge project actually puts into practice the *equalizing* model so strongly recommended by government papers such as the report on women's mental health (DoH 2002) and implicit in much writing about psychotherapy and social change:

1   The way the project is organized involves *equal* partnership between all the workers.
2   The respect given to clients provides a sense of *equality* between them and the workers.
3   The whole project is working towards general *equalizing* processes in the society at large by focusing, first, on women.
4   Then, *specifically* on disadvantaged groups such as refugees and single mothers.
5   In its clinical methods, it also encourages women to *equalize* the different sides of themselves by accepting the unacceptable 'shadow' sides, the vulnerable sides and the child sides as well as the strong, acceptable adult sides.
6   By helping women to raise their self-esteem the project enables them to have more *equal* relationships with their families, friends and with statutory bodies such as social services.

14 How to create social activism: turning the passive to active without killing each other
Katie Gentile and Susan Gutwill

Introduction

On a cold January morning of 2002, in a room overflowing with partici-pants, a panel of psychoanalysts discussed the US response to 9/11. It was 7 am and the International Association of Relational and Related Psycho-therapies (IARRP) had added the panel to their conference. The attendance signalled an important need on the part of therapists to form a community in order to discuss the impact of 9/11 and US policies on the profession and how we could collectively respond.

This chapter is a synopsis of the efforts we made to create a group of psychotherapists to work for socially responsible action; to support each other in holding the growing pain and trauma of our patients and ourselves; and to generate a relevant, non-reductive analysis of the govern-ment's tactics of manipulating fear, war-mongering and closing the possi-bility for public reflection and dissent. We will describe how we organized, the activities and community work we initiated, as well as our understand-ing of why our task was difficult in the face of American ideology and how that ideology impacted on us as a group. Last, we will look at the internal psychodynamics that challenged us as a group.

Therapists mobilize after 9/11

In New York City, mental health workers immediately mobilized to respond to 9/11. Individually professionals went to firehouses, police stations, hos-pitals and places of worship. Therapists also participated in institutionally organized efforts with Safe Horizon (a victims' service agency) and the Red Cross on phone banking (calling victims' families with service information) and assisting at sites designated for survivors and victims' families. Training institutes, clinics and graduate programmes were contacted by unions and financial companies from the World Trade Center to work with survivors. Therapists were also contacted to go on site visits with survivors and family members in order to help process the experience. Indeed, therapists were thoroughly involved in the post-traumatic effort. However, we, too, were impacted. As the identified processors of the traumatic experience for our patients and the community, we were often overwhelmed. This trauma was exponentially heightened by the aggression exercised by the government and what we experienced as a crackdown on efforts to symbolize and speak what was going on.

In the aftermath of 9/11, our President was granted the power to make war without congressional approval. The government quickly attacked US citizens' civil rights with the Patriot Act and the Health Insurance Portability and Accountability Act (HIPAA)[1], each of which attacked the right to privacy, freedom of speech and religion and enabled the arrest, detention and deportation of thousands of people, many of whom were US citizens. Daily security alerts and details of potential terrorist plots crammed the news, heightened fear and created conditions for a perpetual post-traumatic atmosphere. The President's language of good versus evil created a frightening sense of national victimization that supported his 'pre-emptive' war and, simultaneously, collapsed any potential space for public reflection. In this atmosphere, negotiation and peaceful action was spurned as unpatriotic and potentially compromising to the security of the country. A reflective and thoughtful response was equated with weakness and even with support for terrorism.

As therapists, we understood the power and danger of splitting off aggression in order to be identified as the good, virtuous victim. We knew that collapsing potential space limits reflection, thinking and the capacity to question. In this atmosphere, all wrongdoing on behalf of the USA, for example, the history of our support for dictators in the Middle East, could be erased, as the Taliban and then Iraq and others were cast as the 'evil enemy' who threatened us. It was this cycle of generating and perpetuating vulnerability, fear, aggression and limiting reflection that most frightened us. As professionals who work to speak the unspeakable, we believed we had an expertise and a responsibility to analyze the mechanisms of the unconscious dynamics of power and control underlying popular support for the Bush administration. This included finding ways of counteracting how the government invaded our psyches on a daily basis by using fear as a tactic of oppressive control. We also discussed when and how to bring politics

---

[1]   HIPAA, like many of the Bush administration's mandates (e.g. the No Child Left Behind and the Clean Air Acts), supposedly promises to protect citizens' liberties, social services and the environment, but actually endangers them and places corporate/government interests first. In regards to HIPAA, it was initially created under President Clinton to protect patient records. However, under President Bush, HIPAA required electronic transmission of all patient records. Under the application of the Patriot Act, this facilitated and justified government surveillance of medical and psychiatric records, compromising the confidentiality of patients and healthcare providers.

into the analytic relationship. Last, we explored how to expand the analytic vision from being an exclusively individualistic form of inquiry, to one more responsive to the escalating political situation and the 'large group' (societal) psychodynamics it created.

From this discussion, we identified a core of 15 people who were interested in forming a steering committee to focus the creation of a unique group that would work towards socially responsible theory and action. We hoped to create an organization similar to Physicians for Social Responsibility, with an inclusive membership dedicated to analyzing and acting in the larger political scene without having to cater to the interests of larger and more conservative professional umbrella organizations.

Our actions

The steering committee immediately reached out to other socially critical and/or activist psychotherapists in order to organize a larger group that would share the following goals:

1   to create a potential space for therapists to talk to one another about frightening current events and the relationship of politics to emotional life
2   To educate people within the profession about the Bush administration's policies in order to mobilize socially responsible action opposing US aggression, governmental attacks on our standard of living, social services and civil liberties from the perspective of the knowledge and moral commitment we shared as therapists.

A speakout for psychotherapists

We began with a speakout about 9/11 and the war in Afghanistan, which was well attended and inspiring. We created a space in which, one by one, people could come up to an open microphone to have the opportunity to hear their own voices and the voices of their colleagues expressing fear, dismay, dissent and alternative visions. The speakout is a frame, a ritual space like the analytic or psychotherapeutic session, where the unthinkable can more safely be thought and put into words. This speakout was our attempt to help the community symbolize what was not being said. It worked.

Launching a new group

We followed the speakout with a developmental meeting where the organization was founded in a more public way. Two members prepared position papers, coalescing the thoughts of the group as a whole, which analyzed the political crisis from both political–economic and psychodynamic perspectives. These papers, on our website now, were both very well received. They seemed to speak, in one way or another, for everyone in attendance.

With the hope and excitement generated, we organized six committees for membership participation:

1   a media committee to bring our message to the media
2   a committee to study and teach about nonviolence as a strong form of 'action'
3   a committee to contribute to the peace process in the Middle East
4   a committee for community outreach
5   a committee to link us to the larger peace movement (especially United for Peace and Justice)
6   a committee to organize peer discussion groups – consciousness-raising groups for therapists.

Educational meetings

- We showed the movie *The Hidden Wars of Desert Storm*. Well over 100 people came and there was a rich discussion.
- We brought in speakers to talk about the Patriot Act and to highlight the way it would affect psychotherapy through HIPAA, which was threatening the rights to privacy for both patients and therapists. While there were many seminars on 'how to' comply with HIPAA, this programme was a critique of it. Our attendance decreased for this meeting.

Uniting psychotherapists in larger protests

Our group also co-sponsored and participated in many protests. For each protest we created a meeting space specifically for psychotherapists to walk together under the banner 'Peace of Mind – Psychotherapists for Social Responsibility'. We participated in many local and national protests including the worldwide effort of February 11 2003.

Online web conferences and discussion and website

Our group also worked with PsyBC to organize an international web conference. This was an attempt to politicize the profession around the way in which the social unconscious and the personal unconscious intersect in two particular ways:

- how and why sectors of the population at large respond to, identify with or oppose the politics of fear and aggression
- how these politics find their way into or are avoided in our clinical work.

PsyBC also donated space on their internet educational service to post announcements, meetings, protest information, educational facts and news updates and facilitated general conversation among members between meetings. This space grew into our own current web page, www.pfsr.org (Psychotherapists for Social Responsibility). The website offers versions of positions papers written by a number of our members. (The online discussion can be be seen in the PsyBC archives.)

Joining the professionals for social responsibility network

We immediately became a member of the Professional Network for Social Responsibility (PNSR), which was the umbrella lobbying organization for Physicians for Social Responsibility, Architects for Social Responsibility, economists, educators, Quaker Friends and other groups. In addition, we met with the national group Psychologists for Social Responsibility and tried to coordinate our activities.

Joining the election effort

As the election neared in the winter of 2003, with a smaller number of people attending our events, the steering committee merged into the whole group, so that whosoever wanted to attend meetings could. We began focusing primarily on the presidential election. We developed and published a position paper describing the kind of leadership we believed would benefit the country. We tried to get this paper into the Democratic Party in order to influence and support the candidates. We also made this position paper available to our members to use in their own local election efforts. We worked with the Kerry Campaign and MoveOn to organize phone banking and bus trips to swing states to help defeat President Bush.

Prior to the election we held another speakout about our fears and hopes about the election and to mobilize action towards defeating President Bush. Although the discussion was profound, it was not as well attended as earlier events.

After the profoundly disappointing election, we organized another meeting as a way of mobilizing people. This event was not well attended. However, a group of about 15 or 20 continue to meet – a largely different membership than the original group. At this point, the group continues to meet and is looking for a focus for its efforts.

What we were up against: merger of politics with the American consumer culture ideology

We attempted to organize psychotherapists within a particular cultural atmosphere. We had come together in the crisis of 9/11 and the administration's subsequent exploitation of citizens' fear. We all agreed that the manipulation of public opinion was designed to frighten people into feeling like innocent victims who would be best and most safely served by a strong uncompromising leader who would stand firm and fight for them by making war. That fight and the all-out aggression that it took, breaking with international law, was justified by the governmental promotion of a state of mind of a Kleinian paranoid–schizoid bifurcation of good and bad. Here, 'the good freedom-loving Americans' would exist only because the government took on the 'axis of evil'. Moreover, taking on this evil would not only save us, it would actually make us righteous defenders of democracy, first in Afghanistan and then in Iraq. With the media being carefully orchestrated to support the government's agenda (see *Outfoxed*, the film by Robert Greenwald, mediamatters.org and *Weapons of Mass Deception: The Uses of Propaganda in Bush's War on Iraq* (Rampton and Stauber 2003) to name but two) and the incapacity of the Democratic Party to fully expose this corporate takeover inherent in the Bush domestic and international agenda, alternative forms of leadership did not materialize.

Beyond the explanatory power of these realities, we wanted to use our perspective to wonder about how people could support the further militarization of the economy against their own interests, at the expense of the stability of the dollar, social services such as healthcare, education, social security and environmental protection and industrial development to provide jobs at home. In writing this chapter, we want to propose that this ideological coup could not have been achieved without the underlying subjectivity characterized by the particular form of commodity fetishism of our time. This ideology inhibits people from seeing the class-based power dynamics (including gender, race, ethnicity) within which they are embedded. More particularly, it inhibits people from seeing both the links between themselves and their political–economic culture and their own potential power to affect their larger social world.

As Marx theorized, in capitalism, social relationships of production are mystified: labour is hidden and the conditions of labour are hidden; in the world of huge conglomerates in which we live, the seller too is hidden and the relationship between those who own the corporations and those who work for them and buy from them are all obscured. But the unique quality of fetishism in this century, and especially as it is shared in this country, is that the goal of consumerism is not bound by the product. We do not simply buy products, we buy lifestyle. And that lifestyle is meant to become our sense of self and self in relation to others. Thus, we can all appear equal, based on the capacity to consume – 'the democratization of surfaces' (Ewen and Ewen 1979). What used to be a Calvinist work ethic has now morphed into the very re-creation of self and body through consumption. Our work now is to create character and identity through the consumption and display of a lifestyle of which we can be proud. Body alterations and attitudes are sought in a never-ending attempt to recreate oneself anew into an improved self, a self with power, a self, above all, beyond contempt. And in the USA after 9/11, that self is neither vulnerable nor guilty. This new 'safe' self is part of an undifferentiated mass, created not only by the exploitation of fear described earlier, but also by the exploitation of commodity fetishism.

After 9/11 President Bush and New York City Mayor Giuliani told the people of the USA to go shopping to show their patriotism, to actively strengthen the economy, to enjoy themselves and not 'give over' to 'what the terrorists wanted'. Flags showed up everywhere: on highway billboards advertising supermarkets, health insurance, cell phones, etc.; on stores of all kinds and then on public buildings, cars and homes. American public life was simultaneously filled with the combination of colour-coded threat levels, the drive to war and flags associated with products, businesses and family life. Inherent in this combination bombarding our unconsciousness and conscious experience, was the notion that we would be safe and strong, proud to be American, primarily through our allegiance to the government and to the products for which it stands.

Splitting other countries into good versus evil, the use of fear and the commodity fetishism whereby one guarantees safety by purchasing patriotism all supported the culture's paranoid–schizoid position. When operating from this Kleinian position, one is impeded in one's capacities to reflect, think or to hold complex ideas. Without these capacities, the media hold even more power than usual to create and sway public opinion. When people cannot reflect and think, media are swallowed whole, with no digestion or analysis. This created an atmosphere where parroting the corporate media became a form of dialogue.

As analytic psychotherapists who were concerned about the intersection of individual and social unconscious experience, we thought it was imperative that our profession observe and find some way to intervene.

Some difficulties mobilizing psychotherapists in this environment

Psychotherapists have shared values of honesty and ethical responsibility and the charge to create ways of speaking what has been rendered unspeakable by the patient's respective history. However, we all exist within this culture of performative identity and lifestyle perfection that depends on attacks on linking. Additionally, psychotherapy and psychoanalysis in particular have been preoccupied by a notion of clinical neutrality that destroys the links between the personal, the cultural and the political. So we were faced with quite a challenge: how do we create these links within our own professional community while helping to create this capacity within the larger surrounding community?

Our plan of action was to illuminate the connection between the political situation and individual suffering. We hoped that speaking and articulating these links would support the capacity to grieve and mourn and then, from this depressive position, we could take responsible non-retaliatory action. As we found, these goals were easier to theorize about than to enact.

External pressures of professional dynamics and hierarchies

As a new group we faced not only the cultural attacks on linking, but also those of our professions. To begin we must provide a brief description of some of the hierarchies that have constituted the evolution of the mental health field in the USA. First, there are distinct splits between the degreed professions of psychiatry, psychology, social work and masters-level creative arts therapies (art, drama, music, dance). Psychiatry, with its basis in medical science, is the most esteemed. Psychologists with licensed PhD status are next, followed by non-licensed psychologists. Licensed social workers and non-licensed social workers follow, with creative arts therapists last. Now, in writing this we are not casting a judgement on the value of these practitioners, only describing what tends to be a hierarchy within our own profession and the US culture at large. This hierarchy is reinforced by our privatized insurance system that defines which practitioners will be covered (licensed only, for the most part) and how much each is worth per session. These professions are quite literally ranked by a monetary value defined by insurance companies. As of this writing, psychoanalysts are working toward being licensed.

This stratification is reinforced by very separate educational tracks, training and level of terminal degree: masters degree for creative arts therapies and social work; doctorate for psychology and some social workers; and medical degree for psychiatrists. While white women and people of colour have broken into the higher ranks of psychology and psychiatry, both these professions continue to be dominated by whites and men constitute the majority of psychiatrists. Social workers and other masters-level practitioners are the most diverse ethnically, racially and by class and are predominantly female. Although institutes may accept people with any of these degrees for psychoanalytic training, they continue to be dominated by white, upper-middle class practitioners.

Each of these professions emerges from distinct theoretical ideologies and training practices that are quite diverse. However, because any licensed practitioner must diagnose according to the Diagnostic and Statisical Manual (DSM), a psychiatric view dominates. Psychiatry emerges from a medical epistemology, where there is an institutionalized destruction of links based on the notion of individual pathology. For instance, the established aetiology of eating disorders describes them resulting from a person's inability to deal with stress or adequately regulate affect. Links to a misogynist cultural atmosphere and commercial exploitation of skeletal beauty ideals are destroyed. So despite variations in graduate training, the epistemology that supports mental health practice in the USA views psychological distress as individual pathology with no links to the social system, the dynamics of which remain hidden.

But this attack on linking to the social does not end with diagnostic categories. The attack is most virulent in the concept of neutrality, which considers political content to be inappropriate in the clinical setting. The psychotherapist who brings in politics is considered invasive and the patient who does so is seen as avoiding talking about personal issues. Additionally, most psychoanalytic journals have considered politics and culture superfluous and shallow, we think, as a defensive reaction against exposing the social unconscious.

All mental health professionals face the opposition of the US culture which has a particular disdain for the unconscious, the unknown and the uncontrollable. US capitalist culture has created a distorted pragmatism where only concrete material experience matters and anti-intellectual and anti-analytic attitudes flourish. Here reflective thinking is considered elitist and analysing issues or one's life is considered a waste of time. This cultural tendency became only more entrenched with the government's policies of fear and unreflective action, outlined earlier. All these external dynamics came to play in the difficult task of reaching out to psychotherapists. As we found, seeing the power dynamics of the culture threatens one's sense of the world. It requires critically rethinking one's theoretical and clinical stance, an upsetting prospect to many.

Internal pressures: let's not talk about it

Our steering committee, as well as the group at large, included representatives from a variety of educational backgrounds. As a group of professionals, these identities were always present in the room with our names (quite literally if our email contacts included titles of doctor, professor, MD or PhD). Additionally, we had the politics of institutes. New York City is home to numerous psychoanalytic training institutes from a variety of theoretical backgrounds and each has garnered a different level of respect and visibility within the field. Because the steering committee was created at a convention of the International Association of Relational Psychotherapists and Psychoanalysts (IARPP) and New York University Postdoctoral Program was central to the development of the IARPP, our steering committee already had a built-in dynamic to deal with: that between members of NYU and the others. Thus, as members we had our names, our degrees, as well as our institutional affiliations each contributing to defining our group membership. While not always conscious or gross, these dynamics impacted people's felt power in the group.

There were also hierarchies of publishing and public reputation, related to years in the field. As a social responsibility group, we had an additional hierarchy of activist experience: who had been to which protests and who had engaged in and lived through which social movements. These various hierarchical identities served as a vehicle for typical group dynamics and power struggles. The leadership that emerged was based not only on transferential and personal histories, but also along these hierarchies. Given this conflation of professional identity and political experience with personal and group dynamics, authority became more difficult to address or challenge for some and more seductive to topple as a professional Oedipal victory for others. Each person's historical relationship to authority, be it competitive, envious or powerless, was magnified. This dynamic is probably inevitable in any professional grouping. We were unprepared to effectively deal with it.

Balancing the dialectic between the real need for strong leadership and creating the conditions for members to grow and be active participants was something we had difficulty conceptualizing, discussing and maintaining. For example, it was a struggle for younger, less esteemed members to assert themselves in order to be heard and recognized in the face of more professionally esteemed members who took leadership to shape the message of the group. This struggle limited the capacity of the group to function as well as it might have and actually caused an attrition of membership in the steering committee.

As a steering committee we did not fully discuss how we might address internal issues or how we would strike the balance between being a task-oriented group and maintaining group morale through the necessary processing of internal dynamics. There was also contention about the steering committee itself. Some believed we should merge immediately into a larger group for the sake of inclusion, while others felt developing a core leadership subgroup would best create the conditions for a functioning larger group.

With these unprocessed dynamics pulsing through the steering committee, group tasks began to be organized in such a way that certain members did the more manual/secretarial ('female') work while others did the intellectual ('male') labour. Which worked very well for some people and caused a conflict for others. Reproducing cultural hierarchies, the intellectual labour defined a form of individualistic leadership. Although the intellectual labour was initiated and overseen by professionally established members of the group at large, there were attempts to delegate these tasks. For instance, a younger member was asked to organize the PsyBC website, which brought with it both writing and administrative responsibilities. Additionally, by delegating tasks into committees, we attempted to engage more diverse voices in writing outreach statements and think pieces. Still, because of our struggle with the group issues described earlier, our desperation to shake US voters out of their media-induced trance in order to create a public potential space for reflection and our desire to be received as a credible and legitimate organization, we had difficulty balancing quality control with censorship.

These undigested dynamics infected the large group around the steering committee, contributing to divisive splits along a variety of lines. First was the issue of the theoretical analysis we wanted to use to advertise the group. On the one side were the members struggling to create an astute, generative, non-reductive analysis and critique of the government's use of fear and force to cohere the public and anaesthetize dissent. On the other side were members who felt alienated by the psychoanalytic language used in the critique. For them, this emphasis would hinder outreach to mental health workers from more diverse settings. This split was evident in our struggle to name ourselves: Psychoanalysts for Social Responsibility, or Psychotherapists and Mental Health Professionals for Social Responsibility.

Second, there was the issue of class. Some felt the centrality of capitalism in our analysis necessitated a critique of our class system, while others felt this critique was too heavy handed and polemical. Even though we were appealing to practitioners who were politically liberal, not all would welcome a challenge to the ideological notion that the USA is a classless society with 'equal' opportunity for all. After all, most of our group members were self-employed psychoanalysts who had class privilege but not necessarily great economic stability or protection from market forces.

Class was also a divisive element within the steering committee itself. In New York City, planning events and finding meeting spaces can be a full-time, entrepreneurial endeavour. Often members of the steering committee had to forward a large sum of money with the faith that enough people would attend the meeting and donate money to cover the charge. When there was a loss, the steering committee initially split the cost. For some members, this was a financial problem that was embarrassing to discuss. Although we were deconstructing the competitive spirit of the culture, it was still difficult not to feel humiliation if one could not equally share the financial burden of social responsibility.

Last, and perhaps most importantly, as our outreach expanded and our events and activities garnered more public recognition, we found ourselves with more people who wanted to participate in shaping the mission and policies of the group. For example, many people wrote statements to be sent to the media. There was no clear chain of command for quality control in order to guarantee the consistency of the message. Some people were hurt and annoyed with editing done by the steering committee, while others just sent letters directly to newspapers and community groups in a spontaneous and helpful way.

While our group interfaced with many organizations on protests, phone banks and voter registration drives in different states, the group lost some of its original spark. The hopeful energy and incisive thoughtfulness regardless of the negative elements of the group dynamics dissipated. So, as the presidential election neared and the desperation for political change mounted, members found themselves over-committed or/and additionally involved in organizations with the potential for more direct action. After protesting the war and working so hard on turning the election, feeling defeated was inevitable. Added to the political sadness was that of having lost the surge of the excited response among psychotherapists that we had for the previous two years. However, a smaller group of members emerged as the constant group. This current group comprises approximately 20 active members who meet regularly and an email discussion list that includes 300 national and international members.

Conclusion

The other side of defeat? Successfully mobilizing for lasting social transformation

In the process of writing this chapter, the two of us were granted the opportunity to analyze what we succeed in creating and the ways in which the group could have been stronger and more effective. Nonetheless, as a professional organization, we continue to be unique. As mentioned in the beginning of the chapter, we sought to form a group that would be independent from training institutes and schools and we did that. We have evolved into a loosely organized large group of mental health professionals committed to critically speaking out and we are aligned with national and international organizations that are working toward social change. We manage a website advertising our own events and those of other related organizations. Thus, we succeeded in meeting our initial goals. We have become psychotherapists not only to individuals in distress, but to a cultural family that is being battered by government deception, the physical violence of war and the violence and neglect that result from capitalist militarism, including under-funded social programmes and schools and a growing number of impoverished communities here at home.

In essence, the evolution of the group created a space to publicly grieve both 9/11 and the resulting actions taken by our government, enabling a transformation of loss into social mourning and collective action. As psychotherapists we joined together in protests, demonstrations and wrote a number of position and clinical papers (available on our website). As of this writing we are observing a number of institute activities focused on our traumatogenic political environment. We do not know but we hope we were some small part of expanding this public potential space and ushering new voices into US psychoanalytic discourse.

Bibliography

Abbott, A. (1988) *The System of Professions: An Essay on the Division of Expert Labor*. Chicago: University of Chicago Press.

Abrams, D. (1997) *The Spell of the Sensuous: Perception and Language in the more than Human World*. New York: Vintage.

Adams, C. (ed.) (1996) *The Soul Unearthed. Celebrating Wildness and Personal Renewal Through Nature*. New York: Tarcher Putnam.

Adams, M.V. (1996) *The Multicultural Imagination: 'Race', Colour, and the Unconscious*. London: Routledge.

Akinsete, R. (2002) *Identiying Barriers to Help-Seeking: A Qualitative Analysis of Black Male Students' Preparedness to Seek Help from University Counsellors*. London: University of Greenwich.

Alford, C.F. (1990) Reparation and civilisation: A Kleinian account of the large group, *Free Associations*, 19: 17–30.

Altemeyer, B. (1996) *The Authoritarian Specter*. Cambridge, MA: Harvard University Press.

Altman, N. (1995) *The Analyst in the Inner City: Race, Class, and Culture through a Psychoanalytic Lens*. Hillsdale, NJ: Analytic Press.

Altman, N. (2003) How white people suffer from white racism, *Psychotherapy and Politics International*, 1(2): 93–106.

American Psychological Association (1992) Ethical principles of psychologists and code of conduct, *American Psychologist*, 47: 1597–611.

Arlow, J.A. (1972) Some dilemmas in psychoanalytic education, *Journal of the American Psychoanalytic Association*, 20: 556–66 .

Arlow, J.A. (1982) Psychoanalytic education, *Annual of Psychoanalysis*, 10: 5–20.

Armstrong, J. (1995) Keepers of the earth. In T. Roszak, M.E. Gomes and A.D. Kanner (eds) *Ecopsychology: Restoring the Earth, Healing the Mind*. San Francisco: Sierra Club Books.

Arrue, O. (1998a) Brief note on the history of Chile in the last thirty years, *International Psychoanalysis*, 7(1): 15–16.

Arrue, O. (1998b) Omar Arrue answers his critics, *International Psychoanalysis*, 7(2): 5.

Arye, L. (2001) *Unintentional Music: Releasing Your Deepest Creativity.* Charlottesville, VA: Hampton Roads Publishing Company.

Atwood, G.E. and Stolorow, R.D. (1984) *Structures of Subjectivity: Explorations in Psychoanalytic Phenomenology.* Hillsdale, NJ: Analytic Press.

Audergon, A. (2004) Collective trauma: The nightmare of history, *Psychotherapy and Politics International*, 2(1): 16–31.

Audergon, A. (2005) *The War Hotel: Psychological Dynamics in Violent Conflict.* London: Whurr.

BACP (2002) *Ethical Framework for Good Practice in Counselling and Psychotherapy.* Rugby: BACP.

Bancroft, J. (1989) *Human Sexuality and its Problems.* Edinburgh: Churchill Livingstone.

Bateson, G. (1982) *Steps to an Ecology of the Mind.* San Francisco: Chandler.

Battaille, G. (1987) *Eroticism.* London: Marion Boyars.

Baumeister, R.F. and Hastings, S. (1997) Distortions of collective memory: How groups flatter and deceive themselves. In J.W. Pennebaker, D. Paez and B. Rimé (eds) *Collective Memory of Political Events.* Mahwah, NJ: Lawrence Erlbaum.

Benjamin, J. (1988) *The Bonds of Love.* London: Virago.

Berke, J. (1989) *The Tyranny of Malice.* London: Simon & Schuster.

Berman, E. (1987) From war to war: Cumulative trauma, *Sihot*, 2: 37–40.

Berman, E. (1988a) Communal upbringing in the kibbutz: The allure and risk of psychoanalytic utopianism, *Psychoanalytic Study of the Child*, 43: 319–35.

Berman, E. (1988b) The silence of the psychologists, *Politika*, 19: 23–5.

Berman, E. (1989) Mobilized psychology and involved psychology. Presentation in Imut conference, Jerusalem (Psychologists and the left, *Ha'aretz*).

Berman, E. (1991) So far only questions, *Sihot*, special Gulf War issue: 3.

Berman, E. (1993) Psychoanalysis, rescue and utopia, *Utopian Studies*, 4: 44–56.

Berman, E. (1995) The day after [unsigned editorial], *Sihot*, 10(1).

Berman, E. (1996) Psychologists who slandered Rabin, *Sihot*, 10: 154.

Berman, E. (1997) Psychology for the rich and psychology for the poor?, *Ha'aretz*, June 1.

Berman, E. (1998) Evil winds are blowing: Public mental health in Israel, *Sihot*, 12, 140–1.

Berman, E. (2004) *Impossible Training: A Relational View of Psychoanalytic Education.* Hillsdale, NJ: Analytic Press.

Berry, T. (1999) *The Great Work.* New York: Bell Tower.

Bersani, L. (1995) *Homos.* Cambridge, MA: Harvard University Press.

Bion, W.R. (1990) *Brazilian Lectures.* London: Karnac.

Biram, H. (2003) The difficulty of transforming terror into dialogue, *Group Analysis*, 36(4): 490–502.

Bloom, S.L. (2000) Our hearts and our hopes are turned to peace: Origins of the ISTSS. In A. Shalev, R. Yehuda and A.S. McFarlane (eds) *International Handbook of Human Response Trauma*. New York: Plenum Press.

Bloom, S.L. (2003) *Understanding the Impact of Sexual Assault: The Nature of Traumatic Experience*. Maryland Heights, MO: GW Medical Publishing.

Bloom, S.L. (2004a) Neither liberty nor safety: The impact of fear on individuals, institutions, and societies, Part I, *Psychotherapy and Politics International*, 2(2): 78–98.

Bloom, S.L. (2004b) Neither liberty nor safety: The impact of fear on individuals, institutions, and societies, Part II, *Psychotherapy and Politics International*, 2(3): 212–28.

Bloom, S.L. (in press) Neither liberty nor safety: The impact of fear on individuals, institutions, and societies, Part III, *Psychotherapy and Politics International*, 3(2).

Boadella, D. (1999) Transference, politics and narcissism, *International Journal of Psychotherapy*, 4(3): 283–311.

Bohm, D. (1980) *Wholeness and the Implicate Order*. London: Routledge.

Borch-Jacobsen, M. (1988) *The Freudian Subject*. London: Macmillan.

Bracken, P. (2002) *Trauma: Culture, Meaning and Philosophy*. London: Whurr.

Brint, S. and Levy, C.S. (1995) Professions and civic engagement: Trends in rhetoric and practice, 1875–1995. In T. Skocpol and M.P. Fiorina (eds) *Civic Engagement and American Democracy*. Washington, DC: Brookings Institution Press.

Brown, A. and Bourne, L. (1996) *The Social Work Supervisor*. London: Heinemann.

Bunzl, J. and Beit-Hallahmi, B. (eds) (2002) *Psychoanalysis, Identity and Ideology: Critical Essays on the Israel/Palestine Case*. Norwell, MA: Kluwer.

Burr, V. and Butt, T. (2000) Psychological distress and postmodern thought. In D. Fee (ed.) *Pathology in the Postmodern: Mental Illness as Discourse and Experience*. London: Sage.

Butler, J. (1990) *Gender Trouble: Feminism and the Subversion of Identity*. New York: Routledge.

Califia, P. (1997) *Sex Changes: The Politics of Transgenderism*. San Francisco: Cleis Press.

Casement, A. (ed.) (2004) *Who Owns Psychoanalysis?* London: Karnac.

Casement, P. (1990) *Further Learning from the Patient*. London: Routledge.

Castoriadis, C. (1997) *World in Fragments: Writings on Politics, Society, Psychoanalysis, and the Imagination*. Stanford, CA: Stanford University Press.

Castoriadis, C. (1999) The psychical and social roots of hate, *Free Associations*, 7(3): 402–15.

Cecchin, B. (1987) Hypothesizing, circularity and neutrality revisited: An invitation to curiosity, *Family Process*, 26: 405–13.

Cecchin, B. (1993) Foreword to L. Hoffman, *Exchanging Voices: A Collaborative Approach to Family Therapy*. London: Karnac.

Chaplin, J. (1988) *Feminist Counselling in Action*. London: Sage.

Chasseguet-Smirgel, J. and Grunberger, B. (1986) *Freud or Reich? Psychoanalysis and Illusion*. London: Free Association Books.

Chodorow, N. (1978) *The Reproduction of Mothering: Psychoanalysis and the Sociology of Gender*. Berkeley, CA: University of California Press.

Clarke, L. (2003) Interview, *Counselling and Psychotherapy Journal*, 14(7): 6–7.

Clarke, S. (2003) *Social Theory, Psychoanalysis and Racism*. Basingstoke: Palgrave Macmillan.

Clarkson, P. (1995) *The Therapeutic Relationship*. London: Whurr.

Clarkson, P. (1996) *The Bystander: An End to Innocence in Human Relationships*. London: Whurr.

Clarkson, P. (2000) *Ethics: Working with Ethical and Moral Dilemmas in Psychotherapy*. London: Whurr.

Clarkson, P. (2004) Everything you ever wanted to know about the seven level model. Available at www.nospine.com

Clarkson, P. and Lindsay, G. (2001) Collegial working relationships: Ethics, research and good practice. In Clarkson, *On Psychotherapy* Vol. 2. London: Whurr.

Clarkson, P. and Nicolopoulou, K. (2003) Developing epistemological consciousness about complexity: Seven domains of discourse. In E. Mitleton-Kelly (ed.) *Complex Systems and Evolutionary Perspectives on Organisations: The Application of Complexity Theory to Organisations*. Oxford: Elsevier Science.

Cocks, G. (1997) *Psychotherapy in the Third Reich: The Goering Institute*, 2nd edn. New Brunswick: Transaction.

Cohen, F.S., Solomon, S., Maxfield, M., Pyszczynski, T. and Greenberg, J. (2004) Fatal attraction: The effects of mortality salience on evaluations of charismatic, task-oriented, and relationship-oriented leaders, *Psychological Science*, 15(12): 846–51.

Cohen, S. and Taylor, L. (1992) *Escape Attempts*. 2nd edn. London: Routledge.

Contratto, S. (1987) Father presence in women's psychological development. In G.M. Platt, J. Rabow and M. Goldman (eds) *Advances in Psychoanalytic Sociology*. Malabar, FL: Krieger.

Cooper Marcus, C. and Barnes, M. (1998) *Healing Gardens: Therapeutic Benefits and Design Recommendations*. London: Wiley.

Coyne, J. and Woods, W. (2002) Constructing subjects and making experts: Reading the politics of the psychotherapy novel, *Social Semiotics*, 12(3): 315–30.

Dalal, F. (2002) *Race, Colour and Processes of Racialization*. New York: Brunner-Routledge.

Dale, P., Allen, J. and Measor, L. (1998) Counselling adults who were abused as children: Clients' perceptions of efficacy, client–counsellor communication, and dissatisfaction, *British Journal of Guidance and Counselling*, 26: 141–58.

Darwin, C. (1859) *On the Origin of Species by Means of Natural Selection*. London: Murray.

Davies, D. and Neal, C. (eds) (2000) *Therapeutic Perspectives on Working with Lesbian, Gay, and Bisexual Clients*. Buckingham: Open University Press.

de Levita, D. (2000) Child psychotherapy as an instrument in cultural research: Treating war-traumatized children in the former Yugoslavia. In A.C.G.M. Robbens and M.M. Suarez-Orozco (eds) *Cultures Under Siege: Collective Violence and Trauma*. Cambridge: Cambridge University Press.

De Mare, P. (1975) The politics of large groups. In L. Kreeger (ed.) *The Large Group: Dynamics and Therapy*. London: Maresfield Reprints.

DeMause, L. (1982) *Foundations of Psychohistory*. New York: Creative Roots.

DeMeo, J. (1991) *Saharasia: The 4000 BCE Origins of Child Abuse, Sex-Repression, Warfare and Social Violence, In the Deserts of the Old World*. Ashland, OR: Natural Energy Works.

Denman, C. (2001) Women's friendships: Theory and therapy. In S. Izzard and N. Barden (eds) *Rethinking Gender and Therapy: The Changing Identities of Women*. Buckingham: Open University Press.

Denman, C. (2003) *Sexuality: A Biopsychosocial Approach*. London: Palgrave Macmillan.

Department of Health (1999) *National Service Framework for Mental Health*. London: Department of Health Publications.

Department of Health (2002) *Women's Mental Health: Into the Mainstream*. London: Department of Health Publications.

Department of Health (2004) *Organising and Delivering Psychological Therapies*. London: Department of Health Publications.

Depression Alliance (2003) Treatment for depression. Available at www.depressionalliance.org

Derrida, J. (1982) *Difference: In the Margins of Philosophy*. Chicago: University of Chicago Press.

Dimen, M. (2003) *Sexuality, Intimacy, Power*. Hillsdale, NJ: Analytic Press.

Dimen, M. (2004) At the crossroads: Feminism, psychoanalysis, politics, *Psychotherapy and Politics International*, 2(1): 32–49.

Dinnerstein, D. (1999) *The Mermaid and the Minotaur*. New York: The Other Press.

Dryden, W. (1996) A rose by any other name: A personal view on the differences among professional titles, *Self and Society*, 24(5): 15–17.

Du Boulay, S. (2004) *Teresa of Avila: An Extraordinary Life*. New York: Rainbow Books.

Durning, A. (1995) Are we happy yet? In T. Roszak, M.E. Gomes and A.D. Kanner (eds) *Ecopsychology: Restoring the Earth, Healing the Mind.* San Francisco: Sierra Club Books.

Eichenbaum, L. and Orbach, S. (1982) *Outside In, Inside Out: Women's Psychology, A Feminist Psychoanalytic Approach.* Harmondsworth: Penguin.

Elias, N. (1994) *The Civilising Process: Sociogenic and Psychogenic Investigations.* Oxford: Blackwell.

Elliot, M., Bishop, K. and Stokes, P. (2004) Societal PTSD? Historic shock in Northern Ireland, *Psychotherapy and Politics International*, 2(1): 1–16.

Elliott, A. (2004) *Social Theory Since Freud.* London: Routledge.

Ernst, S. and Goodison, L. (1981) *In Our Own Hands: A Book of Self-Help Therapy.* London: Women's Press.

Ernst, S. and Maguire, M. (eds) (1987) *Living with the Sphinx: Papers from the Women's Therapy Centre.* London: Women's Press.

Ewen, S. and Ewen, E. (1979) *Channels of Desire: Mass Images and the Shaping of American Consciousness.* New York: McGraw-Hill.

Fanon, F. (1986) *Black Skin, White Masks.* London: Pluto Press.

Ferenczi, S. (1932) Confusion of tongues between adults and the child. In *Final Contributions.* New York: Brunner/Mazel, 1980: 156–67.

Fernando, S. (2002) *Mental Health, Race and Culture*, 2nd edn. Basingstoke: Macmillan.

Figlio, K. (2000) Registration and ethics in psychotherapy, *British Journal of Psychotherapy*, 16(3): 327–34.

Fortune, C. (1993) Sandor Ferenczi's analysis of 'R.N.': A critically important case in the history of psychoanalysis, *British Journal of Psychotherapy*, 9(4): 436–43.

Foster, R., Moskowitz, M. and Javier, R. (1996) *Reaching Across Boundaries of Culture and Class: Widening the Scope of Psychotherapy.* Northvale, NJ: Aronson.

Foucault, M. (1980) *Power/Knowledge: Selected Interviews and Other Writings. 1972–1979.* (ed. C. Gordon). New York: Pantheon.

Foucault, M. (1981) *The History of Sexuality, Vol. 1: An Introduction.* Harmondsworth: Pelican.

Foucault, M. (1987) *Mental Illness and Psychology.* Berkeley, CA: University of California Press.

Fox, M. (2002) Finding a way through: From mindlessness to minding. In R.K. Papadopoulos (ed.) *Therapeutic Care for Refugees.* London: Karnac.

Freshwater, D. (2003) Researching mental health: Pathology in a post-modern world, *NT Research*, 8(3): 161–72.

Freshwater, D. (2005) *Mental Illness: Questions and Answers for Counsellors and Therapists.* London: Whurr.

Freshwater, D. and Rolfe, G. (2001) Critical reflexivity: A politically and ethically engaged research method for nursing, *NT Research*, 6(1): 526–37.

Freshwater, D. and Rolfe, G. (2004) *Deconstructing Evidence-Based Practice.* London: Routledge.

Freud, S. (1905) Three essays on the theory of sexuality. *Standard Edition* Vol. 7. London: Hogarth Press, 1953.

Freud, S. (1930) Civilisation and Its Discontents. *Penguin Freud Library* 12: 251–340. Harmondsworth: Penguin, 1985.

Friedson, E. (1970) *The Profession of Medicine: A Study of the Sociology of Applied Knowledge.* New York: Dodd Mead & Co.

Fromm, E. (1995) *The Essential Fromm: Life Between Having and Being.* Bury St Edmunds, Suffolk: St Edmundsbury Press.

Frosh, S. (1989) *Psychoanalysis and Psychology: Minding the Gap.* London: Macmillan.

Frye, M. (1983) On being white: Thinking toward a feminist understanding of race and race supremacy. In M. Frye (ed.) *The Politics of Reality: Essays in Feminist Theory.* Freedom, CA: Crossing Press.

Gabriel, Y. (1993) Organizational nostalgia – reflections on 'The Golden Age'. In S. Fineman (ed.) *Emotion in Organizations.* Thousand Oaks, CA: Sage.

Gampel, Y. (2000) Reflections on the prevalence of the uncanny in social violence. In A.C.G.M. Robbens and M.M. Suarez-Orozco (eds) *Cultures Under Siege: Collective Violence and Trauma.* Cambridge: Cambridge University Press.

Gampel, Y. (2002) A view of Israeli society through the link between Israelis and Palestinians in the context of psychoanalytic psychotherapy training. In J. Bunzl and B. Beit-Hallahmi (eds), *Psychoanalysis, Identity and Ideology.* Norwell, MA: Kluwer.

Gampel, Y., Canestri, J., Diatkine, D., Braun, J. and Puget, J. (1998) The history of Chile? [letters to the editor], *International Psychoanalysis*, 7(2): 4–5.

Garnets, L., Hancock, K.A., Cochran, S.D., Goodchilds, J. and Peplau, L.A. (1991) Issues in psychotherapy with lesbians and gay men, *American Psychologist*, 46: 964–72.

Gay, P. (1995) *Freud: A Life for Our Time.* London: Papermac.

Gergen, K. (1994) *Realities and Relationships: Soundings in a Social Construction.* Cambridge: Harvard University Press.

Gergen, K. and Gergen, M. (eds) (2003) *Social Construction: A Reader.* London: Sage.

Gilbert, D. (1997) *The American Class Structure*, 5th edn. Chicago: Dorsey Press.

Gilbert, P. (1992) *Depression and the Evolution of Powerlessness.* Mahwah, NJ: Lawrence Erlbaum.

Greer, G. (1999) *The Whole Woman.* London: Doubleday.

Guattari, F. (1984) *Molecular Revolution: Psychiatry and Politics.* Harmondsworth: Penguin.

Guggenbuhl-Craig, A. (1978) *Power in the Helping Professions*. Zurich: Spring.

Haaken, J. (1998) *Pillar of Salt: Gender, Memory and the Perils of Looking Back*. London: Free Association Books.

Halbwachs, M. (1992) *On Collective Memory*. Chicago: University of Chicago Press.

Hatfield, E., Cacioppo, J. and Rapson, R. (eds) (1994) *Emotional Contagion*. New York: Cambridge University Press.

Hazell, J.E. (2000) Private sector downsizing: Implications for DOD, *Acquisition Review Quarterly*, March 22.

Health Professions Council (2004) *Standards of Proficiency for Arts Therapists*. London: HPC.

Heinl, P. (2001) *Splintered Innocence: An Intuitive Approach to Treating War Trauma*. Hove: Brunner-Routledge.

Herberg, W. (ed.) (1961) *The Writings of Martin Buber*. Cleveland, OH: Meridian Books.

Hermann, J. (1997) *Trauma and Recovery: The Aftermath of Violence from Domestic Abuse to Political Terror*. New York: Basic Books.

Hillman, J. and Ventura, M. (1992) *We've Had a Hundred Years of Psychotherapy – and the World's Getting Worse*. San Francisco: Harper.

Hinshelwood, R.D. (1985) Questions of training, *Free Associations*, 2, 7–18.

Hinshelwood, R.D. (1997) *Therapy or Coercion?* London: Karnac.

Hocquenghem, G. (1978) *Homosexual Desire*. London: Alison & Busby.

Hofstede, G. (1980) *Cultures' Consequences: International Differences in Work-Related Values*. Beverly Hills, CA: Sage.

Hogan, D.B. (1979) *The Regulation of Psychotherapists* (4 vols). Cambridge, MA: Ballinger.

Hoggett, P. (2004) Strange attractors: Politics and psychoanalysis, *Psychoanalysis, Culture & Society*, 9: 74–86.

Holland, S. (1988) Defining and experimenting with prevention. In J. Marmor (ed.) *Psychiatry in Transition*. London: Pluto Press.

Hopper, E. (2003) *Traumatic Experience in the Unconscious Life of Groups*. London: Jessica Kingsley.

Horowitz, M.J. (2003) *Treatment of Stress Response Syndromes*. Washington, DC: American Psychiatric Association Press.

House, R. (2003) *Therapy beyond Modernity: Deconstructing and Transcending Profession-centred Therapy*. London: Karnac.

House, R. and Totton, N. (eds) (1997) *Implausible Professions: Arguments for Pluralism and Autonomy in Psychotherapy and Counselling*. Manchester: PCCS Books.

Hymes, D. (ed.) (1977) *Pidginization and Creolization of Languages*. Cambridge: Cambridge University Press.

Illich, I. (1976) *Limits to Medicine*. Harmondsworth: Penguin.

Inskipp, F. and Proctor, B. (1995) *The Art, Craft and Tasks of Counselling Supervision. Part 2: Becoming a Supervisor*. Twickenham: Cascade Publications.

Isay, R. (1996) *Becoming Gay: The Journey to Self-Acceptance*. New York: Pantheon Books.

Jacoby, R. (1977) *Social Amnesia: A Critique of Conformist Psychology from Adler to Laing*. Hassocks, Sussex: Harvester.

James, O. (1997) *Britain on the Couch*. London: Century.

Janis, I.L. (1982) Decision making under stress. In L. Goldberger and S. Breznitz (eds) *Handbook of Stress: Theoretical and Clinical Aspects*. New York: Free Press.

Janis, I.L. (1983) Groupthink, *Small Groups and Social Interaction*, 2: 39–46.

Janis, I.L. and Mann, L. (1977) *Decision Making*. New York: Free Press.

Janoff-Bulman, R. (1992) *Shattered Assumptions: Towards a New Psychology of Trauma*. New York: Free Press.

Jenkins, P., Keter, V. and Stone, J. (2004) *Psychotherapy and the Law: Questions and Answers for Counsellors and Therapists*. London: Whurr.

Johnson, S. (2001a) Family therapy saves the planet: Messianic tendencies in family systems literature, *Journal of Marital and Family Therapy*, 27: 3–11.

Johnson, S. (2001b) Saving the planet – or ourselves!, *Journal of Marital and Family Therapy*, 27: 23–5.

Josephson, B. (2001) First-person experience and the scientific exploration of consciousness. In D. Lorimer (ed.) *Thinking Beyond the Brain*. Edinburgh: Floris Books.

Kanner, A. and Gomes, M.E.. (1995) The all-consuming self. In T. Roszak, M.E. Gomes and A.D. Kanner (eds) *Ecopsychology: Restoring the Earth, Healing the Mind*. San Francisco: Sierra Club Books.

Kareem, J. and Littlewood, R. (eds) (1992) *Intercultural Therapy: Themes, Interpretations and Practice*. Oxford: Blackwell.

Kauffman, K. (2004) *Co-Counselling*. London: Taylor & Francis.

Keinan-Kon, N. (1998) Internal reality, external reality, and denial in the Gulf War, *Journal of the American Academy of Psychoanalysis*, 26: 417–42.

Kennedy, R. (1998) *The Elusive Human Subject: A Psychoanalytic Theory of Subject Relations*. London: Free Association Books.

Kernberg, O.F. (1986) Institutional problems of psychoanalytic education, *Journal of the American Psychoanalytic Association*, 34: 799–834.

Kernberg, O.F. (1992) *Aggression in Personality Disorders and Perversion*. New Haven: Yale University Press.

Kernberg, O.F. (1996) Thirty methods to destroy the creativity of analytic candidates, *International Journal of Psychoanalysis*, 77(5): 1031–40.

Kirsner, D. (2000) Unfree associations: Inside psychoanalytic institutes. Available at www.human-nature.com/kirsner/

Klein, M. (1975) *Envy and Gratitude and Other Works*. New York: Delta.

Kovel, J. (1978) *A Complete Guide to Therapy*. Harmondsworth: Penguin.

Kovel, J. (1988) *White Racism: A Psychohistory*. London: Free Association Books.

Kovel, J. (1995) On racism and psychoanalysis. In A. Elliot and S. Frosh (eds) *Psychoanalysis in Contexts*. London: Routledge.

Krause, I. (1998) *Therapy Across Culture*. London: Sage.

Krystal, H. (1988) *Integration and Self-Healing: Affect, Trauma, Alexithymia*. Hillsdale, NJ: Analytic Press.

Kurtz, S. (1989) *The Art of Unknowing: Dimensions of Openness in Analytic Therapy*. Northvale, NJ: Jason Aronson.

Lacan, J. (1966) *Ecrits*. Paris: Seuil.

Laclau, E. and Mouffe, C. (1985) *Hegemony and Socialist Strategy*. London: Verso.

Lago, C. and Thompson, J. (1996) *Race, Culture and Counselling*. Buckingham: Open University Press.

Langer, M. (1989) *From Vienna to Managua: Journey of a Psychoanalyst*. London: Free Association Books.

Langs, R.J. (1982) *The Psychotherapeutic Conspiracy*. Northvale, NJ: Aronson.

Lees, J. (2001) Reflexive action research: Developing knowledge through practice, *Counselling and Psychotherapy Research*, 1(2): 132–8.

Leitner, M. (1999) Pathologizing as a way of dealing with conflicts and dissent in the psychoanalytic movement, *Free Associations*, 7(3): 459–83.

Lewes, K. (1989) *The Psychoanalytic Theory of Male Homosexuality*. London: Quartet.

Leys, R. (2000) *Trauma: A Genealogy*. Chicago: Chicago University Press.

Linden, S. and Grut, J. (2002) *The Healing Fields: Working with Psychotherapy and Nature to Rebuild Shattered Lives*. London: Frances Lincoln.

Lindsay, G. and Clarkson P. (1996) Ethical dilemmas of psychotherapists. *The Psychologist*, 12(4): 182–5; reprinted as Chapter 1 in Clarkson, 2000.

Luepnitz, D. (1988) *The Family Interpreted: Psychoanalysis, Feminism, and Family Therapy*. New York: Basic Books.

Macpherson, Lord (1999) *The Steven Lawrence Inquiry*. London: The Stationery Office.

Macy, J. (1995) Working through environmental despair. In T. Roszak, M.E. Gomes and A.D. Kanner (eds) *Ecopsychology: Restoring the Earth, Healing the Mind*. San Francisco: Sierra Club Books.

Macy, J. and Brown, M. (1998) *Coming Back to Life: Practices to Reconnect Our Lives, Our World*. British Columbia: New Society Publishers.

Magee, M. and Miller, D. (1997) *Lesbian Lives: Psychoanalytic Narratives Old and New*. Hillsdale, NJ: Analytic Press.

Maiello, S. (1999) Encounter with an African healer, *Child Psychotherapy*, 25(2): 217–38.

Mann, D. (ed.) (1999) *Erotic Transference and Countertransference: Clinical Practice in Psychotherapy*. London: Routledge.

Marcuse, H. (1970) *Eros and Civilization*. London: Allen Lane.

Marquis de Sade (1966) *The 120 Days of Sodom, and Other Writings*. New York: Grove Press.

Marx, K. (1844) Economic and philosophical manuscripts of 1844. In D. Caute (ed.) *Essential Writings of Karl Marx*. London: Panther, 1967.

Maslow, A. (1970) *Motivation and Personality*. New York: Harper & Row.

Masson, J. (ed.) (1985) *The Complete Letters of Sigmund Freud to Wilhelm Fliess*. Harvard: Belknap.

Masson, J. (1990) *Against Therapy*. London: Fontana.

Mcaskill, A. (1999) Personal therapy as a training requirement: The lack of supporting evidence. In C. Feltham (ed.) *Controversies in Psychotherapy and Counselling*. London: Sage.

McDougall, J. (1995) *The Many Faces of Eros*. London: Free Association Books.

McIntosh, P. (1988) White privilege and male privilege: A personal account of coming to see correspondences through work in women's studies. In M.L. Andersen and P.H. Collins (eds) *Race, Class and Gender: An Anthology*. Belmont, CA: Wadsworth.

McKenzie, R. (2002) The importance of philosophical congruence for therapeutic use of self in practice. In D. Freshwater (ed.) *Therapeutic Nursing*. London: Sage.

McWhorter, J. (ed.) (2000) *Language Change and Language Contact in Pidgins and Creoles*. Amsterdam: John Benjamins.

Mearns, D. and Thorne, B. (1988) *Person-Centred Counselling in Action*. London: Sage.

Mellor-Clarke, J. (2000) *Counselling in Primary Care in the Context of the NHS Quality Agenda*. Rugby: BACP.

Menzies, I.E.P. (1975) A case study in the functioning of social systems as a defense against anxiety. In A.D. Coleman and W.H. Bexton (eds) *Group Relations Reader I*. Washington, DC: Rice Institute Series.

Mindell, A. (1986) *River's Way: The Process Science of the Dreambody*. New York and London: Viking-Penguin-Arkana.

Mindell, A. (1989) *The Year I: Global Process Work with Planetary Myths and Structures*. London: Penguin Arkana.

Mindell, A. (1992) *The Leader as Martial Artist: An Introduction to Deep Democracy; Techniques and Strategies for Resolving Conflict and Creating Community*. San Francisco: HarperCollins.

Mindell, A. (1995) *Sitting in the Fire: Large Group Transformation Using Conflict and Diversity*. Portland, OR: Lao Tse Press.

Mirousky, J. (1989) *Social Courses of Psychological Distress*. New York: Aldine de Gruyter.

Mitchell, J. (1974) *Psychoanalysis and Feminism*. New York: Vintage Books.

Modena, E. (1986) A chance for psychoanalysis to change: The Zurich psychoanalytical seminar as an example, *Free Associations*, 5: 7–22.

Mohr, R. (1992) *Gay Ideas: Outing and Other Controversies*. Boston, MA: Beacon Press.

Moses, R. (1982) The group self and the Israeli–Arab conflict, *International Review of Psycho-Analysis*, 9: 55–65.

Mowbray, R. (1995) *The Case Against Psychotherapy Registration: A Conservation Issue for the Human Potential Movement*. London: TransMarginal Press.

Murray, C.J.L. and Lopez, A. (1997) Mortality by cause for eight regions of the world: Global Burden of Disease Study, *Science*, 274: 740–3.

Musil, R. (1937) Helpless Europe. In B. Pike and D. Lufts (eds & trans), *Precision and Soul: Essays and Addresses*. Chicago: University of Chicago Press, 1990.

Nairn, K. and Smith, G. (1984) *Dealing with Depression*. London: Women's Press.

NewsBriefs (2000) More knowledge: Song strikes chord, *Computing Canada*, May 12.

Newton, J (2004) *From Panthers To Promise Keepers: Rethinking The Men's Movement (The New Social Formations)*. New York: Rowman & Littlefield.

Nobus, D. (1998) Splitting images: Lacan, institutional politics and the social authorization of psychoanalysis, *ps: Journal of the Universities Association for Psychoanalytic Studies*, 1: 53–67.

Noel, B. and Watterson, K. (1992) *You Must Be Dreaming*. New York: Poseidon Press.

Norberg Hodge, H. (1991) *Ancient Futures: Learning From Ladakh*. New York: Random House.

O'Connor, N. and Ryan, J. (1993) *Wild Desires and Mistaken Identities: Lesbianism and Psychoanalysis*. London: Virago.

O'Connor, P. (1992) *Friendships Between Women: A Critical Review*. New York: Guilford Press.

Orange, D. (1995) *Emotional Understanding*. New York: Guilford Press.

Orange, D., Atwood, G.E. and Stolorow, R.D. (1997) *Working Intersubjectively: Contextualism in Psychoanalytic Practice*. Hillsdale, NJ: Analytic Press.

Orbach, S. (1982) *Understanding Women*. Harmondsworth: Penguin.

Orbach, S. and Eichenbaum, L. (1987) *Bittersweet: Facing Up to Feelings of Love, Envy and Competition in Women's Friendships*. London: Century.

Parker, I. (1996) Postmodernism and its discontents: Psychotherapeutic discourse, *British Journal of Psychotherapy*, 12(4): 447–60.

Parker, I. (1997) *Psychoanalytic Discourse*. London: Sage.

Parry, G. (1996) *Using Research to Change Practice*. In T. Heller, J. Reynolds, J. Gomm, R. Muston and S. Pattison (eds) *Mental Health Matters: A Reader*. Basingstoke: Palgrave.

Parsons, T. (1951) *The Social System*. London: Routledge & Kegan Paul.

Paul, S. and Pelham, G. (2000) A relational approach to therapy. In S. Palmer and R. Woolfe (eds) *Integrative and Eclectic Counselling and Psychotherapy*. London: Sage.

Pearson, G. (1983) *Hooligan: A History of Respectable Fears*. London: Macmillan.

Peck, M.S. (1987) *The Different Drum*. London: Rider.

Pennebaker, J.W., Paez, D. and Rimé, B. (eds) (1997) *Collective Memory of Political Events*. Mahwah, NJ: Lawrence Erlbaum.

Perls, F. (1955) Morality, ego boundary and aggression. In J.O. Stevens (ed.) *Gestalt Is*. New York: Bantam Books.

Perls, F. (1969) *Ego Hunger and Aggression*. New York: Vintage Books.

Perls, F., Hefferline, R.F. and Goodman, P. (1973) *Gestalt Therapy: Excitement and Growth in the Human Personality*. Harmondsworth: Penguin.

Perry, B.D. (2002) Childhood experience and the expression of genetic potential: What childhood neglect tells us about nature and nurture, *Brain and Mind*, 3: 79–100.

Perry, B.D. and Pate, J. (1994) Neurodevelopment and the psychobiological roots of post-traumatic stress disorder. In L. Koziol and C. Stout (eds) *The Neuropsychology of Mental Disorders: A Practical Guide*. Springfield, IL: Charles C. Thomas.

Perry, B.D., Pollard, R.A., Blakley, T.L., Baker, W.L. and Vigilante, D. (1996) Childhood trauma, the neurobiology of adaptation and use-dependent development of the brain: How states become traits, *Infant Mental Health Journal*, 16: 271–89.

Person, E. (1999) *The Sexual Century*. New Haven, CT: Yale University Press.

Phillips, A. (1988) *Winnicott*. London: Fontana.

Phillips, A. (2002) *Equals*. London: Faber & Faber.

Pingitore, D. (1997) The corporatization of psychotherapy: A study in professional transformation, *Free Associations*, 7(1): 101–27.

POPAN (2004) *Ten Years is Too Long: Proposals for Interim Public Protection Measures in the Talking Therapies*. London: POPAN.

Pope, K.S. (2001) Sex between therapists and clients. In J. Worrell (ed.) *Encyclopedia of Women and Gender: Sex Similarities and Differences and the Impact of Society on Gender*. Burlington, MA: Academic Press.

Pope, K.S., Keith-Spiegel, P. and Tabachnik, B.G. (1986) Sexual attraction to clients: the human therapist and the (sometimes) inhuman training system, *American Psychologist*, 41: 147–58.

Pope, K.S. and Vetter, V.A. (1991) Prior therapist–patient sexual involvement among patients seen by psychologists, *Psychotherapy*, 28: 429–38.

Poster, M. (1978) *Critical Theory of the Family*. London: Pluto Press.

Postle, D. (1998) Gold into lead: The annexation of psychotherapy in the UK. *International Journal of Psychotherapy*, 3(1): 53–83.

Postle, D., Musgrave, A., House, R., Burchell, S. and Piohtee, S. (2004) The Independent Practitioner's Network: Special issue, *Self and Society*, 32(14), 5–28.

Prechtel, M. (2002) *The Toe Bone and the Tooth*. London: Thorsons.

Prescott, J. (1975) Body pleasure and the origins of violence, *Bulletin of Atomic Scientists*, November: 10–20.

Prozan, C.K. (1993) *The Technique of Feminist Psychoanalytic Psychotherapy*. Northvale, NJ: Aronson.

Pyszczynski, T., Solomon, S. and Greenberg, J. (2003) *In the Wake of 9/11: The Psychology of Terror*. Washington, DC: American Psychological Association.

Rachman, A. (1997) *Sandor Ferenczi: The Psychoanalyst of Tenderness and Passion*. Northvale, NJ: Aronson.

Rampton, S. and Stauber, J. (2003) *Weapons of Mass Deception: The Uses of Propaganda in Bush's War on Iraq*. New York: Tarcher/Penguin.

Rangell, L. (1962) Prospect and retrospect: An interim report by the President, *Journal of the American Psychoanalytic Association*, 10: 227–57.

Rangell, L. (1982) Transference to theory, *Annual of Psychoanalysis*, 10: 29–56.

Reich, W. (1967) *Reich Speaks of Freud*. London: Condor.

Reich, W. (1975) *The Mass Psychology of Fascism*. Harmondsworth: Penguin.

Reich, W. (1983a) *Children of the Future*. New York: Farrar Straus Giroux.

Reich, W. (1983b) *The Function of the Orgasm*. London: Condor.

Renik, O. (1995) The ideal of the anonymous analyst and the problem of self-disclosure, *Psychoanalytic Quarterly*, 64: 466–95.

Richards, B. (ed.) (1984) *Capitalism and Infancy: Essays on Psychoanalysis and Politics*. London: Free Association Books.

Ridley, M. (2003) *Nature Via Nurture: Genes, Experience and What Makes Us Human*. London: Fourth Estate.

Robertson, C. (1993) Dysfunction in training organisations. Available at www.re-vision.org.uk

Rogers, C. (1951) The problem of diagnosis. In *Client-Centred Therapy*. London: Constable.

Rogers, C. (1973) *Encounter Groups*. Harmondsworth: Penguin.

Rolnik, E. (2002) From Vienna to Jerusalem: The reception of psychoanalysis in Palestine. In J. Bunzl and B. Beit-Hallahmi (eds), *Psychoanalysis, Identity and Ideology*. Norwell, MA: Kluwer.

Rose, N. (1989) *Governing the Soul: The Shaping of the Private Self*. London: Routledge.

Rose, N. (1990) *Governing the Soul: The Shaping of the Private Self*. London: Routledge.

Roudinesco, E. (1990) *Jacques Lacan and Co: A History of Psychoanalysis in France 1925–1985*. London: Free Association Books.

Rowan, J. (1976) *Ordinary Ecstasy*. London: Routledge.

Rustin, M. (1991) *The Good Society and the Inner World*. London: Verso.

Ryde, J. (1997) *A Step Towards Understanding Culture in Relation to Psychotherapy*. Bath: BCPC Working Papers.

Ryde, J. (2000) Supervising across difference, *International Journal of Psychotherapy*, 5(1): 37–48.

Ryde, J. (2004) *Racialising Whiteness: White Racial Identity and Intersubjectivity in Psychotherapy*. Bath: University of Bath.

Ryle, G. (1984) *The Concept of Mind*. Chicago: University of Chicago Press.

Samuels, A. (ed.) (1986) *The Father: Contemporary Jungian Perspectives*. New York: Guilford Press.

Samuels, A. (1989) *The Plural Psyche: Personality, Morality, and the Father*. London: Routledge.

Samuels, A. (1993) *The Political Psyche*. London: Routledge.

Samuels, A. (1994) Replies to an international questionnaire on political material brought into the clinical setting by clients of psychotherapists and analysts, *International Review of Sociology*, 3: 7–60.

Samuels, A. (1996) From sexual misconduct to social justice, *Psychoanalytic Dialogues*, 6: 295–321.

Samuels, A. (1997) The political psyche: A challenge to therapists and clients to politicise what they do. In J. Reppen (ed.) *More Analysts at Work*. Northvale, NJ: Aronson.

Samuels, A. (1999a) Working directly with political, social and cultural material in the therapy session. In *Clinical Counselling in Context: An Introduction*. London: Routledge.

Samuels, A. (1999b) From sexual misconduct to social justice. In D. Mann (ed.) *Erotic Transference and Countertransference: Clinical Practice in Psychotherapy*. London: Routledge.

Samuels, A. (2001) *Politics on the Couch: Citizenship and the Internal Life*. London: Profile Books.

Sands, A. (2000) *Falling for Therapy: Psychotherapy from a Client's Point of View*. London: Macmillan.

Sands, A. (2003) Seeking professional help. In Y. Bates and R. House (eds) *Ethically Challenged Professions: Enabling Innovation and Diversity in Psychotherapy and Counselling*. Hay-on-Wye: PCCS Books.

Schaverien, J. (1995) *Desire and the Female Therapist*. London: Routledge.

Schimel, J., Simon, L., Greenberg, J., Pyszczynski, T., Solomon, S., Waxmonsky, J. and Arndt, J. (1999) Stereotypes and terror management: Evidence that mortality salience enhances stereotypic thinking and preferences, *Journal of Personality and Social Psychology*, 77(5): 905–26.

Seed, J., Macy, J., Fleming, P. and Naess, A. (1988) *Thinking Like a Mountain: Towards a Council of All Beings*. British Columbia: New Society Publishers.

Segal, H. (1988) Silence is the real crime. In H.B Levine, D. Jacobs and L.J. Rubin (eds) *Psychoanalysis and the Nuclear Threat: Clinical and Theoretical Studies*. Hillsdale, NJ: Analytic Press.

Seligman, M. (1992) *Helplessness: On Depression, Development and Death*. New York: W.H. Freeman.

Shalev, A. and Berman, E. (1988) Exchange on 'From war to war: Cumulative trauma', *Sihot*, 2: 147–8.

Sharaf, M. (1984) *Fury on Earth: A Biography of Wilhelm Reich*. London: Heinemann.

Shepard, P. (1995) Nature and madness. In T. Roszak, M.E. Gomes and A.D. Kanner (eds) *Ecopsychology: Restoring the Earth, Healing the Mind*. San Francisco: Sierra Club Books.

Sloan, T. (1996) *Damaged Life*. London: Routledge.

Smail, D. (2003) Psychotherapy, society and the individual. In Y. Bates and R. House (eds) *Ethically Challenged Professions: Enabling Innovation and Diversity in Psychotherapy and Counselling*. Hay-on-Wye: PCCS Books.

Smith, D. (1999) *Hidden Conversations: An Introduction to Communicative Psychoanalysis*, 2nd edn. London: Rebnus Press.

Socarides, C. (1996) Major advances in the psychoanalytic theory and therapy of male homosexuality. In I. Rosen (ed.) *Sexual Deviation*, 3rd edn. Oxford: Oxford University Press.

Solomon, Z., Garb, R., Bleich, A. and Gropper, D. (1987) Reactivation of battle reactions among Israeli soldiers during the Lebanon war, *Sihot*, 2: 31–6.

Some, M.P. (1998) *The Healing Wisdom of Africa: Finding Life Purpose Through Nature, Ritual and Community*. New York: Tarcher Putnam.

Steiner, C. (1981) *The Other Side of Power*. New York: Grove Press.

Steiner, R. (1916) Psychological distress and the birth pangs of the consciousness soul. In R. Steiner, *The Meaning of Life*. London: Rudolf Steiner Press, 1999.

Steltzer, J. (1986) The formation and deformation of identity during psychoanalytic training, *Free Associations*, 7, 59–74.

Stoller, R.J. (1991) *Pain and Passion: A Psycoanalyst Explores the World of S & M*. New York: Plenum Press.

Stolorow, R.D. and Atwood, G.E. (1984) *Structures of Subjectivity*. Hillsdale, NJ: Analytic Press.

Stolorow, R.D. and Atwood, G.E. (1987) *Psychoanalytic Treatment: An Intersubjective Approach*. Hillsdale, NJ: Analytic Press.

Stolorow, R.D. and Atwood, G.E. (1992) *Contexts of Being*. Hillsdale, NJ: Analytic Press.

Stolorow, R.D., Atwood, G.E and Brandchaft, B. (1994) *The Intersubjective Perspective*. Northvale, NJ: Aronson.

Stolorow, R.D., Atwood, G.E. and Orange, D. (2002) *Worlds of Experience: Interweaving Philosophical and Clinical Dimensions in Psychoanalysis*. New York: Basic Books.

Sue, D.W. and Sue, D. (1990) *Counselling the Culturally Different*, 2nd edn. New York: Wiley.

Suttie, I. (1936) *The Origins of Love and Hate*. Harmondsworth: Penguin.

Taylor, T. (1997) *The Prehistory of Sex*. London: Fourth Estate.

Thomas, L. (1992) Racism and psychotherapy: Working with racism in the consulting room, an analytic view. In J. Kareem and R. Littlewood (eds) *Intercultural Therapy*. London: Blackwell.

Thompson, A. (1990) *Guide to Ethical Practice in Psychotherapy*. New York: Wiley.

Thompson, H.S. (1995) *Better Than Sex: Confessions of a Political Junkie, Trapped Like a Rat in Mr Bill's Neighborhood*. London: Black Swan.

Todd, J. and Bohart, A.C. (1994) *Foundations of Clinical and Counseling Psychology*. New York: HarperCollins.

Todres, L. (2003) Humanising forces: Phenomenology in science; psychotherapy in technological culture, *Counselling and Psychotherapy Research*, 3(3): 196–203.

Totton, N. (1997a) Not just a job: Psychotherapy as a spiritual and political practice. In R. House and N. Totton (eds) *Implausible Professions: Arguments for Pluralism and Autonomy in Psychotherapy and Counselling*. Manchester: PCCS Books.

Totton, N. (1997b) The Independent Practitioners' Network: A new model of accountability. In R. House and N. Totton (eds) *Implausible Professions: Arguments for Pluralism and Autonomy in Psychotherapy and Counselling*. Manchester: PCCS Books.

Totton, N. (1999) The baby and the bathwater: 'Professionalisation' in psychotherapy and counselling, *British Journal of Guidance and Counselling*, 27(3): 313–24.

Totton, N. (2000) *Psychotherapy and Politics*. London: Sage.

Tuckwell, G. (2002) *Racial Identity, White Counsellors and Therapists*. Buckingham: Open University Press.

Turkle, S. (1979) *Psychoanalytic Politics: Jacques Lacan and Freud's French Revolution*. London: Deutsch.

Turnbull, C.M. (1972) *The Mountain People*. New York: Simon & Schuster.

van der Kolk, B.A. and Ducey, C.P. (1989) The psychological processing of traumatic experience: Rorschach patterns in PTSD, *Journal of Traumatic Stress*, 2: 259–74.

van der Kolk, B.A., Hopper, J.W. and Osterman, J.E. (2001) Exploring the nature of traumatic memory, *Journal of Aggression, Maltreatment & Trauma*, 4(2): 9–31.

Villela, L. (2001) Cale-se, the chalice of silence: The ethics of psychoanalysis and the return of the repressed in Brazil. Available at www.etatsgeneraux-psychanalyse.net/archives/texte32.html

Volkan, V. (2002) September 11 and societal regression, *Group Analysis*, 35(4): 456–83.

Voloshonov, V.N. (1976) *Freudianism: A Marxist Critique*. New York: Academic Press.

Wehowsky, A. (2000) Diagnosis as care: Diagnosis as politics, *International Journal of Psychotherapy*, 5(3): 241–55.

Werbart, A. (2000) Our need of taboo: Pictures of violence and mourning difficulties, *Free Associations* 8(2): 21–48.

Wilkinson, H. (1999) Psychotherapy, fascism and constitutional history, *International Journal of Psychotherapy*, 4: 117–26.

Winnicott, D.W. (1945) Primitive emotional development. In *Through Pediatrics to Psycho-analysis*. New York: Basic Books, 1975: 145–56.

Winnik, H.Z., Moses, R. and Ostow, M. (1973) *Psychological Bases of War*. New York: Quadrangle.

Wittig, M. (1981) One is not a woman, *Feminist Issues*, Winter: 47–54.

Witztum, E., Levey, A., Kotler, M., Granek, M. and Solomon, Z. (1989–91) Battle reactions in Israel's wars, 1948–1982. Series of papers, *Sihot*, vols 4–5.

Young, R.M. (1994) *Mental Space*. London: Process Press.

Young, R.M. (1996) The culture of British psychoanalysis and related essays on character and morality and on the psychodynamics of psycho-analytic organisations. Available at www.sheffield.ac.uk/uni/academic/N-Q/psysc/staff/rmyoung/paper53.htm

Young, R.M. (1999) Psychoanalysis and psychotherapy: The grand leading the bland, *Free Associations*, 7(3): 437–58.

Zizek, S. (1989) *The Sublime Object of Ideology*. London: Verso.

Zizek, S. (1993) *Tarrying with the Negative*. Durham, NC: Duke University Press.

Index